FAIRBREAK

noun: equality, opportunity, diversity, inclusion, movement

Karen Motyka and Shaun Martyn

FairBreak envisions a world where people have fair and equal access to opportunities that enable them to succeed in their chosen endeavour, independent of gender or geographical location. The mission is to create opportunities that progress gender equality on a global scale, using cricket as a primary vehicle. By doing so, they aim to provide a "FairBreak" for all: to create opportunities across sport, health, business, media, arts and education to empower women to pursue success.

Every corner of the planet matters. From Vanuatu, Brazil and Australia to Afghanistan, Bhutan and Rwanda. The organisation is committed to creating opportunities and pathways.

FairBreak started with cricket, building on founder Shaun Martyn's passion for the sport and his role in performance coaching both on and off the cricket field.

Cricket is a team game played in over one hundred countries around the planet. It is not gender specific. It is not body type specific, and it is not bound by culture, religion or ethnicity. Most importantly, it is a game that is traditionally built on partnerships.

Founded in 2013 under the name Women's International Cricket League, FairBreak was originally created to be a standalone tournament for women to advance their playing opportunities and remuneration in cricket. Since then, the movement has evolved to tackle systemic barriers to gender equality around the world.

FAIRBREAK

ISBN: 978-0-6456583-0-9 (Paperback)
ISBN: 978-0-6456583-1-6 (E-Book)

Cover and interior design: Andy Meaden meadencreative.com

Front and back cover photographs and all Dubai match images by Neeraj Murali.

First printing edition 2023.

DEDICATION

This book is dedicated to all #fairbreakers

Everything Karen Motyka knows about cricket she has learnt through researching and writing this book. That is exactly how it should be because this book is not about cricket. It's about the FairBreak movement and the incredible people who have come together to nurture that movement and keep it always moving forward.

Karen began writing player announcements and press releases for us in the lead-up to the FairBreak Invitational in Dubai in early 2022. It was obvious, very quickly, just how good her writing and research skills were. It then came to my attention that she harboured a desire to write more, even to try her hand at a book!

We are all about opportunity at FairBreak so I asked Karen if she'd be interested in writing the FairBreak story and so we began. It's been an absolute delight working with her on this project. I know that everyone she has interviewed has thoroughly enjoyed the experience and her attention to detail is second to none.

This is Karen's first book. Congratulations and thank you from all #fairbreakers.

Shaun Martyn

CONTENTS

FOREWORD

I am incredibly proud to serve as Patron of FairBreak Global.

Working together, our organisation is advancing the cause of women and the iconic game of cricket.

FairBreak is fundamentally about disruption and innovation. We are disrupting the barriers that lock women around the world out of our sport. We are giving young women and girls from developing nations the chance to live up to their potential and to play opposite and alongside the elite.

We are innovating by offering a T20 cricket tournament that is shorter, pays better and lets players balance the demands of participating in the competition with their need to keep working or looking after their families.

FairBreak is building excellent global teams. These teams are not based on nationality. Instead, FairBreak is bringing together emerging and talented players, no matter where they live on the planet, to compete with the very best.

The FairBreak format means a young woman from Bhutan, Namibia or Argentina gets the chance to meet and play on the same team as the great Sana Mir or Suzie Bates.

Along with millions of fans on television and social media, watching a young Rwandan woman take multiple wickets during our first major tournament, The FairBreak Invitational in Dubai, was thrilling and one of the great joys of my life.

FairBreak is achieving all of this whilst ensuring that women's cricket is a beacon of ethical sport and does not rely on advertising money from gambling or tobacco companies.

It is a wonderful privilege to work with FairBreak as it changes lives. This is an organisation that is transforming the lives of women, transforming the game of cricket and opening up the economic opportunities it can deliver to women across the globe.

This is sports diplomacy at its finest.

Jennifer Westacott AO
Patron of FairBreak Global
Chief Executive, Business Council of Australia

PREFACE

Dear Reader,

I hope that you have you picked up this book because you are drawn to the captivatingly joyful photograph on the front cover. Who is this young, female, Asian athlete? Let me tell you about her. Winifred Duraisingam is from Malaysia. She first started playing cricket in the street when she was eight years old. The boys in her neighbourhood, including her brothers, would not let her hold their precious cricket bat, never mind give her a go at batting. Observing how unfair this situation was, Wini's uncle taught her how to bowl a cricket ball to the boys instead. At fourteen years old, she was selected to play for Malaysia's national cricket team and at age twenty-one she became their captain.

Earlier this year, in February 2022, a friend asked me to assist her with some administration tasks. I knew, vaguely, that she worked for the founder of a company called FairBreak. Professionally, I had some spare time on my hands, and I was happy to help them out. I would never have guessed that within a few months of rocking up to her home with my laptop that I'd have written a book and I would be arranging to have it printed and published. I had fallen, like Alice, down a rabbit hole into the thrilling world of women's cricket.

When my friend's employer, Shaun Martyn, asked me to write the story of FairBreak, I questioned his wisdom. I am a woman who has managed to traverse life without watching sport on TV nor reading the sports pages of a newspaper. I enjoy playing social tennis, hiking in the mountains, cycling, skiing and swimming in the ocean. I don't particularly excel at any of these activities. I do them for fun and to be outside in nature.

With furrowed brow I asked Shaun whether I was a suitable candidate for such a task. I am not a journalist. I am not a cricketer. I have never even been to a cricket match. Surely I was not an appropriately qualified person to be writing a book about women's cricket? Shaun assured me that he wanted the story written by a woman. Moreover, he wanted it written by a woman who has not been steeped in cricket her whole life. He wanted it written by a woman who could be objective and make the story accessible to all readers; those who follow cricket and those who are new to the subject. Ultimately, he was offering me a chance to shine. Through writing this book, I have discovered that this is Shaun's superpower. He sees talent and skill in an individual and he presents them with opportunities they may never have been given ordinarily. He changes lives.

The FairBreak story features all the familiar aspects you might expect in a compelling narrative. A theme that involves adversity, inequality and empowerment of the underdog. A determined protagonist and a diverse cast of supporting characters who give the story its life force. The settings are various international locations and, in a broader sense, a period of modern history during which women's cricket emerges from obscurity to take its rightful place in the pantheon of global sport. There's a tense plot that lasts two decades. The stakes for our protagonist escalate leading to an inevitable and successful resolution. Underlying this tension is our story's conflict. Externally, we have various antagonists; the decision-makers of cricket's establishment, blinkered sports marketeers and numerous hurdles including sanctioning, lack of financial backing and a global pandemic. Throughout, our leading character stays true to his sense of purpose and internal moral compass - striving for gender equality in a world ripe for change.

Interviews and perspectives from a broad range of professionals and stakeholders will surprise, engage, frustrate and uplift you as the world of women's cricket and the delivery of a global tournament are brought into clear focus.

Women's cricket is growing at a phenomenal rate globally and is the fastest growing sport in Asia. Viewing of the Women's T20 World Cup in 2020 set new records, and the final at the MCG on International Women's Day was the most watched women's cricket event ever. Women's cricket has arrived. Never before has this sector of the sport been so accessible.

The world deserves to read the FairBreak biography. Female cricketers must be properly represented, valued, remunerated, sponsored, broadcast and celebrated for being the incredible athletes they are.

Karen Motyka

PROLOGUE

This is not a book about me. Although I started the whole adventure, it will live on long after me and be carried forward by anyone and everyone who is a #fairbreaker.

I have, however, been asked to set the scene; how we arrived at the place we now find ourselves.

Cricket has always been my first love in terms of sport. Golf is a close second. I have many other interests, but I always come back to sport as the great leveller.

Growing up in Bowral, a small country town in the NSW Southern Highlands, south of Sydney, in the late 1960s and early 1970s, everyone played a great deal of sport. There was nothing else to do, other than sit at home and watch black and white TV.

I was seven years old when my cricket coach, Mr. Jack Thompson, took me aside and told me I was now "playing the game of life". Never were truer words ever spoken. I would front up every Saturday morning to, what is now, Bradman Oval in Bowral, and train the house down. I always loved training. Still do.

I attended Chevalier College at Burradoo near Bowral, a Catholic co-educational secondary day school offering a wide range of sport including cricket. All the girls I went to school with also played sport. Multiple sports. And the girls played sport with the boys. I considered the girls to be good athletes. I never once thought they were inferior to the boys as was often the mindset of the time.

I was obsessed. I ate, drank, slept, watched and read cricket. I drew field settings in class and threw rocks at telegraph poles on the way to school to practice my fielding. This continued throughout my school life. I read every cricket book in the Chevalier College library. Twice. And snuck my transistor radio into bed at night to listen to The Ashes from England.

The first live Test match I ever attended was the same one as Geoff Lawson. We were both at the Sydney Cricket Ground in 1969 to watch Australia play the West Indies. Sir Wesley Hall and Sir Garfield Sobers were my cricketing heroes. In those days you could run onto the field at the end of the day's play. I still remember reaching up to touch Wes Hall on the shoulder. I offered my hand to Gary Sobers and he shook it. I'm sure he still remembers that. Okay, maybe not!

Cricket was also played at Frensham, a day and boarding school for girls in nearby Mittagong and at Sydney Church of England Grammar School for Girls (SCEGS) in neighbouring Moss Vale. My first girlfriend played cricket for SCEGS.

I first played against an all-girls team in 1970 when Chevalier College played the Frensham 1st XI. I was twelve years old. Playing against girls seemed perfectly normal. I can honestly say that gender wasn't an issue for me. They were all cricketers and that was all that mattered.

I remember that one of the Chevalier players went out to bat without wearing a box. He said they were "just girls" bowling. More fool him, because he copped one right in the Jatz Crackers and went down like he'd been shot. I thought it was very funny at the time. It's even funnier when I think about it now.

I competed in multiple sports at school including athletics. My sprint coach was the legendary Jean Coleman who was the 1938 British Empire Games Gold Medalist. This wonderful athlete could undoubtedly have won many medals at the Olympics had World War II not ended her running career.

I benefited from strong male and female role models at home. Both my parents were excellent sports people, and my father always spoke positively about my mother's sporting ability. My father was always encouraging and supportive, and both my grandmothers were strong, independent women. Sadly, both my grandfathers were deceased by the time I was two years old, so I never knew them.

My closest aunt travelled as a clerk on one of Australia's first political delegations to China. She was a Supreme Court recorder and had a strong influence on my education. A pioneer of further education, in retirement, she returned to Sydney University at sixty-five years of age to study Japanese.

I fell out of love with cricket after my father died in 1978. He had been away supporting me again while I captained an Under-23 Rep team. He passed away the night we got back. My plan had been to go to England in 1979 with my teaching qualifications and to try and further my cricket career, but my sister was still at school and my mother needed me to stay. Grief does strange things to you. I blamed cricket and drifted away from the sport. It was a big mistake. I should have kept playing both for him and for me.

After my father died, I saw how strong my mother was, and I had a better appreciation of the vital role she played in our family. I also observed how she managed the rest of her life, and I was inspired by her inner strength and resilience.

In the 1990s, I worked with Raelene Boyle who represented Australia at three Olympic Games as a sprinter, winning three silver medals. She started to educate me about the massive discrepancy between the meagre sports funding for women and the proportion of medals won by them.

I also worked with Heather Turland, the Australian long-distance runner who competed in road running events, and whose greatest achievement was a gold medal in the marathon at the 1998 Commonwealth Games. I saw, first-hand, the problems Turland experienced with sponsorship and financial support.

I have been incredibly fortunate to have benefited from positive sporting influencers, male and female, in my career. They have helped shape my thinking such that I don't see gender in sport. I just see athletes.

A chance meeting with some old mates from school at a Test match in Brisbane got me involved with cricket again. From that encounter grew a charity cricket club, the Wish I Was Cricket Connection, then the Women's International Cricket League (WICL) and finally FairBreak.

Once I started collaborating with the Australian Women's Cricket vice-Captain, Lisa Sthalekar, my frustration with the inequality in women's sport really kicked up a gear. Helping Lisa write her autobiography *Shaker. Run Maker. Wicket Taker* and dealing with Cricket Australia made me angry.

I have never been good with injustice, and there is too much injustice facing female athletes. I figured I might as well have a go at making things better. So my mission has not been motivated by 'white saviour' syndrome, nor by the fact that I have two daughters.

Lisa and I naively thought that the cricket establishment would endorse the Women's International Cricket League (WICL). Sadly, the cricket establishment did not support it, such that our push to make an impact around fairer remuneration and more playing opportunities became increasingly difficult. Nonetheless, our campaign prompted Cricket Australia to start the Women's Big Bash League (WBBL) and the England & Wales Cricket Board to commence the KIA Super League (KSL). Despite the push-back, we got traction, and made change happen.

When Lisa left WICL to pursue her post-cricket career in commentating, I understood the reasons behind her decision, and was faced with the dilemma of letting go of the gender equality campaign or pressing on with it. I decided to keep going. The number of people who had invested their time, passion and expertise into the whole concept meant I had to continue. Today, I feel an enormous debt to them all and an absolute obligation to keep striving to make a difference.

Everyone at FairBreak knows what this movement means to the female cricketers we work with and their families. Cricket is an inclusive sport. I am enormously proud of the fact that FairBreak has many more women involved in management roles than when we first started out. FairBreak is constantly learning and evolving, and that is what I enjoy.

I am often asked why FairBreak has become so important to me. Only through working with Karen Motyka on this book have I had the opportunity to reflect and formulate an answer.

Initially, it was important because what I saw while working with Lisa and other female cricketers was just so wrong on every level. What started with a purity of intention ran into so many roadblocks that it turned into a personal challenge. Today, what is important to me are all the people who have helped drive this movement forward. The FairBreak management team, the players, and all the supporters and advocates who call themselves a #fairbreaker. This book is for them and about them. It's a celebration of their work.

Shaun Martyn

ACKNOWLEDGEMENTS

This book was written on Walbunja country, part of the Yuin Nation, and I pay my respects to their Elders past, present and emerging. I also wish to acknowledge the Elders of the Gundungurra and Dharawal people, the traditional owners of the lands on which I grew up and learnt to play cricket.

I would like to thank Annette Pendergast, Professor Shirley Randell, Alistair Cane, Rajiv Podar, Vicki Waters, Simon Rothery and family, Adrian Wegryzn, Shakti Gounden, Maher Magrabi, Adam Spencer, Nicole and Matthew Wilcock, Gary and Saira Digby, John Cunningham, Peter Shortle, Paul Clarke, Simon Doble, Katey Martin, Mariko Hill, Sterre Kalis, Selina Solman, Shameelah Mosweu, Isabelle Duncan, Simon Taufel, Colin Tennant, Anoop Gidwani, Ravi Nagdev, Mark Farmer, Tony Melloy, Shane Deitz, Lisa Sthalekar, Lesego Pooe, Georgie Heath, Annesha Ghosh, Ebba Qureshi, Maila Reeves, Steve van der Horst, Roshni Krishnan, Adam Collins, Lara Richards, Azhar Habib and Wildtrack TV, Manvi Dhodi, Sam Charnley, Renee Montgomery, Julie Abbott, Sue Strachan, Bruce Hanson, Yash Mehotra, Charles Cowper, Kym Livesley and his team at Dentons, Andrew Walton, Rina Hore, Associate Professor Deirdre McGhee, Elyse Potter, The Hon. Kristy McBain MP.

Thank you to Saba Nasim for her management and commitment. Evan Lawrence, our web designer, for his outstanding work. John Blondin for always challenging my ideas and pushing me forward. Tony Wright for never letting any of us forget the message and always keeping us in the fight. David Sexton for his unwavering support and guidance. Greg Shipperd for his guidance, counsel, and creativity. Verona Kite for everything she has done. Roy Burton for his constant support and friendship. Roy has more skills than I can list here. Lindsay Brown for his political nous, dedication to the project, attention to detail and infectious enthusiasm.

Thank you to Suzie Bates who captained our first FairBreak XI at Wormsley in 2018 and turned up again in 2019 to run the water for the team. Suzie has been a huge supporter of me and everything FairBreak since Day One. By lending her name and support, Suzie has given our movement credibility and wider acceptance. She is an outstanding contributor.

Mignon "Minx" Van der Merwe (née du Preez) has been one of the world's greatest players over the last 15 years. I am delighted that she is now our Head of Marketing based out of South Africa. She is always enthusiastic and full of wonderful ideas. Everyone at FairBreak is looking forward to working with Minx.

I thank my family for their love and encouragement.

I would like to particularly acknowledge the contributions of Geoff Lawson, Alex Blackwell and Sana Mir.

Geoff 'Henry' Lawson holds a special place in the FairBreak family. As one of Australia's and the world's most celebrated players, commentators, coaches and cricket writers, Geoff brings a gravitas to what we do that is impossible to quantify. His friendship, counsel, support, enthusiasm, and positivity constantly inspire us all. I try, every day, to live up to the standards he sets. Geoff has had a positive impact on every player, coach, commentator and manager who has been a part of FairBreak thus far.

Alex Blackwell and Sana Mir hold positions in world cricket as revered players and captains of their respective countries, Australia and Pakistan. Over and above all that, their contributions to the advancement of women's cricket are a legacy they continue to build upon. It has been one of the great honours and pleasures of my life to work with them and have them as integral members of our management team.

Paul Harvey is always the smartest man in the room. I don't care what room you are in. FairBreak does not run without Paul. We go a long way back. We met at Chevalier College in 1970. He was catching the school bus every day from Picton, and I was catching the bus from Bowral. We were both 'day bugs', as the boarders, priests and brothers liked to call us. It was not a friendly environment. Everything was a competition, and it was definitely "survival of the fittest".

We both played cricket, although not together, at any stage, in the same team. Before school, at recess and lunchtime, it was a race to the nets and cricket was all that we spoke about. Many years later, Paul and I reconnected through old school friends in Brisbane at a Test match and over dinner. A charity cricket club was formed and so began a cricket journey that has led to FairBreak.

Paul has incredible attention to detail. He can pull apart and construct a contract better than anyone, and he has a strategic mind. We have our own language around FairBreak. I'm always talking about 'setting my traps'. Paul always talks about building the business like you build an innings - ones and twos with the occasional boundary. I'll often want to charge ahead. He pulls me into line. It's a great combination. We bat in partnership, and we bowl in partnership, very often with contrasting skills. It works and I love him to death.

I first met Vidya Rao in India in 2013. What an amazing person she is. Vidya has devoted herself to FairBreak. She is the head of our operations in India and our strongest advocate in that vast cricketing nation. Vidya displays grace and dignity every day. There is no task that is too big or too small for Vidya to attend to. I am in awe of her ability to engage and influence at all levels. Her mentorship of young female players and businesspeople in India is outstanding.

Kimberley Lee and Sucheta Gorolay are two dynamos who have driven the bulk of the branding and messaging for FairBreak. Exceptional in everything they do, always keeping me on my toes and continuing to educate me in this space. They are very much the conscience of FairBreak. We have all learnt so much from them and we continue to learn from them.

Claudia Lamb is our videographer and social media driver. Claudia has a great eye for design and our 'look and feel'. She is a delight to work with, and a person I have total confidence in. It has been a joy to watch Claudia's interaction with the players and her calm, considered and supportive interviewing style.

Although Elle Williams has only been with us for less than two years, it feels like she has been here since the beginning. Elle came into her role with no background in cricket at all. She is now steeped in it. Professional to a tee, kind, compassionate, always working to bring out the best in all members of our team and every player she engages with. Elle is very much the engine room of FairBreak. Her counsel has been invaluable.

Finally, I must thank Venkat for his dedication to this project. I have no words for the passion, commitment and force he brings to FairBreak. His friendship goes way beyond his work with us, and I am in awe of what he has achieved both in cricket and in life.

Shaun Martyn

INTRODUCTION

Paul Harvey
School Friend and "Wish I Was" Founder

Shaun and I have known each since we were thirteen years old. In 1970 we both started high school at Chevalier College in Bowral, the Australian town where legendary cricketer Sir Donald Bradman lived for many years.

Our birthdays are two weeks apart and we have shared a lifelong interest in sport, especially cricket. We used to spend every lunchtime in the nets at school, testing one another and the other boys with our skills.

As a day student, I travelled by bus from the town of Picton, nearly fifty kilometres away. Living so far from the school meant I could not play weekend sport for the College. Instead, I played tennis, cricket and soccer around the wider Picton area, including U/16 Representative Cricket for Macarthur District. In local cricket circles I was known as "Bumper Harvey" for my fast, short-pitched bowling. It brought many a batsman undone.

Travelling long distances for inter-district cricket was a problem. I could not play at Rep level for long because it was difficult for me to get a lift to games if no other local boys had been selected. My parents played competitive district tennis on weekends and could not drive me to the matches.

Meanwhile, Shaun had blazed his own trail around the Bowral district, playing high-level inter-school and inter-district sport, particularly cricket and athletics.

After graduating from Chevalier College, we moved on in separate directions; Shaun chose to study at the University of Wollongong to be an

English teacher, while I took up Civil Engineering at the University of NSW. I ended up withdrawing from that course and started work. Later, I completed a Business and Marketing degree.

For many years we pursued our careers and started families without crossing paths. We maintained strong connections with our school mates, most of whom loved cricket. During those years, Shaun became heavily involved in sports team coaching and management outside of his teaching role and he eventually set up Shaun Martyn & Associates. He specialised in delivering management training, team building, event management and celebrity speakers to corporate groups. Using aspects of high-performance sports coaching and development, he established a wide network of international business, sports and celebrity contacts.

My career path took me into business and marketing operations, strategy, R&D, contract management and procurement roles across multiple sectors including international telecommunications, energy and IT. I also developed the practical skills to organise and manage websites and imagery for cricket clubs and small businesses. In the late 1990s, I resumed playing cricket, and I saw how clubs could benefit from the use of technology to improve member communication. My return to local cricket also involved grassroots club management of junior and senior players.

In 2000, Shaun and I reconnected through several cricket-loving friends from Chevalier College, and we spent three days together in Brisbane watching Australia play England in the Orange Test Series. During that trip, our thoughts turned to how we could use cricket as a force for good and to raise money for charity. Having enjoyed a certain level of success in our professional fields, we all wanted to give back while having fun playing our favourite sport.

As a result, the Wish I Was Cricket Connection (WIWCC) was founded. We arranged cricket matches as fund-raisers for good causes. Participants could play as the cricket legend they "wished they were". Those legends' names were printed on the playing shirts, written in the score book, appeared on the scoreboard, and were announced over the PA. WIWCC Founders always had a place in the team. Shaun's far-reaching connections with cricket personalities ensured our events always had real life cricket legends participating to add to the fun and on-field banter. One and all had to "Play Like a Legend".

Memorable matches were held in various locations around Australia, and we raised money for numerous good causes. Grounds in Cairns, Melbourne and Sydney hosted us. Naturally, we also played at Bowral's Bradman Oval. Male Australian legends including Geoff 'Henry' Lawson, Merv Hughes, Kerry O'Keeffe, Dean Jones, Rodney Hogg and Colin 'Funky' Miller competed with us. Emerging legends from Australia's female ranks, Alex Blackwell and Lisa Sthalekar, also appeared in our charity games.

The demands of domestic and professional life led to some WIWCC founders retiring leaving Shaun and I to form 14 Degrees International Pty Ltd in 2008. While the Wish I Was Cricket Connections faded away, the underlying philosophies of "cricket for good" and "greater opportunity through cricket" continued to evolve and they still underpin our FairBreak values.

Through 14 Degrees, Shaun and I organised other events to provide greater playing opportunities in circumstances where cricket matches might never happen. For example, we fielded an opposition for the Australian Transplant Cricket Club, an offshoot of Transplant Australia, whose cricket-loving members had all undergone medical transplants and wanted to enjoy a "second innings in life". It was a privilege and pleasure to take the field with ATCC members whose commitment to the game were second-to-none.

During this time, Shaun had been managing Lisa Sthalekar, and together they formed WICL in 2013. Their concept involved establishing a privately-run T20 Women's International Cricket League aimed at rapidly advancing the playing and income generating opportunities for female players. I provided commercial and operational support and guidance where needed.

WICL's journey and the hurdles are described elsewhere in this book, but it became obvious that it was an idea ahead of its time. In terms of elevating women's cricket, it was a concept far ahead of what the "powers that be" in world cricket wanted anything to do with. It would take many years of frustration and the equivalent of crawling across broken glass to advance that concept. In leading cricketing nations, there was an element of "not invented here" in the attitude of well-paid cricket administrators, including elite female administrators, to the WICL model. Beyond that, there were deliberate strategies of appearing to be supportive. WICL was sent up blind alleys to waste time and money in the hope they would run out of steam and just go away.

Shaun and I had many conversations during this time about how progressing opportunities for the women's game was like living through episodes of the British television drama series *Upstairs Downstairs*, from forty years earlier. The analogy being that cricket administrators seemed intent on keeping female players "Downstairs" in the place assigned to them, and not letting them "Upstairs" into the world of opportunity and comfort enjoyed by male players. The administrators seemed intent on holding up the pace of change, even when operators like WICL were knocking on their doors offering to help share the effort of bringing female players into the light.

The desire to make a difference to women's cricket was always too strong to be put off by disruption and stalling from laggard cricket administrators. As the proud fathers of accomplished daughters, Shaun and I found it galling that anyone would seek to hold girls and women back from any pursuit of their choosing. It made us even more determined to think through how to move around and past the veiled but evident obstructions. It became a very personal mission for us and our Chevalier College motto, "Strength in Faith", underpinned our efforts.

Drawing on my background in marketing strategy, in 2014, I put it to Shaun that the "front-on" approach to administrators needed to change. And the player targets for our improvement initiatives needed widening. Even if this took longer to deliver the benefits to female players than would be the case had administrators been more receptive, innovative, and conscientious about improving the women's game. We could only see tokenism happening.

We decided to re-position our initiatives as a "movement". We wanted to build on the groundswell of understanding and support for greater opportunity and benefits in the women's game. I had deduced that while equality and opportunity for female cricketers in Tier 1 nations still needed improving, they were starting to benefit from better access to facilities, infrastructure, and coaching, as well as minor increases in remuneration. The noises Shaun and WICL had been making publicly about that topic had not gone unnoticed.

We could see the rapid growth in the women's game globally, so it was obvious that unrealised potential existed amid the ranks of Associate Nation players. However, development activities in that arena were receiving little attention internationally. Even less so around player remuneration, exposure and broadcasting. Cricketers in Associate Nations and Tier 1 countries seldom crossed paths and were rarely cross promoted. A glass ceiling between Associate Nations and Tier 1 countries was apparent. The sustained status quo was not conducive for the future of the women's game globally, nor was it benefiting the aspirations of the burgeoning numbers of Associate Nation players.

Our discussions around these issues included trusted advisers Alex Blackwell and Geoff Lawson, and between us we germinated the following:

- Female players were not getting enough of a "fair break", drawing on the Australian vernacular of a "fair go".

- The issue was widespread all over the world. It was a global problem.

- The opportunities afforded to female players were inequitable and skewed in favour of Tier 1 players. Administrators appeared oblivious to the growing numbers of Associate Nation cricketers.

- The apparent and continued suppression of opportunities for female players had become, by the mid-2010s, an anachronism.

- Enormous potential existed for unearthing a plethora of talented players by organising a tournament that would mix Associate Nation and Tier 1 players in combinations permitted under ICC sanctioning rules. This would also achieve fairer playing opportunities, skills development and cultural awareness.

The prospect of taking on such a mission was daunting in the face of ongoing cricket establishment resistance, but our team felt compelled to press on. Ideas percolated over time. Various strategies and programs were attempted. Eventually WICL morphed into FairBreak Global. As with previous ventures, I established the website, communication channels and operational aspects of the company. The ongoing player market research I set up through the website continues to provide visibility into the ongoing disparity in the opportunities and playing facilities for female players around the world. This research continues to inform FairBreak's plans and programs.

In the years since FairBreak's formation, I have continued to be involved, on a consultative basis, as nominal Chief Operating Officer. I contribute across most aspects of systems and processes, including commercial, legal, and operational matters. I endeavour to "keep the wheels on" the FairBreak "wagon" as the movement positions itself for growth and expanded player support.

There is still much work to be done for the global improvement of women's cricket. FairBreak's agenda is far-reaching, and our management team remains determined to achieve our goals.

"FairBreak has been a life-changing experience for me personally. From getting exposed to a world-class playing environment to learning from the greats of the game. An inclusive environment and tournament like FairBreak is the only way to develop the women's game...I look forward to more opportunities...to inspire more girls back home."

Sita Rana Magar, Nepal

1ST INNINGS
THE EARLY DAYS

"FairBreak has spent every moment of its existence fuelling the movement that enables female athletes to believe that equality of opportunity is a genuine right. History will bear testimony to the considerable impact FairBreak has had on the pursuit of equality."

Tony Wright

Lisa Sthalekar and the Women's International Cricket League

FairBreak was first conceptualised nearly two decades ago. A couple of years into the new millennium, Shaun Martyn was running corporate networking events around Australia for CISCO Systems, the USA based information technology conglomerate. CISCO's staff and clients were organised into teams, and they played together in cricket matches to foster stronger business relationships, team building, problem solving and strategic thinking. Martyn was assisted in these endeavours by his associate and old school friend, Paul Harvey. The pair also organised cricket tournaments to raise money for several charities.

In 2003, Martyn was introduced to Lisa Sthalekar, a leading Australian international cricketer, by former Australian men's team fast bowler Geoff Lawson. Martyn had been looking for a female guest speaker for one of his dinner functions. Martyn was also introduced to Alex and Kate Blackwell and Charlotte Anneveld. He decided to enlist the cricketing prowess of these top Australian female cricketers, along with male former Test players, and to showcase their skills in his corporate networking events.

He did this for several reasons: firstly, to highlight just how good these women were as cricketers, and secondly, to supplement the women's incomes because these talented players were not getting paid for training or representing Australia in professional cricket matches. And if they were being paid, it was a ludicrously modest amount. Martyn elected to pay these female players appearance fees to take part in the corporate networking cricket matches he and Harvey were organising.

As a result of this working relationship, Martyn began to manage Sthalekar's professional cricket career and offered her a partnership in a company they named the Women's International Cricket League (WICL). It was not the usual type of relationship that a manager might normally have with an athlete; it was not based on Martyn taking a management fee, it was more about how and where he could assist or help female cricketers, and what opportunities they could look for.

During 2011-2012, as her manager, Martyn assisted Sthalekar with the writing, editing, publishing and launch of her autobiography, *Shaker. Run Maker, Wicket Taker*. The period it took them to write Sthalekar's book in the lead up to her retirement from professional cricket on the day after the ICC's Women's World Cup final at the Brabourne Stadium in Mumbai on the 7th of February 2013 was significant, and there were notable events they chose not to include in her book for fear of being too contentious.

There were other developments happening in Australian cricket around that time. Martyn recalls having a meeting in the Cricket Australia offices in Jolimont in Melbourne and talking to senior executives about a payment structure for the top twenty Australian female players. Martyn was suggesting that the female players be paid at a rookie Sheffield Shield or first-class contract rate of $52,000 per year. A sum still insultingly low compared to what the male players were being paid, but substantially better than what the women had been receiving up until then.

To illustrate the point, at the end of her career in 2013, Lisa Sthalekar, vice-Captain of the Australian Women's Cricket Team, was being paid the paltry sum of $15,000 per year by Cricket Australia. This included fifteen public appearances. A proposed pay rise to the "generous" annual sum of $52,000 sounded like a fortune in comparison.

In order to survive, Sthalekar needed another job. She was also employed as the High Performance Manager for Female Cricket at Cricket NSW. But when she represented Australia internationally, she had to take holiday leave and sick leave to travel and play as the vice-Captain of the nation's women's team. For Martyn, the premise that Australia's top female cricketer, working for one of the biggest regional cricket organisations in the world, was expected to take sick and holiday leave in order to play for her country was disgraceful.

When Sthalekar's autobiography was released at the prestigious Cricket Club of India in Mumbai in 2012, Geoff Lawson, former Australian fast bowler, and former Indian cricketer Dilip Vengsarkar were in attendance. Also on hand was Sachin Bajaj, the Indian businessman who had been instrumental in helping them publish, print, and launch the book in India, the country of Sthalekar's birth.

An underlying reason for producing Sthalekar's book was to shine a light on the as yet unseen world of leading female cricketers, and to start a conversation, globally, about the inequitable remuneration female cricketers were expected to accept. Sthalekar's book was a marketing tool for the WICL's nascent campaign to shine a light on this inequality.

Martyn tried to secure cricket bat sponsorship for Sthalekar in the lead up to the 2013 ICC Women's World Cup tournament. He almost had Reebok signed up for US$10,000, but regrettably it never came to fruition. It was incredibly difficult to obtain any sort of endorsement deal for a female player at that time. While it was possible to get equipment, to try to secure money from any cricket body or cricket equipment supplier for a female player was problematic. The harsh and ludicrous reality was that despite being the world's top ICC ranked all-rounder, Sthalekar could not get money for a new cricket bat.

Martyn also talked to several different bat manufacturers about producing a specific "female only" cricket bat, something slightly shorter and lighter than what was in general use. Even the grip size was critical. But these conversations were falling on fallow ground. It was still an alien concept that a female cricketer might need a slightly different bat to that used by a male player, so it was impossible to get any type of deal done.

After the ICC's 2013 Women's World Cup final at Brabourne Stadium in Mumbai and Sthalekar's retirement announcement, discussions around the formation of WICL, the Women's International Cricket League developed further. Sthalekar and Martyn knew that the potential worldwide audience for the women's form of the game was growing rapidly, and the quality of the play was exceptional.

Consequently, the concept was devised that they start a global T20 tournament to showcase female players from all around the world into multi-national teams where the brand rights were owned by sponsoring companies. The aim was to attract the world's best women cricketers and provide more playing opportunities and improved remuneration for female players. This was considered revolutionary stuff in the lead up to FairBreak's Dubai tournament in 2022, so back in 2013, such innovation was beyond the comprehension of most.

In 2013, after Sthalekar had retired from playing professional cricket, she and Martyn began to direct their energies into getting the Women's International Cricket League off the ground.

Unfortunately, what they failed to realise was that because there had been a men's International Cricket League (ICL) created in opposition to the India Premier League (IPL), and because they had named their venture the Women's International Cricket League (WICL), this immediately established in people's minds the idea that they were similar to the ICL, which of course they were not. Martyn admits, in hindsight, it was a naïve mistake that set their movement back significantly.

On the 10th of May 2013, Martyn wrote to Clare Connor who was the Chair of the Women's Committee at the ICC and based in the offices of the England & Wales Cricket Board (ECB) at the hallowed Lord's Cricket Ground in London. In his letter [see Further Reading] Martyn outlined what WICL wanted to do and achieve for the women's game. He then flew to London to have a meeting with Connor in the offices of the ECB.

He recalls the meeting very clearly, and that Clare Connor's comments during the discussion indicated that his proposal would be a "game-changer for women's cricket". He left the ECB offices feeling optimistic and supported by ECB. That what he was embarking upon would be seen as a positive step in world cricket. Not a negative. And certainly not the scheming of a "rebel" organisation.

WICL were not looking to break away from established cricket. They were looking to create a vehicle to further enhance the women's game, and to expand the playing opportunities for leading and emerging female cricketers around the world.

While in London, Martyn gave an interview to Alison Mitchell on BBC Radio 4's breakfast program about what WICL were proposing. This subsequently generated some negative press in the UK. As a result, WICL and Martyn's management team were falsely branded as a breakaway organisation by members of the ECB and the cricketing establishment.

The WICL proposal was not supported by either the ICC or any of its members. In early June 2014, Clare Connor said, "...from an ECB perspective this competition is not on our agenda." The following day, Pat Howard, the then Executive General Manager of Team Performance at Cricket Australia, confirmed it saying, "...CA has not endorsed the [WICL] competition in any way". [See relevant letters and newspaper articles in Further Reading]

Who were Martyn and Sthalekar turning to for help and support during this time? There were several people involved in structuring and advising WICL. Firstly, there was Lisa's partner, Tracy Scott, who was in the legal department at Cricket Australia. Secondly, Tony Wright, senior marketing executive at CISCO, who was a strong public advocate of everything Martyn had been highlighting from the start.

Martyn was also spending extended time in India working with Mr. Rajiv Poddar, Mr. Yash Mehrotra and Mrs. Vidya Rao, who had all become very important contributors and patrons of WICL in India around 2013. The venerable Vidya Rao is still working with FairBreak Global today, as Head of Operations in India, and my interview with her features in this section. While Mehrotra no longer has an active involvement with FairBreak, he and Martyn are still in touch.

WICL formulated a plan proposing a tournament that looked similar to a tennis grand slam: One City. One Venue. Seventeen games. Martyn had spent considerable time researching other sports around the world such as Japanese rugby, ATP and WTA Grand Slam Tennis, and the Tour de France, and was talking to the participants and organisers of these major sporting events.

Martyn did not consider a six-to-eight-week-long tournament for women appropriate. He envisioned an event more like Grand Slam tennis or a golf tournament where competing involved a shorter period away from home and work, and where the players could bring their partners or families. Many of the female players were not full-time cricket professionals and had demanding careers outside of their sport, so they needed to maximise their income over a shorter period. Hence the notion of a briefer, more intense event.

Furthermore, in his WICL tournament, Martyn did not advocate a team franchise ownership model. In the India Premier League (IPL), team ownership is a geography-based model, where each team is owned, affiliated with, and supported by a city in India. Martyn did not believe that such a model was appropriate for a women's cricket tournament.

In 2013-14, no individual person or company was willing to sponsor a women's team anyway. They could not see the value in it. Martyn believed that it needed to be a brand partnership. A particular brand, like Unilever or Sony for example, would be much better aligned with women than having a franchise team ownership model. Martyn could not see team ownership working financially nor how it could be argued to be beneficial for the players.

In the Tour de France, individual competitors from different nations are arranged into teams and those teams are owned by one or more brands. For example, Bora Hansgrohe, Jayco, B&B Hotels, Intermarche, etc. Spectator loyalty in the Tour de France is based on the brand(s) the cyclists are riding for and the individual athlete. Martyn believed that this type of model would better suit female cricketers because women are excellent brand ambassadors,

Once Martyn and Sthalekar got the structure of the WICL tournament conceptualised in terms of one city, one venue, 78 players, 6 teams, 17 games, the International Cricket Council (ICC) instructed them to get a host nation's cricket board to back, approve and endorse their event. This would then pave the way for the ICC to formally "approve" the tournament. In the absence of this approval, the ICC indicated that the notion of what they called "approved" or "disapproved" cricket was applicable. Without the backing of a host nation board, WICL would be considered "disapproved", and as such, the ICC would not "release" cricketers to play in the tournament.

From the very beginning, Martyn envisioned that the tournament had to be played in an Associate Nation country, and not in a major Full Member Nation such as Australia, England, India, or South Africa. WICL's primary motive was to create playing opportunities for emerging female cricketers in the Associate Nations.

Articles have since been written suggesting that the formation of WICL pushed Cricket Australia to start the Women's Big Bash League (WBBL) and for the England & Wales Cricket Board (ECB) to accomplish more with their female program. WICL was the catalyst for those changes to happen.

Martyn and Sthalekar decided that Singapore might be an appropriate venue to host the inaugural WICL tournament. The city had an historic sports ground and an enclosed stadium named The Hub. Whilst it did not have a cricket wicket in it, that problem could be easily resolved with a "drop in" pitch. It also benefited from hydraulic seating, meaning that the seating could be moved closer to the boundary. One of the major issues troubling Martyn at this time was the fact that the women's games were being played on grounds that were too big for them. And that the boundary ropes had to be moved so far in that the resulting distance negatively affected the relationship between the crowd and the players and the building of an entertaining atmosphere in the ground.

Once they settled on the idea of Singapore, Martyn travelled to the city to meet the heads of the Singapore Cricket Association (SCA). He had, what he believed to be, a productive initial meeting with them. The WICL tournament concept had not been rejected out of hand, and Singapore Cricket's attitude was, on the face of it, encouraging.

Martyn toured The Hub, inspected the whole facility, and began to formulate a plan around Singapore being an appropriate host. In the meantime, he was told by the SCA to return to the ICC and get approval from them first before anything else could proceed. When he did this, the ICC told him, again, to go and secure the endorsement of a host nation's cricket board. Which is what he had already tried to do in Singapore and had been flicked back to ICC for their approval first. This uncooperative "ping-ponging" arrangement continued for some time.

In June 2014, Sthalekar travelled to Singapore with Martyn for a second meeting with Singapore Cricket. A member of the board of the SCA happened to also head up a law firm in central Singapore. Martyn and Sthalekar were given an audience with him at the law firm's offices, and they were seated on the opposite side of an imposing boardroom table.

Martyn clearly remembers the SCA board member saying to Sthalekar, "So I assume you are here because you play cricket?" Lisa Sthalekar, at this stage, had just retired from being the world's number-one-ranked all-rounder in women's cricket and was the former vice-Captain of the Australian national team. Martyn was offended on Sthalekar's behalf by the ill-informed question and can clearly remember Sthalekar nudging his leg under the table to warn him not to react.

Martyn attempted to explain the reality of what was going on in women's cricket and used an analogy. He suggested, quite cheekily, that the SCA board member should call all the female lawyers in his law firm into the room and tell them that he was going to pay them $15,000 per year even though all the male lawyers would continue to be paid whatever their current salaries were. Furthermore, that not every female lawyer would get $15,000 per year. Only the BEST female lawyers would get $15,000 per year. Martyn then challenged him to speculate what his staff's reaction to such news might be. Obviously, this hypothetical scenario was met with incredulity.

Martyn followed it up by adding, "This is exactly the situation that the world's leading female cricketers find themselves in. They are doing the same amount of work. They are spending as many hours at their tasks as the male players. The expectations on them as international players are the same. But the remuneration for all their effort is nothing".

Martyn and Sthalekar recall leaving that meeting with the representative of Singapore Cricket feeling extremely disillusioned. They decided that this "ping-ponging" arrangement between a potential host nation's cricket board and the ICC was just not going to work. They returned to Australia and attempted to come up with a new game plan to move things forward and around the increasing number of roadblocks being put in the way of progress. [See Further Reading for a letter from SCA]

Compared to today, in 2014, there were no podcast conversations and only scant press or social media commentary about women's cricket and the meagre amounts of pay female players were receiving. So, Martyn started to contact a few fringe journalists to promote what he, Sthalekar and WICL were attempting to do to alter the status quo, and to discuss with the media how they could better approach the matter.

Coverage started to emerge. Martyn specifically remembers some Women's Cricket blog posts by Martin Davies in England [see Further Reading]. They followed an interview Davies had had with Clare Conner at Wormsley Cricket

Ground wherein she had stated that cricket had to be wary of privately-run organisations like WICL because there was potential for "inherent corruption", and that a WICL tournament would be "uncontrolled" and "unsanctioned" by the ICC.

This interview and blog post triggers memories for Tony Wright, who was a senior executive at CISCO at the time and a strong advocate of the WICL cause. Wright was affronted by the interview's implications. He had been conducting a substantial amount of advisory and mentoring work for Martyn and was very passionate about the WICL mission. Wright felt disparaged due to his close association with WICL. I interviewed Tony Wright and extracts from my conversation with him are up next.

"For me, the highlight was being around the other squad players, learning from them on a cricket level (invaluable) and getting to meet very charismatic but also very different women from across the globe."

Poppy McGeown, France

Tony Wright
Leading Advocate

Tony Wright has held senior sales and marketing positions with IT companies such as CISCO, TechnologyOne, Symantec and Riverbed. He has been influential in the advice, guidance and mentoring of FairBreak over the years. His connections in the software space have also been invaluable to the organisation, and he is a strong public advocate for FairBreak's cause.

"I was there when it first began, as a concept, twenty years ago. I was head of marketing for CISCO Systems in Australia. In 2002 or thereabouts, Shaun was in event management and he helped me host corporate networking cricket matches between CISCO and its partners.

"Every man and his dog did golf days back then. At a golf day, you get to talk to three people for six hours. We decided to be innovative. And that is how it started, as a corporate networking exercise to increase the contact that CISCO's managers had with our business partners. Everyone got to bat and bowl. The camaraderie was great, everyone was competitive. Shaun used to run three or four events per year for us. We played at excellent venues, either quality school grounds or first grade cricket grounds. We even played the Barmy Army one year when they came out to Australia. We had baggy greens made and we played them at the University of NSW. We put these events on regularly for at least four or five years.

"Shaun used to invite professional cricketers to take part. We would pay $1,000 cash to each of them to play cricket with us. He would arrange a cricket match, in Melbourne for example, with high profile male cricketers like Merv Hughes, Geoff Lawson, Damien Wright or Damien Fleming for example. We would have 40 overs in the morning. Then have lunch, and then we would have another 40 overs in the afternoon. It was a very productive networking opportunity for fifty people. There'd be a sports dinner the night before with a guest speaker to talk about cricket. It was great, except everyone was so hungover the next morning, the cricket was a debacle!

"We started to get female cricketers involved. They were reticent at the start, until Lisa Sthalekar led the way. At the time, Lisa's total salary for playing professional cricket for Australia amounted to $5,000 per annum. When we paid her $1,000 to run around at our corporate networking events, she was earning one fifth of her annual wage in just one day. We paid the cricketers in cash and that is how the conversation first arose. I had just handed over, in an envelope, 20% of Lisa Sthalekar's entire annual salary, and she was the best female cricketer in the world at that time. I could not believe it. I was appalled. And so, I became Shaun's militant voice. We were outraged by the injustice of it all.

"I had no idea that this was the reality facing female athletes in Australia at the time, and in cricket especially. Lisa was also employed by Cricket NSW, and when she went away on tour to play for Australia, she had to take annual leave. It was wrong. So, we set about trying to do something about it.

"We decided to run a cricket tournament, and to invite female players, and we would pay them. But it quickly became apparent that the relationship the International Cricket Council (ICC) had with its players, females in particular, meant that this was going to be very difficult and we couldn't get any sanctions to play.

"Consequently, we decided to tinker with the focus and turn it into a movement. Because to make it work, it had to be about more than just cricket. It could not just be about the game, it had to be about equality of pay and opportunity. Every other field of endeavor was making progress on this front except cricket and female sport.

"We need to tell the story of the journey and share the reality of the obstacles that were overcome; it took years to get sanctioned by ICC, that is true. It took years of negotiations with the England & Wales Cricket Board to get sanctioned, that is true. Cricket Australia didn't want a bar of us, that is true.

"It was ironic that after having detailed conversations with Cricket Australia around the establishment of a professional tournament for females, in the following year, the Women's Big Bash appeared! The ECB wanted our tournament strategy before they would sanction us. Our financials, our strategy document, our plan, where our players were coming from. They wanted to know everything. We were placed in a situation where, without being clandestine, it was hard to challenge the establishment. And if we had not challenged the establishment, none of this would ever have happened. It would have been pushed into the background.

"I firmly believe that without Shaun Martyn, the Women's Big Bash League would never have happened. He unsettled Cricket Australia with his concept, and so our conversations became more about opportunity than the game. We knew we had to stop talking about cricket and start talking about opportunity. Because if we talked exclusively about cricket, the powers that be would shut us down. But they can't shut us down if we're not talking about it. They can't shut us down for creating opportunity, which is all we wanted to do. And that's why it had to become much bigger than cricket.

"I can remember having lots of meetings with Shaun and Lisa in the early days about how we could make this work. It quickly became obvious that it wasn't going to be easy. It had to be about more than female cricket to get attention, and over the last two or three years it has gone gangbusters in terms of the attention. But the first seven years were arduous. Shaun has staked everything he has on this mission.

"Shaun started to focus on female players outside of the Test playing nations. He had discovered some young women in Vanuatu who could really play. We started to hear stories where grants given to Associate Nations such as Vanuatu Cricket, for example, never made it to the women. The men would take all the money, while the women did not even have their own kit. Female players were not able to play because they didn't have any bats.

"Hearing this made me angry. This is not what handing out grants is all about. I was involved in Corporate Social Responsibility programs for CISCO at the time, and we focused heavily on indigenous health and education, particularly in Cape York. CSR programs are about creating sustainable opportunities for disadvantaged communities. That's what FairBreak is doing.

"It took a long time for FairBreak to be taken seriously as an organisation that was looking to improve the lot of female athletes across the world. Not just female cricketers in Australia, or female cricketers in the UK or New

Zealand for that matter. The West Indies were in a similar boat. There were even worrying stories and innuendo about the Sri Lankan national women's cricket team being forced to give sexual favours to earn or keep their places in the squad.

"We decided that this had to be a movement. A campaign to generate a level of understanding and interest that would fire people up to want to do something to fix the injustice. It took a long time to create momentum, but in the last two years progress has been outstanding and we've got some very high-profile supporters, patrons, and activists for FairBreak.

"Let's talk about pay. Probably 20% of female cricketers make their living exclusively from the game. Most female cricketers have a career outside of cricket in order to pay the bills. The difference in pay between the highest paid Australian men's player compared to the highest paid Australian women's player is absurd. The highest paid male cricketer in Australia in 2022 is probably Pat Cummins. His contract is $2 million a year. That's not his IPL money. That's not his Hundred money. That's just what Cricket Australia pays him. He probably earns another $2million from the IPL. So that's $4million. By the time he has done endorsements, he's perilously close to $6 million.

"In comparison, the highest paid Australian female cricketer is a different story altogether. Several sources say Ellyse Perry and Meg Lanning earn roughly $300,000 a year across international and domestic commitments.

"The minimum wages for Australian women in sport domestically are dramatically lower than the men. The average base salary for a woman who holds a contract in both WBBL and the WNCL is just over $65,000. Compare that to an average of $198,000 a year for a male player who plays all formats at domestic level.

"Meg Lanning, the captain of the Australian women's cricket team, and Ellyse Perry, who has the highest profile, are earning around $300,000 as a base salary. Pat Cummins is earning $2million. The captain of the men's team earns $2million and the captain of the women's team earns $300k. Granted there is still some disparity in the salaries of male and female senior executives in boardrooms, but the delta is not on this scale. The corporate ladder is levelling out slowly, but only because of the focus and attention that has been shone on it. [For more discussion on pay and conditions for female players see *Choose to Challenge* by Laura Jolly in Further Reading]

"Some sports are starting to wake up. Basketball. Women's soccer. The AFLW in Australia. But across all sports, there's still a really big gap in the parity of pay between male and female players. But at least there is profile about it now in cricket. And young girls have got a pathway, but they are all in the Tier 1 countries. FairBreak's point is there are hundreds more players out there who do not have this pathway. They don't have the role models, they don't have the opportunities, and it does not take much to give it to them.

"Shaun gave athletes from countries like Rwanda, Bhutan, and Nepal $10,000 each for playing in the FairBreak cricket tournament in Dubai. That's a lifetime's earnings for some of them. It changes lives. Huge sums are not needed. And that is the point FairBreak has been trying to get across to cricket boards over the years. It does not take much to transform countless lives, to make a difference, and to give female cricketers in Associate Nations the opportunities to play and the role models they don't have. The Pakistan Cricket Board get it. They think FairBreak is brilliant.

"Another point to make when it comes to money, is that FairBreak does not want franchisors owning players. FairBreak wants involvement and opportunity that is NOT being sponsored by cigarette companies, alcohol companies or gambling companies, and Shaun has managed to achieve that.

"The Dubai tournament was quite challenging financially, but the message was clear, it was a quality product. It was picked up on televisions around the world. Thirty-five countries were represented, which is more than at the Soccer World Cup. It was the climax of fifteen years of heartache for Shaun. His journey has been very long. The only role I have played in it all has been one of encouragement for him.

"FairBreak has half a dozen nations represented in each of their teams. They have increased the profile of second tier cricketing nations by taking them on tour and giving them opportunity in front of television audiences running into the millions. The data coming out of the Dubai tournament is massive. It is better than the Big Bash League here in Australia. The Women's World Cup sold out at the Melbourne Cricket Ground in March 2020. There were 86,000 people at the #FilltheG final in Melbourne. People love watching women's cricket.

"The battle for content is a no brainer. Every syndicated television channel on the planet is in an arm wrestle for content. Content is king, and there is no question that women's cricket is a high-quality product. Where the problem lies is how are those players who produce the product being remunerated? How are they being paid for their time, effort, and skills?

"I have been passionate about this subject for some time, and I am so proud of Shaun. This is a cause, not a game, and as soon as we got our heads around the fact that to be successful, it had to be about more than just a game, things started to change. Do you want to be involved in the mission? Do you want to sponsor a cricket team? Does your organisation want to be part of this movement? These questions are a long way from where we started.

"We are entitled to tell the story, and to share with the world Shaun's devotion to this project. The story is worth telling. The cause has been everything to him and it continues to be. The sacrifices that he has made to fight this battle are only the beginning.

"I have had plenty of conversations with Shaun over the years where he has wanted to give this up. It was so hard. He has put everything on the line for a cause. Not for a game. Shaun has now got many well-connected humans involved and this cause, hopefully, will keep going. But the ten years it has taken to get to this point have been heavy lifting. It is testament to Shaun's determination. Most people would have walked away by now because it has been so difficult. It has taken a toll on him personally and financially. He has given it everything. I always say you never get out what you deserve, but you always get out what you expect, and I have an expectation that FairBreak will fly in the next two years."

Vidya Rao
FairBreak's Head of Operations in India

*A small body of determined spirits fired
by an unquenchable faith in their mission
can alter the course of history*

Mahatma Gandhi

Mrs. Vidya Rao is FairBreak's Head of Operations in India. She is an economics graduate and has worked in India's corporate sector for over 25 years. She assists FairBreak with brand awareness and seeking sponsorship, not just in India, but globally. As a consultant and advisor for the movement, she builds relationships with potential corporate sponsors, advocates and patrons. She also oversees FairBreak's corporate social responsibility (CSR) initiative, Solar Buddy, which provides lights for energy impoverished women and children in India. Vidya is a treasured and tireless member of the FairBreak team who travels many miles in India spreading the FairBreak message. Vidya epitomises what it means to be a #fairbreaker.

"I have been with FairBreak from Day One. I was the first person Shaun onboarded when it was still WICL. He had come to India in 2013. He was in Mumbai, and back then, I was working for a private investment firm as vice president of customer relations. Somebody brought Shaun in to meet my boss saying that he wanted to talk about women's cricket, and that he was looking for people who would connect with the cause. I sat in the meeting and thought his presentation was wonderful.

"My boss decided that we didn't have the bandwidth to go ahead and do any work for him, but we could give advice. I thought the venture was unique and that we should support it. So, my boss gave me the go-ahead to take on the WICL work independently, outside of my job, so I have her to thank for giving me that opportunity.

"Shaun needed a list of people he could speak to about the project. He needed introductions in India's corporate sector. Not many people knew about women's cricket back then. They said nice things about it, but most people did not know how many countries played cricket nor the names of anyone who played. Alot of awareness had to be created. Shaun has done a fantastic job talking about women's sport, specifically women's cricket, in India.

"We started to build awareness in India that women's cricket must be looked at differently to men's cricket. Sport cannot be looked at just from a male's perspective. Women must have equal opportunity and status. Women's cricket is a different product. It is not a biproduct of the men's game.

"I gave Shaun a list of people and companies to meet with. Potential sponsors and backers in the Indian corporate world. Because I was in customer relations and I knew all the people, I set up the meetings for Shaun to go and pitch his message. I don't know how many people I sent him to see. I've lost count.

"Everyone was very positive, but they always wanted to know what return on investment they could expect. They all viewed it as a business venture. They could never understand that it was a movement that needed support to grow and stand on its own.

"Shaun has come to India many times over the years, and he has met with many people. We've come so far and that feels good. I'm not a cricketer and I don't understand cricket, but I understand what FairBreak is about; creating opportunities, giving equal status and opportunity to women so they can excel in any field. And we are using cricket as a medium to do that.

"I was married very early. I was told I could have a job, but a career was not possible. If I had been given the opportunity to excel as a younger woman, maybe I could be in a different space. I have no regrets now because I'm with FairBreak and I'm happy to be able to have a small influence on people's lives. That's more satisfactory than changing my own life. I'm happy where I am and I'm very thankful to Shaun and FairBreak.

"My family used to be a part of the cricketing world. I was married into a family who ran a cricket club in Delhi. I came from a small town called

Mangalore and I moved to Delhi after my marriage. My family ran a cricket club in Delhi where their boys would play. Back then, in 1988, I knew only a few names in cricket from hearing them on the radio. I didn't see women play the game, but I would go to the men's games. I would take and serve the lunch for their matches. My father-in-law ran the club, and he would arrange for the funding of the game and the lunch. That was my first connection with cricket. There was never cricket for the women and I always wished I could play. My mother understands the game better than me. She watches it on TV.

"Women are very strong, but sometimes they need support. FairBreak are creating opportunities for girls who have not been seen or heard before now. It has excited me so much to be reconnected with sport. My son used to play cricket, but he gave up. It's not easy to continue because there are too many people playing cricket in India.

"So that is my journey with FairBreak since 2013. When the first ball was bowled in Dubai, I was weeping. People were looking at me and asking me why I was weeping. Most people are not aware of the connection between FairBreak and me. But the people who know, came and hugged me and said, "Vidya, it's all right. You can feel happy. You can feel proud of what has been achieved". It was a moment I remember with such fondness.

"In the lead up to Dubai, my role was to talk to people and create awareness. I tried to get sponsors and investors in India and beyond. I have connections globally from working in a private bank, so I have arranged meetings about sponsorship with people in Canada, USA and London.

"While I was at the tournament in Dubai, I spoke to all the people who were there. The parents and the guests of the players. I asked them to spread awareness to others in their circles so that more people can get to know about FairBreak and what we are doing. As many people as possible, globally, need to know what we do. The close circles around the players, and people connected with cricket know about FairBreak, but beyond cricket is where we need to reach out and create awareness.

"I want people to talk about the brand, FairBreak, and know that it is an initiative using cricket as a medium to promote gender equality and create opportunity for women. That's my primary goal. To build brand awareness and to share how FairBreak is impacting the lives of players and their families. So that is what I'm doing: talking to people about FairBreak and trying to get sponsorship so that we can take the game to the next level.

"The Indian girls not being allowed to play at FairBreak at the last minute is a politically sensitive topic. It was very disappointing. Whatever was said and done, the players were looking forward to playing with some of the world's finest female cricketers. It impacted the Associate Nation girls in a different way. They all look up to the Indian players as their idols. For them, it was a wonderful opportunity missed.

"For our Indian girls, they missed out on being part of an initiative which is totally unique. All women should be supporting this cause, not just cricket players. I know the Indian players would have been very happy and proud to be a part of FairBreak. But without permission to play from the Board of Control for Cricket in India, the BCCI, they could not play. They could not break the rules. We did our best reaching out to the authorities. They didn't listen.

"I really don't understand the reasons why the Indian girls were not allowed to play at FairBreak. There was an opportunity lost for both sides. The Indian girls missed out on playing in a distinctive type of team. I watched all the training and all the games during the tournament in Dubai, and every player improved over the fifteen days. That's what I noticed. And I am not a cricketer. If I noticed it, then I am sure others who know cricket much better than me observed it also. A vital opportunity was lost to build the confidence of our Indian girls. Every player at the Dubai Tournament grew in confidence over those fifteen days. They blossomed.

"I spoke to one of the Associate Nation girls, she was from Nepal or Bhutan, I cannot remember which. She was so excited to be playing with or facing Suzie Bates. It was beautiful that she was so keen to have the chance to learn from Suzie and the other big-name players.

"When I think about the roadblocks FairBreak has faced over the eight years I have been involved, there are two that come to mind. Firstly, businesspeople I speak to believe that FairBreak is a good concept and a fantastic initiative. But funding is always an issue. I am still not able to understand why we are not able to get the right kind of funding for a global initiative like this.

"FairBreak has all the right principles, and it is a perfect product. Promoting gender equality and creating opportunities for women, everybody always agrees with that. Initially, everyone looked at it very sceptically. But today, the question marks have gone. They believe and understand that it is a good initiative, but when it comes to funding, I still cannot crack it. What is it that's stopping them?

"Secondly, when I talk to people, the main thing they focus on is the media. Everybody is hungry for publicity, a portrayal of who they are, and what they are. The key question is always about our media coverage. Everybody asks if we are on television. Social media platforms have taken off in a big way globally. Even in India, social media is huge. But people in India always ask if FairBreak is on television.

"I need to meet a few people from the media sector and understand what needs to be done for a product like ours to crack into the media and increase visibility globally. Then getting sponsors or supporters to come on board will be easier. I think the platform FairBreakX, needs to target the student demographic. Anybody and everybody who is interested in cricket should be on that platform. We need to work on that."

I asked Vidya Rao how she thinks the marketing of women's cricket needs to change to grow audiences globally. Millions of female social media users are not aware of women's cricket, even those in cricket playing nations. I live in Australia, home of the Women's Big Bash League, but until I started writing for FairBreak, I was completely ignorant of women's cricket and that there is such an enormous disparity in how female cricketers, and other female athletes for that matter, are remunerated or broadcast compared to their male counterparts.

We need to capture the attention of women globally who will have powerful opinions on this subject. Even though they may have never played cricket, women love to hear inspiring stories about what other females are achieving in sport.

We must find a way to reach those women who don't play or watch cricket, but who will connect with the essence of the FairBreak movement. We need to find a way to share the fascinating and empowering back stories of FairBreak's female cricketers. Vidya Rao believes the answer to this lies in the power of the influencer.

She said, "The India Premier League is into its twelfth season and there is a huge amount of money associated with it. More importantly, the visibility of the IPL is tremendous. There is a film industry in every region of India, and we have film stars all over the country. I have approached a couple of these celebrities and talked to them about helping FairBreak build brand awareness. Many of our Indian film stars have hundreds of thousands of followers. Social media impact comes from having the right set of influencers and the right communication. We need powerful influencers to be sharing the essence and the mission of FairBreak.

"Also, a static social media post isn't enough anymore. FairBreak needs to move more into posting reels and engaging visual content. Some of our players are celebrities in their own country with millions of followers. They need to keep posting and talking about FairBreak in their respective countries after they've gone home or moved on to another tournament. We need those players, the physios, the coaches, the managers and everyone to spread the FairBreak message".

"It was amazing exposure for Associate Nations to grow under legendary coaches and players and playing with such nice players for the first time; all were so humble and supportive throughout the tournament. I'm looking forward to more opportunities. It opened new opportunities as other nationals are now aware that there are players from Sweden. It's an amazing feeling to get to know players from different countries; there's a lot to learn and admire."

Gunjan Shukla, Sweden

The South Pacific Training Camp
Auckland, October 2015

The term FairBreak first emerged in 2015. Martyn recounted, "We embarked on a training program in Auckland for a select group of players from Vanuatu, Fiji, New Caledonia, Papua New Guinea and Singapore.

"We invited other nations from the South Pacific region, but they chose not to send players. Their view at the time was that we were not an approved body so there might be some blow back on them if they sent players.

"We even found it hard to find an opposition team to play in some practice games because of this perception that we were not an ICC approved body. Eventually a group of New Zealand based female cricketers came together to play us and it was a fantastic experience for our WICL players to have that opportunity to test themselves against players of a much higher standard.

"The South Pacific Training Camp in Auckland served several purposes. Firstly, to provide visibility on playing standards, approaches, and current coaching methods. Secondly, to collect footage and interviews for a documentary film. Thirdly, to build awareness of what was then WICL and what we were attempting to do.

"We called the documentary *Fair Break*. A play on the Australian expression of a 'fair go' while mashing it with the leg-break and off-break delivery terms used in cricket. The documentary was never fully realized but the seeds of FairBreak had been sown.

"During that training camp, the colours of our playing and training kit were also selected. A United Nations blue, black and white and magenta. Not pink. Later, we simplified the organisation's base colours to just black and magenta."

[Further Reading contains a WICL letter to Vanuatu Cricket from Lisa Sthalekar dated 27th October 2015 detailing the successful outcomes of the South Pacific Training Camp]

David Sexton
Friend and Advisor

David Sexton is the Chief Executive Officer of WeFlex Pty Ltd, an organisation that connects people with a disability to mainstream fitness and health providers. WeFlex facilitate training to ensure confidence in health professionals and they leverage the power of technology to change lives.

Sexton is also the Chair of the What Ability Foundation, a not-for-profit working towards better community access for people living with a disability or diminished capacity and the families who love and care for them. The Foundation offers a range of opportunities by partnering with companies providing ticketed sport, adventures, accommodation, dining and entertainment experiences. By breaking down barriers and unlocking experiences for individuals and families living with disability, they are given equality of access to the communities in which they live.

Shaun Martyn first met David Sexton through conferencing and his event management roles in consulting and training. They have known each other for nearly twenty years.

When the Women's International Cricket League was first established, they explored synergies because Sexton was the General Manager at Pymble Ladies College (PLC) on Sydney's North Shore. There was an opportunity to get the students involved because it is an extraordinarily strong sporting school. Ellyse Perry, currently Australia's most high-profile female cricketer, attended Pymble Ladies College. Sexton and Martyn discussed the objectives of WICL and they formed a strong connection.

Sexton is enthusiastic about sport. He is passionate about equality and pushing the agenda. He is a father of three daughters and was happy to help. At the time, Martyn and Sthalekar were both driving WICL, and Sexton assisted them by acting as a sounding board, providing strategic advice, opening networks and connections within PLC and elsewhere, and supporting them wherever he could.

In October 2015, Sexton and the school's deputy principal, Julie Shaw, went to New Zealand to support the WICL South Pacific Training Camp at King's College in Auckland. King's College is a co-educational secondary day and boarding school. Twelve female cricketers from South Pacific nations and Singapore were invited to attend. The intensive cricket training camp was run by Martyn, Sthalekar and Lawson. Two students from Pymble Ladies College also travelled to Auckland to shoot some videography for a short documentary about WICL called *Fair Break*, and to write blogs and social media posts for the event.

Sexton and Shaw supported the WICL team and the students during the Auckland trip and he expanded on this when he stated, "The principal of PLC at the time was Vicki Waters and she was very encouraging and receptive to the project because I was heavily involved. Vicki also had a zeal to drive gender equality, and to be a global thought leader when it came to the college and its outlook, so WICL resonated with her straight away.

"There was no financial commitment from Pymble Ladies College to WICL. What Shaun was looking to do was leverage capacity through the students and staff. Having a couple of students and a staff member go over to New Zealand to support the digital and social aspects of the training camp was mutually beneficial. The South Pacific Training camp was a way to integrate and get the students involved in an important mission. When they came back, the girls spoke to the rest of the school about their experiences, what they did and how they supported the event. Vicki then continued a dialogue with Shaun after I left the college, and she continued supporting him until she left the college."

Sexton assisted with logistical support on the ground in Auckland in terms of the students and the cricketers on the tour. He and Julie Shaw formally represented Pymble Ladies College at the event. Shaw took care of student management. Sexton supported the camp logistically and practically and wherever Martyn needed him to by driving the minibus, filling water bottles, and putting up stumps.

Sexton declares that the organisation's drive, intent, and purpose has remained almost unchanged over the years. Now that it is known as FairBreak, it is all about pushing opportunity and gender equality through sport and through cricket particularly.

Today, Sexton's involvement with FairBreak is light touch. Occasionally, he acts as a sounding board for Martyn who now benefits from having "lots of excellent people around him". In the early days, Sexton introduced Martyn to Kimberly Lee, who was doing some work for him at PLC. Lee has been supporting Martyn in a marketing capacity ever since.

When asked for his views on how far Martyn has come, David Sexton said, "I watched some of the Dubai Tournament, the highlights, and all the social media content. It was fantastic to see Shaun's vision come to life. He is a remarkable guy. He has poured so much of himself into this cause; emotionally, financially, his career. To see the tournament finally take place is a credit to his resilience and his inner drive. I am sure it has taken quite a toll on him. These events are hard work, and he has been fighting this battle for nearly a decade.

"Shaun is the lone voice out there trying to run an event at scale globally from the start. He is not piloting it in one country. He is bringing cricketers from places like Namibia, USA, Singapore, the UK, the Netherlands, New Zealand, Bhutan, Nepal, and Vanuatu. It has been a global effort right from the start. It needs to be, to showcase the mission. And that is incredibly challenging logistically, dealing with countries on every continent. But he is tenacious, and he has kept on battling, having the conversations, and getting the message out to more people.

"There have been diverse levels of roadblock. Getting endorsement from the ICC for this tournament was the biggest roadblock and getting the message across to them that FairBreak is not a breakaway, rebel organisation. Getting financial backing has also been difficult. It is problematic to get financial support at scale if you do not have a tangible product or an offering to show to a sponsor. Now that the first Invitational has been successfully delivered, and the metrics are in place, it will be much easier to sell future events."

Blog Post – *Dreams Do Come True*
by Lisa Sthalekar

After WICL's South Pacific Training Camp at King's College in Auckland, Lisa Sthalekar posted the following reflection to her personal blog, dated 13th November 2015.

"Inspired, exhausted, elated, emotional, motivated, sleep deprived, passionate, and relieved are just some of the emotions that I am feeling after completing Women's ICL's first cricket program in Auckland, New Zealand.

"Playing cricket at the highest level for Australia for over twelve years afforded me some amazing opportunities that I will be forever grateful for. These included the opportunity to travel the world, the opportunity to meet a diverse range of people, the opportunity to be treated like I really mattered, the opportunity to learn and the opportunity to do what I love with passionate, generous, and driven people. I have made lifelong friends. I have been taken care of and it has meant that I have always had a support network around me.

"Therefore, when I retired from international cricket in February 2013, I wanted to give back to the game which has given me so much. Anyone who knows me, or who has followed my career, knows how much I love the game of cricket. So post-retirement I knew that I would stay involved in some way, and I knew that what I was most passionate about was finding a way to engage with female players across the world and to find a way of giving them a chance, even if it is just a brief chance, of experiencing what I have been fortunate enough to experience.

"It was about two years ago I teamed up with my manager at the time, Shaun Martyn, and we both set about starting the business, Women's ICL. Our vision was (and still is) to create Opportunity, Performance and Education, through the vehicle of women's cricket. It is my passion, as it's my chance to leave the game in a better place than when I came into it.

"Not only is our goal to support female cricketers on the field, but also to create opportunities for players who are less fortunate than myself. Having had a brief chance to work with the Argentinean Women's cricket team (Flamingos) in 2011, it was evident that they hadn't had the chance to be exposed to the intensity and standard of women's international cricket. If you were not lucky enough to be eligible to play for the national team of one of the Full Member ICC countries, your potential exposure to elite cricket as a female was virtually non-existent.

"Like all startup ventures, there were and still are, so many lessons that you learn along the way, not only about yourself, your business partner, but also the world of business and the politics that are inevitably involved.

"Have we made some mistakes along the way? No doubt we have. If we had our time again there would be some things which we may approach differently with the benefit of hindsight.

"That being said, whilst standing at King's College in Auckland, with twelve players from Associate ICC countries running around, with WICL having been able to fund their attendance at a two-day high performance camp, enjoying each other's company, using great facilities, learning more about the game of cricket and being filmed by a group of talented Pymble Ladies College students, I caught myself feeling briefly overwhelmed by the realisation that my dream had come true.

"Earlier this week, WICL's 'Fair Break' program came to life. The impetus for its birth arose when I was lucky enough to watch a documentary earlier this year about Team SCA, the first all-female team since 2002 to complete in the toughest ocean race in the world, the Volvo Ocean Race. The documentary covered the selection process that took place in finding the fourteen team members from five nations and then of course the race itself.

"This instantly resonated with me as being something we could do in the context of cricket and Shaun and I decided it would be great opportunity to provide players from Associate ICC countries with a chance to come together, meet other skilled cricketers and continually learn about the game of cricket in a high performance environment they had not necessarily been involved with before. In addition, we entered into a partnership with Pymble Ladies College (PLC), to have four students attend WICL's camp to provide real life learning experiences for their students. The students will be actively engaged in the creation and delivery of the WICL *Fair Break* documentary and supporting the creation of other online content.

"Sport has such a unique capacity to bring different cultures together and through the language of sport, break down so many barriers. I certainly witnessed this firsthand, not for the first time, earlier this week.

"As you would expect, I have been a part of probably over a hundred cricket camps in my time as a player and a coach, but what made this one extremely special to me was that we had players from five different countries (Papua New Guinea, New Caledonia, Fiji, Vanuatu, and Singapore) and within a matter of less than twenty four hours they had bonded like a team.

"The love of cricket certainly bound them, but it was also their singing and dancing that completed the unification. It was evident that music is something so strong in each of their cultures that helped the process immediately. Even more special was seeing how the players and the students bonded instantly through sport, singing and dancing. Within no time, the girls were all starting to absorb and learn each other's native language.

"Thank goodness one of the PLC students spoke fluent French, as the two players from New Caledonia hardly spoke or understood a word of English. There were constant cries out for Zoe to come and help translate what we were saying from a coaching point of view.

"During my career, I was fortunate enough to train and play at the best facilities. It came as a huge shock to me that there were five players that had never played on turf before, despite representing their country. Plus, a number of players didn't own cricket gear, such as a bat or pads, making it difficult to train.

"As many of you know, nearly all high performance cricket camps will involve a component of cricket match play as a way of facilitating tactical learning opportunities. We were fortunate enough to provide valuable match time for the players, with an Invitational XI consisting of Provincial Representative players to play against.

"Even just that opportunity to play against a stronger opposition allowed us to assess the players more meaningfully from a tactical perspective and to rate their performance under pressure. The most pleasing thing from my point of view was the players improved in such a short amount of time.

"Of course, projects like this cannot happen without the generous support of people behind the scenes. We could not have run the program and funded all of the players to attend the camp without our very generous sponsors, Hertz, Rudy Project, NicStar, New Balance and Yaru Water for making it happen. Plus, a very special thanks to FitBit and SKINS who provided gear and a FitBit watch to each of the players to take home with them and hopefully inspire more female players to pick up a bat and ball in their regions.

"I can't wait to share with you what we were able to achieve in such a small time. Please start to follow our Facebook, Twitter (@WICLNews) and now Instagram (wiclnews) to catch all the news of this last camp and us building towards our next camp. Where will the next one be?"

"I was happy at the end that I was in a team where I could feel comfortable. I could just be myself, and just play cricket and have fun and enjoy it. Everyone was very encouraging and gave support like, "go out there and have fun". It was exciting, so I was very happy to be part of the Barmy Army family."

Selina Solman, Vanuatu

Isabelle Duncan
Women's Cricket Historian and Commentator

"FairBreak is a tale of gritty determination"

Isabelle (Izzy) Duncan is a highly respected English cricket writer, MCC player, coach, and a commentator for BBC Radio 5's Sports Extra. She first met Shaun Martyn during the Men's and Women's Ashes Series in England in August 2013. Martyn had just read Duncan's book *Skirting the Boundary – A History of Women's Cricket* and had contacted her for a meeting. He was in London to meet Clare Connor at the England & Wales Cricket Board (ECB), so the pair caught up over a coffee at The Oval Cricket Ground.

During their meeting, Martyn explained the concept of WICL which Duncan considered "a fantastic idea for the Associates, affiliates and all the female players around the world who do not get a look in, because there is no money, or money does not reach them. Nothing was happening for the female players in the Associate Nations. Nobody was unearthing the raw talent hidden there."

Duncan was impressed with Martyn's vision. She said, "Shaun had really big ideas right from the start. Whether it was to do with the use of technology or the stadium. I thought all his ideas were really appealing and very different. He was almost, I hate to say it, like the Kerry Packer of women's cricket. But his motivations were different. Kerry Packer was in it for the money, whereas for Shaun it was about revealing the quality of talent and reaching those female players globally who were getting no opportunity to play.

"Shaun was getting no traction with the ECB. Cricket Australia hadn't really given him the time of day, and the ICC were hopeless. So as a private enterprise, he needed to get allies on board. Influential people. Companies. Because he knew it was going to be a long haul; that it would take time to make change happen."

With Martyn in England, Duncan set about introducing him to suitable patrons, setting up meetings and getting some big names on board. First up, was Sir John Major, the UK's former Prime Minister, who loves women's cricket and has always been supportive of it. He was very happy to endorse WICL as a patron. Former cricketers, Mike Brearley and Mick Gatting, were also happy to sign up as patrons.

"Shaun is great when he is in front of individuals, selling the movement and persuading people it's a good idea, even though it was very much "off-piste" as far as cricket was concerned. We went to see a friend of mine at Goldman Sachs and had one or two other meetings. And then Shaun took off to visit the Singapore Cricket Association.

"These meetings did not, particularly, come to anything back then, but it was all about spreading the word, getting people talking about WICL, and getting some commercial interest. But it was such a novel concept. People were distrustful of a private enterprise like this. They thought Shaun was in it just for the money. We really had to persuade them that this was not about him.

"Shaun's personality and passion made it work. Basically, he has given up his life for this project. I first met him in 2013, and he has always been single-minded, determined, and full of self-belief in the concept, the project, the dream, the vision that this is going to work. But there was negativity, and constant knockbacks from the boards and the cricket establishment. Shaun was not looking to compete with them. He was trying to get their support and endorsement."

Duncan recalls flying out to Dubai in 2015 to meet with the ICC about the FairBreak movement and to attempt to lobby the organisation on Martyn's behalf. She said, "The ICC were not keen for various reasons. Essentially, they like control. They want to be in charge. They don't like mavericks. They don't like people doing their own thing. They could see that FairBreak would embarrass them, because at that point the ICC were doing very little for the women of the Associate Nations. There was no funding reaching them. No opportunities to play were being created. The world was unaware of all the raw talent in the Associate Nations. The ICC had other projects happening and unearthing female talent wasn't a priority for them."

Duncan met with Holly Colvin, the former England bowler who was working at the ICC in Dubai after retiring from her international cricket career. Colvin had just started with the ICC and was employed as a Women's Development Officer, the first time the ICC had put somebody in that role. Duncan also met with a male Development Officer who was higher up in the organisation. She could detect that they were defensive and paying her lip service.

"I was not really getting anywhere. I was trying to sell them a story they already knew. They were a bit hostile. They had already discussed it behind closed doors. And this is what happened to Shaun all the time. Met with a brick wall. No co-operation. It was a shame. It was very frustrating."

In the meantime, Martyn had started to organise a few exhibition matches and invited women from around the world to play. He organised a training camp in Auckland, New Zealand with some players from the South Pacific region and hosted minor events that did not require the ICC's involvement or permission.

On the 30th of May 2018, Duncan commentated the very first Sir Paul Getty XI v FairBreak XI match at Wormsley Park in England. It was named the Day of Gender Equality. She recalled, "Sponsorships, funding, interest, and some media exposure followed. The match was live streamed worldwide. Henry [Geoff] Lawson, Australia's former test bowler was commentating with me. He believes wholeheartedly in the project. Shaun has picked up some great allies along the way. He is very persuasive, and the whole movement is a great idea.

"It has taken so long. Most people would have just given up and accepted that it was going nowhere. They would have retreated and moved on to something else, got a job and made some money. But Shaun has stayed with it. I have admired that over the years. Of course, I had my doubts too. Five years went by, and I saw little happening. But then suddenly in 2021, FairBreak got ICC sanctioning for a tournament in Hong Kong and it was action stations! To get the endorsement of the ICC was fantastic. It came from nowhere really. And then the COVID-19 pandemic hit the world.

"In terms of the hurdles and opposition that Shaun and FairBreak have faced up until now, the biggest has been dealing with the individual boards, like Cricket Australia and the ECB. Without their endorsement, he could not get the big-name players like England's Charlotte Edwards or Australia's Nicola Carey. They are all professionally contracted and without the permission of their boards they are not allowed to play. He needed the boards' endorsements, as a bare minimum, for the ICC to sanction any FairBreak tournament.

"The ECB and Cricket Australia were the two major boards Shaun needed to get on side. And he worked very hard to convince both. But he was continually knocked back. Sometimes executives on these cricket boards would not see him or would ignore him. The ICC even had somebody on staff who was tasked with preventing Shaun from progressing anything and keeping an eye on him, WICL and later FairBreak.

"Obviously, they saw Shaun as a threat at first. But now it has worked out well with the ICC's endorsement, as we always knew it would. With the ICC on board, you would expect the other Member Nations to follow suit. But it is still difficult. There are still hurdles to be overcome.

"With the ICC, it's all about control. I'm not involved with the ICC. I am not an insider. There is nobody on the inside of the ICC we can talk to about it. So, I am guessing that they want to be in control, that they ultimately want their own tournament under their own banner. An ICC tournament that they organise. But they haven't done that. They seem to have other priorities elsewhere.

"Ultimately that is probably what they want to do. Rather than having an outsider like Shaun disrupting the status quo, Packer style. Kerry Packer, and his World Series Cricket, was seen as the "anti-Christ" in the late 1970s. But in fact, all Packer had was a distant and fantastic vision, which eventually turned out to be the future of cricket. He just got there a lot earlier than everybody else. And that is what Shaun is trying to do for women's cricket, but without the Packer cheque book."

Isabelle Duncan was invited to join the commentating team for the FairBreak Invitational in Dubai in May 2022. She speaks glowingly of the experience, "The tournament in Dubai was incredibly successful and exciting.

There were all these players no none had heard of who will, no doubt, get contracts. They will end up in the Women's Big Bash League, the Charlotte Edwards Cup, or The Hundred. Or the Women's IPL which needs to happen soon. It will not be long before we see a female player from Japan or a young girl from Vanuatu playing in one of these tournaments and getting paid big bucks. It's exciting to think that it was FairBreak who made that happen.

"It was fantastic, progressive, and positive to have all these women playing together. The learning curve in Dubai was exceptional. Women who had never played with or against international players before; never been paid to play under lights with a little bit of a crowd and TV cameras. All of that was new to many of these players. As well as playing with women from the Full Member Nations. It was fantastic for them to learn from the likes of Mignon du Preez or Heather Knight. In Dubai there was opportunity; the vibe was, "It does not matter who you are, we believe in you".

"It did not matter if the player was unknown, a small fish, or if they were a big name. Everybody got the same bite of the cherry. And it was like that across the board. Whether you were a commentator or in charge of social media. Whether you were a player, a coach or a manager, everybody received the same level of respect and a chance to get immersed into it.

"I thought that was brilliant. From my own personal perspective, I got the chance to do a pitch report. I've never done a pitch report before. I was very happy to do it. It was all incredibly nerve-wracking because tens of millions of people were watching the whole tournament on TV. It was wonderful that FairBreak believed I could do this.

"It is the belief that FairBreak has in you that gives everyone the confidence to go forward. This philosophy applies to everybody. There were players who were told, "You are opening the bowling today. We think you have huge potential".

"Shaun motivates people to get outside of their comfort zones. Most people would have been well out of their comfort zones. For many participants it was their first chance at having a go.

"For me, it was the first time I had been in a TV studio previewing a game live. The FairBreak team told me I could do it. That is their attitude. To give people who are not well-known a chance to shine. And that is what it is all about. It isn't about big names at the box office. It's about empowering people. Imagine what that does for the confidence of a twenty-one-year old cricket player from Sweden or Tanzania? To have an organisation backing them and paying them professionally?

"To be professionally paid to play cricket shows complete appreciation and value in what you do. This will sink deep into those players who have been ignored. In many countries, these female players are not treated with the respect they should be. To get paid and to play on a global stage, and for viewers in their country to see them doing so, it's transformative. Everybody's outlook, view and perception of women's cricket has changed. It is very powerful.

"There was a wonderful buzzy positiveness happening behind the scenes of the Dubai tournament. As the first major tournament that FairBreak had put on, there was bound to be trepidation about how it might turn out. But from day one, bang, off it went and we all thought, "Wow! This is going very well. It's entertaining." It was great cricket and the quality of play was amazing.

"Right from the first coin toss, there were players from Associate Nations taking wickets, and scoring runs. This was exactly what we wanted. It worked well. Shaun had obviously carefully hand-picked his operational people. The people employed by FairBreak to deliver the event did so very professionally. And the next tournament will be even better because they will have learned tricks from the first tournament. They will tighten up and sharpen operations. It will be a slick machine.

"Roberta Moretti-Avery, who is the Captain of Brazil's women's cricket team is in the UK right now [I interviewed Isabelle Duncan in early August 2022] and she is giving a number of interviews about FairBreak to the media. She is here in Europe to play cricket in the FairBreak XI exhibition matches in England, Scotland, and the Netherlands. She was on *Tailenders* yesterday, that's the biggest cricket podcast in the UK, hosted by Jimmy Andersen."

Duncan planned to attend the FairBreak XI exhibition games during August 2022 and to do some networking on behalf of FairBreak. She intended taking her friend Shayam Bhatia, a Dubai contact she has known since her 2015 trip to the United Arab Emirates to lobby for Martyn at the ICC. Shayam

Bhatia is an Indian steel magnate who is very supportive of cricket. He has a charity, his own foundation, and FairBreak are keen to get him on board as a patron. Duncan hoped to take Bhatia along to a couple of the FairBreak XI matches at the Wormsley Estate and Arundel Castle in England.

She revealed, "During the FairBreak Invitational, we all had dinner with Shayam and visited his cricket museum in Dubai which houses the world's largest privately owned collection of cricket memorabilia. It's incredible. It now features some FairBreak pieces donated by Shaun. Shayam did the coin toss for the final of the tournament. He arrived in his Bentley, got out and ran out into the middle of the pitch, spun the coin, and had a chat with the players and officials. He was treated like a king. He loved the whole experience."

In terms of how the marketing of women's cricket needs to change and adapt, Duncan said, "I think the Dubai tournament was a very good example of how the marketing should happen. We all know that social media plays a massive role. So, if you have, for example, highlights of Shizuka Miyaji, the Japanese girl taking her five wickets, and the celebrations of some of the players, that really captures the imagination. People will watch it, but their concentration span is only about five seconds. Engaging reels on social media work very well, and of course good quality TV broadcasting. Spinning it out to all those territories - FairBreak hit 142 countries - and getting the very best social media people on board and projecting all these engaging characters.

"From an Indian point of view, because India is the leading cricket nation with all the money in the world. People in India are fixated on players rather than teams. They get obsessed with the players as individuals, and the players have millions and millions of followers on their social media accounts. I think that's the way that women's cricket should go, and it's certainly the way I think the Dubai tournament went. It was all about the characters. And we had some very special characters from different countries doing all sorts out there on the pitch. It worked really well.

"For the next tournament, you don't need to have the same teams exactly. But you don't want to change them too much because a team in itself has a personality and a character. I think it is about the individuals and their heroics, and I think that is what went down really well globally during the tournament.

"In terms of the future of women's cricket as a whole, it will be good when we get the women's IPL going, because up until now they've just had exhibition matches on the side. They've got some sort of a tournament going on out there, but it's not really getting noticed and needs to be a proper women's IPL. It will probably look a lot like the Men's IPL in terms of marketing, getting it out there, the crowds and the TV. India is now realising, very late in the day, that their women players have a massive following. They're getting into T20 finals. They're getting into 50-over finals. And millions of people are watching and following the players. They've realised that there's money to be made out of the women.

"India will make it happen. They're just so slow out of the blocks. This could have happened years ago and everybody would have benefited from it. They need to get the Women's IPL going and invite the best players from around the world just like they do for the Men's IPL, and that will be massive exposure that will boost the women's game even more.

"We have The Hundred in England, which has been a huge success for the women. I'm a bit dubious about the Men's Hundred, but the Women's Hundred here has been a massive launchpad for the development players. It's a bit like the Associate players getting their time in the sun and their opportunities.

"With The Hundred, there is a rule, that they need to have perhaps three, I'm guessing, development players in their side. The Hundred has brought forward some new players who've been really exciting to watch and you've got the internationals coming in too.

"It's those sorts of tournaments that are going to boost the women's game. Sadly, Test cricket is not going in the right direction for women. I want it to because it's the pinnacle of the game and the women who play cricket at the highest level want to play and are hungry for it. But they don't play enough. Look at India, they probably play once every four or five years, which is criminal really, and it's to do with TV rights, and them not wanting to cover it for four days.

"The Ashes for the women, is part of a multi format system which works quite well. There are three ODIs, three T20s and one Test match. That's the brainchild of Clare Conner. It works well because it gives context and meaning to the Test match rather than just a stand-alone Test match which would be a bit meaningless. You gain points for each match and everything's linked up. So that works and could work well across the board. And we [England] did play a Test match against South Africa this year. South Africa haven't played Test cricket for years and years, which is sad, but they played superbly. Most of their team had never played a Test match before and it went for four days. It was a great game. To perform like that having had no experience of playing the long game, most of those players had probably only played T20 and 50-overs. There's no doubt, women are very capable and their Test cricket can be entertaining.

"But the ICC and the boards are not focused on that. FairBreak will want to play a Test match to show that this can be done, that this can be entertaining, that TV will cover it and that people will watch it. There's talk of a warm-up Barmy Army, but I don't think they're playing a four-day game against the Barmy Army. There has been talk of FairBreak playing a Barmy Army XI and turning it into a Test match. The whole Women's T20 format around the world just needs to get more established, so that countries have their own franchises. It's looking quite positive.

"The Lionesses recently winning the UEFA European Women's Championships will boost the watching of women's sport as a whole. And right now [August 2022], we have the Commonwealth Games happening, so they'll have a lot of younger, development players in their T20 sides. It's a good place for them to flourish and attract attention.

"We had to work hard to lobby to get women's cricket into these Commonwealth Games, which is a big deal. Because not since 1998, in the Kuala Lumpur Commonwealth Games when the men played a 50-over competition, has cricket been in the Commonwealth Games. Which is an oddity considering it's the most widely played sport in the Commonwealth.

"Once we get a foot in the door with the Commonwealth Games, next will be the Olympics. If we get women's cricket into the Olympics that would be fantastic! What a great global market! Everybody in the whole world watches the Olympics and it is a sport that some people won't have really watched or understood before. And if it was just the women's game in the Olympics, even better, because the focus will be on them."

The FairBreak XI Tours to England in 2018 and 2019

Throughout 2014 and 2015, WICL continued trying to get approval from the ICC with no success. In late 2015, Sthalekar decided that she needed to move out of the business because she felt her brand, position and future job prospects were being compromised, and that the upper echelons of the cricketing establishment might shut her out. She was already on the board of FICA, the Federation of International Cricket Associations, so advocating for change around employment rights and player welfare was still her on her radar. She felt that the WICL business venture was not proceeding in the direction it should be, that they were getting the run around, and that she needed to move on. And so it was amicably agreed that Martyn would take over the business.

The first thing Martyn did was to change the company's name from WICL to FairBreak Global Pty Limited, a private company registered in Australia. He then took the organisation through a process of rebranding. Kimberly Lee came on board to consult around branding and PR, and Sucheta Gorolay around strategy. Paul Harvey and Martyn spent time thinking through how the business could work from this point forwards.

During these years, there was much happening behind the scenes in India. Martyn was conducting numerous meetings on the sub-continent, with the assistance of Vidya Rao, to garner support, to find patrons, sponsors and partners, and to promote the value of women's cricket. It was a very challenging period.

In 2018 an invitation to play the first Sir Paul Getty Women's XI on the Wormsley Cricket Ground arrived courtesy of Alistair Cane. Cane had played club cricket with Geoff Lawson in Sydney and was now the Director of Operations at Wormsley in Buckinghamshire, one of the most beautiful cricket grounds in England.

Paul Harvey and Martyn had always shared the view that they needed to get an exhibition game on the ground to demonstrate to the world what FairBreak was all about, and what they were trying to achieve. This would be a landmark event for FairBreak.

On the 30th of May 2018, FairBreak launched their inaugural Day of Gender Equality with a cricket match on the picturesque grounds at Wormsley between the Sir Paul Getty Women's XI and the newly formed FairBreak XI. The match was livestreamed internationally and was a tremendous success in terms of demonstrating exactly what FairBreak was all about; bringing together the best female cricketers to be found in different parts of the world to compete as one.

The first ever Sir Paul Getty Women's XI was skippered by the revered English Captain, Charlotte Edwards, England's greatest ever player, and included many stars from England and New Zealand. Suzie Bates agreed to lead a FairBreak XI that included Shamilia Connell from the West Indies and Australia's most capped female player at that time, former Women's Captain, Alex Blackwell.

It was a wonderful experience for all participants and the first example of what a FairBreak Global XI could look like. The forerunner to the teams in a global tournament. That first FairBreak XI team had seven current or past national captains in it.

Energy levels were high with the excitement, nerves and gratitude felt by players from around the globe meeting for the first time, some having experienced their first ever international flight to get to the event. The FairBreak Global management team had worked tirelessly to bring to life their vision of gender equality. The day kicked off with a summit involving key advocates for gender equality and FairBreak supporters participating in a robust discussion about the need to progress gender equality globally. Many key stakeholders shared their insights and thoughts around tackling major issues including equal pay and governance.

The Sir Paul Getty Women's XI v FairBreak XI T20 exhibition match on the 30th of May 2018 was a world first and accomplished several notable ambitions; it was the first time a women's cricket team had comprised women from ten countries across five continents. It was the first time the Sir Paul Getty Foundation had fielded a women's team at Wormsley Estate, now affectionately known as "Sir Paul Getty's Ground". It was the first time a global team of female cricketers had the opportunity to connect with like-minded athletes from across five of the world's seven continents. It was the first time a match of this nature had been livestreamed and freely accessible for fans across the world to watch. The inaugural FairBreak XI team comprised of players from Australia, Canada, Hong Kong, India, New Zealand, Oman, Singapore, USA, Vanuatu, and the West Indies.

In 2019, the FairBreak XI returned to the UK for a four-game tour including a match at the Wormsley Estate. It turned out to be a wonderful week of cricket for fourteen players from ten countries. Six past or present national captains participated.

The coach, Khyati Gulani from Delhi, the manager, Saba Nasim from the UK, and senior players Sana Mir (Pakistan) and Alex Blackwell (Australia) challenged the team to play with consistency across all four games. All players responded to the challenge and worked hard as individuals and as a team.

There were excellent 'Player of the Match' performances on field from Sterre Kalis (Netherlands), Shameelah Mosweu (Botswana), Akanksha Kohli (India) and Ryana Macdonald-Gay (England). The 2018 FairBreak XI captain, Suzie Bates, also made an appearance at Wormsley to mentor the players and run the drinks.

Other wonderful #fairbreaker efforts were made by Stephanie Frohnmayer (Germany) and Celeste Raack (Ireland). Frohnmayer, a gynaecologist, returned to Germany on the team's weekend off to deliver four babies before flying back to London to play the Marylebone Cricket Club in back-to-back T20 matches. Raack made a lightning trip back to Dublin to her physiotherapy practice before returning to deliver more leg breaks, flippers and googlies.

The looping spin and bounce from Ruchitha Venkatesh (Hong Kong) proved a handful for the opposition, and Laura Mophakedi (Botswana) was reliable behind the stumps. Lydia Greenway and her *Cricket 4 Girls* program introduced English players Chelsey Rowson, Grace Scrivens and Ryana Macdonald-Gay to FairBreak. All proved themselves as outstanding young players and made significant contributions to their team and results.

It was during this 2019 tour that FairBreak formed an important association with Mr. Ramasamy Venkatesh and his pharmaceutical company,

Gencor. Martyn was introduced to Venkatesh by the Cricket Hong Kong player, Mariko Hill, whom he had first met in Sri Lanka several years earlier. Hill worked for Gencor and she predicted that Venkatesh might be the perfect fit as a FairBreak sponsor because of his background in cricket, his role as an ICC umpire, and his passion for women's cricket. And so began FairBreak's remarkable association with Venkatesh. His influence, financial support and enthusiasm have been crucial to the movement's survival and success.

The Sir Paul Getty XI v FairBreak XI at Wormsley in 2019 turned out to be yet another successful exhibition match. Martyn recalls it being a particularly memorable experience because the players were invited to attend an operatic performance after the game. The Wormsley Estate is home to Garsington Opera. Concerts take place in the 600 seat, specially designed seasonal pavilion from which it is possible to view the beautiful surrounding landscape.

Operatic performances begin in the early evening, allowing for a long dinner during the interval. On this occasion, not only bring did the players have to bring their cricket gear to the ground, but also their evening wear to attend the musical performance afterwards. One can imagine the excitement and anticipation of a night at the opera after playing cricket on the grass of one of England's finest country estates. Another demonstration of the life-changing opportunities and experiences that FairBreak has delivered to female cricketers.

Don't tell me what to do…

The lead up to the 2019 FairBreak XI tour was also particularly significant for one player and highlights the type of roadblocks that are often put in place for women and the development of their game.

Sterre Kalis from the Netherlands had been invited to play as she had been on the FairBreak radar for some time as an emerging star of women's cricket. She was excited to receive the invitation and set about preparing and informing KNCB, the national cricket board of the Netherlands. She was informing them as a matter of courtesy. At this time, Sterre was not a contracted player with her country, and she was not paid. Her cricket development, in the main, had been funded by her family.

"Nobody was prepared for the phone call to Sterre from the KNCB to advise that they would not allow her to travel to England to play in the 2019 FairBreak XI", recalls Martyn. "Even though it was an exhibition tour, permission would not be forthcoming because the tour was not sanctioned by the ICC nor the ECB. Remember, this was only a private tour to develop female players and showcase their talent.

"Sterre was distraught and telephoned me in tears not knowing what to do. Communication was entered into with the Netherlands Board on Sterre's behalf, but it was not encouraging. I was in Singapore when a Dutch number appeared on my phone. Thinking it was a member of staff at KNCB calling me back, I answered it. It wasn't the Netherlands Board, it was Sterre's mother, Pauline.

"Pauline was incensed and calling me to say that Sterre would be playing at Wormsley, and that she was calling the KNCB to inform them that Sterre would not be playing for the Netherlands again.

"Subsequently, the situation was resolved and Sterre has become a prominent #fairbreaker. She has gone on to sign contracts with both the Northern Diamonds and Yorkshire in England, she was a star of the FairBreak Invitational 2022 in Dubai and is now a full-time professional cricketer.

"This is a significant story and not uncommon for many female players. In numerous cases, uncontracted, unpaid players are held back from opportunity and development when there should be a duty of care to all players to ensure they are afforded every opportunity to develop their game and themselves.

"Sterre is just one of many #fairbreakers now connected to a global community of players, coaches, and mentors with whom she interacts daily. That's what this is about. That's the FairBreak movement".

"You can't start a fire without a spark"

Bruce Springsteen

Sucheta Gorolay
Organisational Psychologist

"I first met Shaun Martyn around 2012-13 at an India Association event in Sydney. We both shared a passion around women in sport, and the role that sport, and specifically cricket, can play in improving gender equality on a global scale. At the time, Shaun was Lisa Sthalekar's manager, and he was in the preliminary stages of formulating the Women's International Cricket League. We met again around 2015 when he wanted to rebrand WICL to FairBreak.

"I worked closely with Kimberly Lee on rebranding the entire organisation and defining what FairBreak stood for - its vision and its mission. What scope of work FairBreak could look at. Who they were targeting and what they were trying to achieve holistically. The communications, the branding, and the positioning of FairBreak as an organisation. Translating Shaun's words and ideas into what the world might want to hear about. For what does FairBreak want to be known? What did FairBreak stand for? What did the movement mean?

"We needed to translate Shaun's concept into a business idea. And a message. The look and feel of the website were also part of it. We helped narrow down his thoughts into a clear value proposition to take to players, potential sponsors, and a wider audience. We needed to clarify what being a #fairbreaker means.

"It has been an exciting journey. It has been fulfilling and satisfying to see FairBreak evolve from our original conversations to where it is now. Shaun always knew we would achieve it. That was always clear in his mind. For us, it has been about how do we help people who have never even thought about cricket and gender equality learn about what FairBreak is trying to do? How do we paint that vision for them?"

Sucheta Gorolay works for a company called Bendelta as a senior manager and organisational psychologist. She looks after the leadership strategy and culture of businesses, provides advisory around and leads their sport practice. She helps sport realise it's human potential.

Specifically how that relates to FairBreak and how her skill set works with FairBreak is in that kind of positioning. What does FairBreak want to be known for? What's their vision? What's their mission? What are their strategic objectives? What does the business plan look like? How do they go forward? How do they organise themselves in a way that is a bit more strategic?

Gorolay is employed full time with Bendelta and her work with FairBreak, up until 2021, was pro-bono support. On her advice, Bendelta took FairBreak on as a client and started to advise them, and she now handles the FairBreak account.

"Alot of the work that I do for Shaun is completely outside of what I do with Bendelta. But I do it because I love it, and I am happy to help and support. I feel impassioned about the mission that FairBreak is trying to achieve".

Gorolay told me there are three powerful factors that motivate her to connect with and stick to FairBreak's cause. She said, "The first is my passion for sport, and that I deeply believe sport to be a powerful vehicle for social change. I see the impact that sport can have on uniting humanity and progressing gender equality on a global scale. It is something that transcends everything that we do in society.

"Another factor is the influence I took from a prior role in the diversity and inclusion space. Specifically focusing on gender equality, but also inclusion broadly. So, if you combine the two: sport plus gender equality, that is what FairBreak does.

"On a personal level, I'd say my family background is another motivator. I grew up in a family that was very cricket focused. I am now married and my husband loves cricket. We both love sport broadly, but the sport that we probably spend most of our time looking at and following and having a real passion for, is cricket. I have a deep understanding about those aspects within it all.

"The element that ties it all together is that I have always believed in the athlete. And the role that athletes play in influencing society. FairBreak empowers women who play cricket. And the role these cricketers play in their villages, in their communities, in leading and inspiring the next generation of females is powerful.

"And what I want to see achieved, which is what FairBreak is doing, is lifting women who play cricket. Lifting their development and helping them realise their potential. And by virtue of the impact that they have in their own community and society, there will be exponential influence and impact. Gender equality is phenomenal.

"The tournament in Dubai is testament to and proof of what we can achieve. The scalability and the people that we have impacted. We have given opportunities to women who have never had them before. We have opened their minds and shown young girls (and boys) all over the world that your potential in life should not be limited by your gender or geographical location. If you have capabilities, then you should have access to opportunities to fulfill that potential.

"A defining moment for me came in 2018 during the first FairBreak XI tour at the Wormsley Estate in England, the first time we brought eleven players from ten different countries across five continents together. I remember sitting in the cafe and hearing these players, these women who had never met each other before, talk about the cricket game and their lives. What really blew my mind was their conversation about the impact that a monsoon has in India, which then influences the weather patterns in Oman. And the knock-on effects felt in parts of Africa. They discussed the impact of physical geography and meteorology on their homes and sport in various parts of the world. They were all learning and growing through realising that in their town and community, the challenges they face, and the opportunities they seek, are just like other players who live thousands of kilometres away.

"The connection of like-minded women who have never had the opportunity to meet in person and learn about the life of Selina Solman in Vanuatu, or Vaishali Jesrani in Oman or Henriette Ishimwe in Rwanda or Stafanie Taylor in the West Indies. The joy that FairBreak had given them global reach and awareness that the world is both vast and yet so small, was palpable.

"Even though it was an informal chat in a café, and they were just talking about cricket and how they play. It was the sudden comprehension that there are similar women all over the world, and they are part of something bigger.

"Another defining aspect of my work with FairBreak was seeing how "closed-minded" the entire cricket establishment was globally. The ICC in particular. And the resistance they put up to redefining how things are done. There was this assumption that the women's game must be the same as the men's game, that it was the same product, the exact same comparison point. And that it was always going to be lesser than the men. But this concept is outdated. Look at tennis for example. Women's tennis is a completely different game to men's tennis and always has been. We do not consider it less important than the male game.

"More importantly, there is proof, and this was highlighted by the record numbers of viewers of the UEFA Women's Championship League in the UK recently, that the audience and the viewership for women's sport exists. This bullshit rhetoric that people are not interested in female sport is wrong. It is a classic chicken and egg situation. Just because people are not watching it, does not mean they do not want to watch it. Could it be because, systemically, they have not been given access to it? They cannot watch it because it has not been broadcast. Give viewers access to a decent broadcast or streaming service that allows them to see the quality of the athletes and the sport. Build it and they will come.

"My husband and his friends, who are all cricket mad, have often said, "We don't care who's playing, or whether they're male or female. If it's good cricket, it's good cricket". So that is another motivating factor for me. Disrupt the rhetoric. The ICC maintain that people are not as interested in watching women's cricket. Yes, they are interested! We must give viewers a platform, a voice, and an opportunity to watch it. And that is exactly what FairBreak is doing.

"At first there was significant hesitation from some players around being involved in the FairBreak Invitational because the ICC was resisting sanctioning a tournament, and some cricketing boards would not allow their players to attend. This was frustrating and disappointing. But understandable given the enormous power of the ICC and some cricket boards. But FairBreak has started a revolution. We have opened the women's eyes to knowing their rights. At some point, these cricket administrators will no longer be able to control and dictate what happens when all female players are demanding the same thing.

"In terms of the future of cricket, what we are starting to see, finally, is a changing of the guard around the power dynamics between athletes and administrators. And this is particularly true for women's cricket. Shaun had this idea years ago, and whilst it's been frustrating that it has taken as long as it has, I think that the world is now ready for what he has been pushing for. We are at a tipping point.

"Women's sport across the world is now at a stage where we are starting to have proper conversations about equality. And a spotlight is being shone on the disparity between the levels of pay, the opportunities to play, the funding, the broadcasting, the exposure. Most importantly, that we can no longer take a tokenistic approach to female sport. When we are talking about achieving equality, it is not solely about pay. It is not solely about broadcasting. It is not solely about the quality of and access to facilities. It is about the systemic challenges. We need to take a systemic approach to equality, and that is what is being illuminated in all sports, cricket in particular.

"If I was transported to 2032, ten years from now, the future of women's cricket will be better no doubt about it. I am not sure that the salaries will be similar. And that is based on gender equality in the workplace. As much as we hope to see a shift, equal pay in the workplace is moving at a glacial pace and sport mirrors that trend. I believe and hope we will see cricket played in more countries. And that there will be more opportunities for girls to play cricket from an earlier age. And that entry level will be accessible in as many countries as possible.

"In a decade, I would be disappointed if the audience sizes have not grown, and the sponsorship and branding have not evolved. But I am certain we will see a seismic shift in sponsorship, individual and team branding, awareness, and influences. Women's cricket is a product that is completely different to its male counterpart, and there is an alternative way of marketing it. National cricket boards have an advertising and marketing formula they deploy for the men and are blinkered about the fact that it does not translate to the women. This is where FairBreak has an opportunity to really disrupt the state of play.

Not for FairBreak's gain, but for the benefit of female cricket itself.

"The influence of female cricketers on social media platforms will continue to grow. Some of them have enormous numbers of followers. What has been powerful is hearing, particularly in the last year or two, the number of female cricketers who have become household names. The exposure of positive female role models in cricket and the impact they can have is limitless.

"As a society, we do not want the women's game to fall into the same traps we have seen with the professionalisation of male sports. Female athletes, aside from the fact that they are physically different, are naturally predisposed to working more collaboratively. We do not want to professionalise women's sport to such a degree that we lose the special ingredient that makes female athletes the multi-disciplined people they are.

"Female athletes have had to deal with a range of issues historically and have managed to achieve balanced lives. Sport has not defined their entire life. Many juggle demanding careers outside of their professional cricket to earn a decent income. This has helped them adapt and flourish within their athletic and post athletic careers, and to remain well-rounded human beings. Of course, athletes want to be fairly compensated for the work, effort, and impact they have. But does it need to be the astronomical sums we see paid to the men? Women's sport, particularly cricket, needs to be mindful of this."

> ...there are girls from villages, and I will tell them, "Yes, you can also do this. It's not about the place you are from. It's about what you want to do as a cricket player and as a woman."
>
> Shubdha Bhosle Gaikwad, India's youngest female umpire

Cricket Hong Kong and ICC Sanctioning

Meeting Ramasamy Venkatesh was a formative moment for FairBreak. His company, Gencor, was the major sponsor of the 2019 FairBreak XI tour. Venkatesh got fully involved, even umpiring some of the games in his capacity as an ICC umpire. His links with Cricket Hong Kong, as their major sponsor, and his involvement in the training of umpires throughout Asia gave FairBreak the pivotal introduction they needed to meet with the Chairman of Cricket Hong Kong, Tony Molloy.

FairBreak also met with Ravi Nagdev, the General Manager of Cricket Development, Mark Farmer, and other team members at Cricket Hong Kong who were looking for an opportunity to make a genuine difference in cricket in Asia and had concluded that the best way to deliver it was through supporting women's cricket. A serendipitous relationship was thus formed aimed at championing the women's game globally. And so Cricket Hong Kong became the FairBreak partner. Both parties signed a three-year agreement for the FairBreak Invitational and set about acquiring the required sanctioning from the ICC.

A challenging period followed where they slowly navigated the sanctioning process with the ICC. Lengthy negotiations were carried out by Nagdev and Molloy at Cricket Hong Kong who corresponded with Clive Hitchcock at the ICC. One of the objections the ICC cited regarding the sanctioning of the tournament was that FairBreak were planning on "paying the women too much money", and that "this would disrupt domestic women's cricket globally". There still seemed to be a sustained effort being made at the highest levels of world cricket to deliberately hold back the remuneration paid to female cricketers.

Ravi Nagdev
Cricket Hong Kong

Like most cricketing nations, Hong Kong used to be part of the British Empire. The first recorded evidence of cricket being played in the city dates back to 1841. Today, the sport is professionally administered by Cricket Hong Kong. The national cricket team has been active since 1866, and the Hong Kong Cricket Association was granted associate membership of the International Cricket Council (ICC) in 1969.

Ravi Nagdev is the General Manager of Domestic Cricket & Development at Cricket Hong Kong. Nagdev is a second-generation Hong Kong resident of Indian heritage. He attended an all-boys school and in his first fortnight at the school was drafted into the school's cricket team based purely on his Indian heritage. He went on to play club cricket and threw himself into the behind-the-scenes organisation of his team, eventually becoming Club Secretary.

In 1992, age twelve, Nagdev attended his first Hong Kong Cricket Sixes match at the Kowloon Cricket Club with his father. Iconic cricketers of the time, including Imran Khan, were playing in the tournament. It was a defining moment in his life and shaped his future career choices.

Nagdev told me that until very recently in Hong Kong, women's cricket has been traditionally packaged and marketed as an "afterthought" or "secondary product" of the men's game. The women's teams used to play as "openers" for the men's matches. He believes that, fundamentally, women's cricket is a very different product to men's cricket and should stand alone as a sport.

Nagdev also revealed that, in Hong Kong, there is separate media coverage for men's and women's cricket. The women's games are covered by the local media, while the men's games are covered by the English media. Also, the number of cameras used for broadcasting a cricket match halve when the women play. Despite this, Hong Kong's Women's Captain, currently Kary Chan, is a household name and recognisable by everyone on the streets of Hong Kong. Conversely, the Captain of Hong Kong's men's squad is virtually unknown.

Nagdev believes that the FairBreak Invitational is defined by its acceptance of different cultures from both the Full Member and Associate Nations, and that FairBreak's player mix is the embodiment of everything Hong Kong stands for. The city has long been a melting pot of cultural backgrounds: Chinese, Indian, Pakistani, British and Philippino, and there are many layers to Hong Kong's society.

"The cricket boards of the Full Member Nations do not comprehend the potential of women's cricket globally. But change is coming," he said. "The FairBreak management team and players are "trailblazers", and the Invitational is a template for how women's tournaments should look. It's high time a tournament like this happened.

"Since coming home from the FairBreak Invitational in Dubai, the players from the Associate Nations say they are "changed" women. They have a new-found confidence in themselves. They have a deeper belief in their own abilities. Essentially, there is no difference in the skills and physique of the players from Full Member Nations compared to those from Associate Nations. The two weeks in Dubai helped all the players to see that. It is only access to facilities, coaching, training and opportunities to play that separate them."

Nagdev was my first interviewee for this book, and I asked him how Cricket Hong Kong came to be a co-host of the FairBreak Invitational. He recounted how Mariko Hill, a Cricket Hong Kong player and former Captain of the national team, had been invited to play in the FairBreak XI Tours to the UK in 2018 and 2019. Mariko works for Gencor as their Global Innovation Manager. Her boss, Mr. Ramasamy Venkatesh, the founder and chairman of Gencor, is a major sponsor of Cricket Hong Kong.

In 2019, Cricket Hong Kong became aware that the FairBreak management team were scouting out suitable cities in Associate Member Nations to hold their inaugural tournament. Furthermore, it was a strategic goal of Cricket Hong Kong to host a major cricket event. The two organisations came together to achieve their goals. Tony Molloy, the CEO of Cricket Hong Kong and Shaun Martyn met up to discuss the possibility of FairBreak holding their inaugural event in Hong Kong. They soon found common ground and had an agreement in place within two months. A fresh take on the global cricket calendar was underway; a fantastic opportunity to showcase the playing abilities of female cricketers from many Associate Nations.

Hong Kong is an international crossroads, and it is the gateway to China, an untapped cricket market. Cricket Hong Kong and FairBreak also had a shared vision about unearthing hidden talent and growing new audiences worldwide. Part of the agreement involved more Cricket Hong Kong players being invited to play than from other Associate Nations. Twelve of Hong Kong's national players were lined up to take part.

Originally, the first tournament's date was set for May 2021. But the COVID-19 restrictions of the pandemic put a stop to that. With the whole world in lockdown, Cricket Hong Kong and FairBreak postponed the date until May 2022, feeling confident that the city and the world would be open again by then.

England hosted cricket matches during the northern summer of 2021 and the Big Bash League (BBL) was played in Australia in the southern summer of 2021-22. Unfortunately, the Hong Kong government's COVID-19 restrictions remained tight, and Cricket Hong Kong knew that hosting a cricket tournament in 2022, in a bubble, would be financially unviable.

Hong Kong Cycling had hosted a bubble event in 2021 and made a substantial financial loss. All media interaction with the competitors was conducted via Zoom. Everything was constantly being disinfected and officials were walking around in full PPE. A major sponsor underwrote the cycling event's loss, and the cost of the event blew out to astronomical sums. They carried on with the event basically because a Hong Kong bronze Olympic medalist needed cycling event points. Similarly, Asian Football was also hosted in Hong Kong in September 2021. The players were brought in on three flights and kept in a bubble. That was another disappointing and costly event.

"We were able to foresee that bringing ninety FairBreak players plus their families, officials and media into Hong Kong from various global locations was just not going to be possible under the prevailing COVID-19 restrictions," said Nagdev. "By mid-December 2021, we decided to shelve the FairBreak Invitational earmarked for May 2022 and we started making plans to do it a different way. The venue mapping, corporate box sales and event planning at

Kowloon Cricket Club were put on ice. It was an emotional moment for me and all the staff at Cricket Hong Kong.

"In April 2021, the India Premier League (IPL) had been forced to switch countries mid-competition due to COVID-19 restrictions. The games were played at the world class International Stadium in Dubai in the United Arab Emirates. Inspired by the IPL's course of action, FairBreak's tournament director and major sponsor, Gencor CEO, Ramasamy Venkatesh and FairBreak's founder Shaun Martyn flew to Dubai to discuss the possibility of the FairBreak Invitational 2022 being held there instead.

"Moving a global sporting event of this scale to a different geographic location five months out from the first coin toss was a stressful and risky proposition. Without people on the ground familiar with the local infrastructure and cultural differences, and a small team of three in the event management company, Oasis Management, it was very difficult to fix problems as they arose. This left the FairBreak management team to carry out many of the tasks themselves. Despite the setbacks, Oasis and FairBreak did a brilliant job in Dubai.

"Cricket Hong Kong are confident that the 2023 FairBreak Invitational in Hong Kong will be a very different experience to Dubai. Sean Moore, a seasoned event manager in the Hong Kong sporting world will be managing the event. He has managed events for the Hong Kong Sixes and the Rugby Sevens. He is well connected in Hong Kong and has a close relationship with the vendors of Hong Kong. Hiring an event management company is all about the experience and contacts they bring to the table.

"The player experience at the Dubai International Stadium was phenomenal. The venue is world class. The dressing rooms, the media rooms and the pitch are outstanding, and it seats 25,000 people. The Kowloon Cricket Club doesn't have quite the same dressing room facilities as Dubai. It's a compact venue, and seats only 4,000 people. However, when it is full, the spectator experience is knock-out. The buzz of the crowd is what Hong Kong will bring to the next FairBreak Invitational. With affordably priced tickets and corporate boxes we will easily fill Kowloon Cricket Club.

"We will bus in Hong Kong's school children during the week. The hotels and nightlife are nearby. The atmosphere and flavour of Hong Kong will make all the difference. The opportunity for players to interact with the sports fans in the bars and restaurants after the matches is traditional in Hong Kong. It works for the Rugby Sevens. Cricket Hong Kong are confidant the 2023 FairBreak players will take home the fun and atmosphere of Hong Kong and the flavour of our city. The adrenaline rush and high of Hong Kong will be very different to Dubai."

Nagdev reminded me that there is a generation in Hong Kong who have grown up unaware of what it was like to be part of a British colony. He also laments that not enough team sports are played in Hong Kong's schools. As a result, the people of Hong Kong no longer get involved in or play team sports as much as they used to. He believes this manifests itself in a mindset where people tend to look out only for themselves because they don't know how to work as a team.

He believes that playing and watching sport unifies the people. Cricket, especially, unifies them. He concluded, "Never underestimate the power of sport to unify people. In 2006, Hong Kong played South Africa in the Asia finals. Everyone was cheering for Hong Kong. The Chinese, the Hong Kong locals, the English expats, the Indians. That year, we had experienced significant political unrest in the city but everyone in Hong Kong was unified by that one cricket match.

"Cricket and other team sports teach important values and skills. They help to develop tomorrow's leaders. Cricket Hong Kong is devoted to advancing the city's community by introducing cricket to all levels of society, providing opportunities for all to benefit from it as a sport."

"I broke 3 cricket bats during the winter hitting millions of balls."

Shizuka Miyaji, Japan

" Q&A with Ramasamy Venkatesh Scientist, Umpire, Gencor Founder and FairBreak Sponsor "

Why are you so passionate about women's cricket?

"I grew up in India where I used to play league cricket. When I moved to Hong Kong, I continued playing league cricket here, but in the year 2000 I ruptured my ACL [anterior cruciate ligament]. And then I chipped a bone and had to have artificial ligament replacement and reconstruction surgery. That put paid to my playing days.

"When my daughter was young, about eight years old, way back in 2004, she started developing an interest in cricket. So, I would take her to the cricket grounds and help her train and practice and throw down balls. At the age of eleven or twelve, she started playing cricket at Hong Kong Cricket Club. And she was chosen to play in their league team. I used to go and watch when she was playing at the lower age group levels. Quite regularly, the umpires wouldn't turn up for the girls' games, so they would request one of the parents to go and stand in the middle.

"That's how I started developing an interest and got into standing in the middle and umpiring the women's games. I found that there was a fascinating amount of talent and passion among the Associate Nation girls to give their very best when playing cricket. And with proper training and exposure, they could be as good as anybody else playing anywhere. All they needed was proper training and opportunities. That gave me insight.

"Over a period of time, I qualified as an International Cricket Council umpire and then I became an international umpire. I'm currently on the ICC's Development Panel. I've umpired over forty One Day and twenty International matches. Fortunately, many of them have been women's matches, at Associate level. So, I've seen plenty of talent in women's cricket and many players who deserve the opportunity to showcase their skills at a much higher level.

"With ICC International umpiring you get sent to whichever tournament you've been rostered onto. When you get chosen, you jump. Initially I was in the Regional Panel of umpires and now I am in the Development Panel.

"Because my business requires me to travel extensively, I limited my umpiring travel to games at a regional level. And at regional level for the Associate Nations, the majority of the games I umpired were for the women. So, it fell by chance that I have umpired many women's cricket matches. Right up to World Cup Qualifiers. It's given me an opportunity to see women from multiple Southeast Asian, Middle Eastern and Pacific nations come out and perform. It's given me an opportunity to see just how good they are.

"I'm also passionate about women's cricket because my daughter plays. Ruchitha got into the Hong Kong U/19 team when she was thirteen. Now, she is twenty-five and she plays for Hong Kong's national team. She also plays Premier League cricket in the UK. She has just completed her Masters in Neuroscience at University College London and she's planning to start a PhD in January 2023. She was in the FairBreak XI Tour during the summer of 2022. Ruchitha is just like me. She has been able to balance her two passions: science and cricket.

"When I saw what was possible for female players with proper playing exposure and opportunity, I realised that there is a large number of girls out there who should be getting the chance to showcase their skills in the arena of international cricket. And get rewarded and recognised for them.

"Cricket builds people into successful human beings. Nothing builds self-belief more than being out there in the field performing. Nothing builds character more than a team game where you realise that it's not all about yourself, it's about the team. And you learn to make sacrifices. There is nothing better than sport for teaching you how to deal with the failures that prepare you for real life. It's not a fair and kind world out there in the real world.

"Sport teaches you that you when you fail, you pay the price and you get dropped. But if you work hard, you can come back. It develops strength of character. It develops teamwork. This is what is needed to get on in the real world. And it teaches players to aspire for higher things without being daunted by setbacks. It teaches them how to face those setbacks, how to fight back and overcome them. That's what increased my passion for women's cricket, I saw it as a tool to help women develop their potential holistically."

You have built Gencor into a quietly successful multinational. How did you end up balancing a career in science and a passion for cricket?

"In India everybody plays cricket all the time. Cricket is in our DNA. I have been playing cricket from the time I was three years old. Children in India collect two sticks for stumps and use a larger stick for a bat. They get any ball they can find and start playing.

"I played cricket at school. I played for my university and then I played in the leagues. In those days, when I was growing up, television was not prevalent in India. But there was cricket commentary on the radio. When I got the chance to watch games live, I went to them, and when the TV started showing cricket, I watched it all the time. It was a natural fit.

"My background is in chemistry. From the mid-1980s, I worked in the pharmaceutical industry in India. I moved to Hong Kong in the early 1990s when I got a job in a pharma company. In 1999 I quit my job and started Gencor. Around 1997-98, this whole region went through an Asian financial crisis when the currencies of all the countries collapsed to less than half, and some of them less than one tenth of their value and it became a serious problem.

"During the Asian financial crisis, countries like Malaysia, Thailand, Indonesia, and Korea were badly affected. Many companies in Asia went through a tough time. Including the company where I worked. For a few years, everyone was in bad financial shape. After years of working and seeing how so many aspects of the pharma business were outside of my control, I decided to do something for myself.

"At the same, the dot-com boom was happening in the computer industry as the internet was introduced and adopted. The software industry was also growing and my uncle, who had been running a small software company, sold it, and wanted to look at investment opportunities in Asia. We got chatting, and within a week, we decided to start a business in Hong Kong in the pharmaceutical sector. I quit my job and started Gencor with him. We built the company up from scratch. We grew it organically. We do not take money out of the company; we reinvest everything back into it.

"Today, Gencor is an organisation with international headquarters in Hong Kong. Our American headquarters are located in Texas, and we have people based in California, New Jersey, and Utah. We also have offices in India and Vietnam and manufacturing facilities in various locations. We have sister companies in Australia. We own pharmaceutical manufacturing operations in Israel and a medical nutrition company in Netherlands. We have a Research & Development company in Ireland. We have invested into multiple areas, and today, Gencor is a small multinational. We fully own the companies and have more than 350 employees worldwide.

"It's been a slog, but we keep Gencor small, neat, clean, and efficient. We have zero debt. We have no borrowings. No equities. No investment from anyone. We started the company as a two man show. I was operating from one of the bedrooms of my apartment in Hong Kong, and my uncle operated from one of his bedrooms in Texas.

"From the first day we started the company, we both worked from home. After a year and a half, we had an office in Hong Kong. We follow a lean, mean, and fit approach. We are not flamboyant. We are science oriented. Our spending is directed into the science rather than marketing or publicity. And that philosophy forms the fundamental DNA of our company. Because of our strength in science and our product range, we grew.

"The company has also been shaped by our upbringing. Both my uncle and I come from a small, middle-class Tamil Nadu family background. We are Tamil speaking and quite traditional. I grew up in a small town that did not have a maternity hospital. Midwives used to come to the home and deliver babies. My uncle and I were born in the same house, in the same room. It was a room that was set aside for baby deliveries only. We were from a joint family. The joint family system is quite prevalent in India. It includes three or four generations, including grandparents, parents, uncles, aunts, nieces, and nephews, all living together in the same household. That's how I grew up.

"My uncle and I entered the pharmaceutical market at the right time. Blockbuster drugs were coming off patent and India and China were developing generics. The companies wanting to develop generic tablets, capsules, injections and formulations needed ingredients. We specialised in getting those ingredients made and delivered. We started with niche active pharmaceutical ingredients. At the same time, we also identified the potential growth in nutraceuticals because the complementary medicine industry was just taking off.

"At first the nutraceutical market was almost like the Wild West. Everybody was jumping on board and selling anything; the discipline that exists in the pharmaceutical industry where years of research work are invested before launching a product was not being applied. We decided to go niche and take a pharmaceutical approach to the nutraceutical business and that has been the backbone of our success. We foresaw opportunities and we invested in them at the right time.

"Today, Gencor provides health solutions for changing needs across the lifespan through clinically proven ingredients. We are driven by scientific research rooted in Ayurvedic tradition and we take a systematic approach to wellness. We offer solutions in sports nutrition, immune health, healthy ageing, mind and mood, metabolic and weight management."

How and why have you chosen to invest your money in FairBreak?

"I have invested because I am passionate about what FairBreak stands for. I teamed up with Shaun in 2019. In 2018, Mariko Hill, who, at the time, was the Captain of Hong Kong's national team, went on the first FairBreak XI Tour to England.

"Shaun had spotted her with the Hong Kong team on a training tour in Sri Lanka a few years prior and had noted her cricketing skills. He invited Mariko on the first FairBreak XI Tour.

"Mariko works for me in my company, Gencor, and I have known her since she was twelve years old. I gave her time off to go and play in the tournament and when she came back, she was gushing about it and how great it was to play with superstars like Suzie Bates, Alex Blackwell, and Charlotte Edwards, how good the atmosphere was and how the Associate girls felt about it.

"Then Mariko introduced me to Shaun. When I saw at first-hand what he was doing, I teamed up with him in 2019, and we took another FairBreak XI Tour to England to play a series of games at Wormsley, the Marylebone Cricket Club, and grounds in Essex and Kent. It was a very interesting and worthwhile tour.

"In February 2020, we were invited by the Bradman Foundation to take a FairBreak XI down to Australia to play a Bradman XI at the Bradman Oval in Bowral. Again, this was a fantastic experience for all the Associate players involved. Sydney Cricket Club sent many of their budding cricketers to it also. They are now in Australia's national squads.

"Players such as Phoebe Litchfield and Georgia Adams played and they are fully professional players now. Linsey Smith was there also and she still plays in England. Sana Mir and Alex Blackwell captained the teams so we had a good mixture of youth and experience, and the whole event set the tone for what was to come.

"At the same time, Shaun was still seeking International Cricket Council permission to host an international tournament for women, but the ICC kept saying that they would not work with private organisations. An application had to come through a Member Board. As I am the chairman of Hong Kong's cricket officials, I collaborated with Cricket Hong Kong and made it possible for them to support FairBreak and for the two organisations to operate as a partnership.

"Cricket Hong Kong applied to the ICC for permission and it was granted. The ICC also wanted to know about the proposed tournament's funding because, at that point, many of the men's T20 leagues outside of the India Premier League, Pakistan Super League and the Big Bash League had financial issues. The stakeholders and players were not getting paid. The ICC was very concerned about it all and they needed somebody to guarantee the financial viability of a FairBreak tournament.

"My pharmaceutical company, Gencor, has been in business for a long time. I had the resources to do it. So, I stood up and said, "I'll back the tournament. My company already works with Cricket Hong Kong as a sponsor in multiple areas. We can't tell you in advance who are going to be the sponsors, but this is our model. We are going to be looking for sponsors from different places, but sponsors will only sign up when the tournament is sanctioned".

"We told the ICC they could be comfortable granting permission because the funding for the tournament to run successfully would be guaranteed by my company, Gencor. Even if FairBreak ended up with no sponsors, we could still run the tournament. It was all about putting down a marker, showing what FairBreak could do and building for the future. I consider it an investment."

Why did FairBreak switch the 2022 Invitational from Hong Kong to Dubai?

"The FairBreak Invitational was originally supposed to be held in Hong Kong in April 2022, but we had to pull the plug on hosting it in Hong Kong in December 2021 because of the ongoing quarantine restrictions.

"Today [early October 2022] was my first trip home to Hong Kong without me having to go into hotel quarantine. The government only lifted the quarantine and isolation policies ten days ago. Every time I have come home to Hong Kong from a business trip, I've done fourteen days, seven days, and three days isolation in a hotel. But today, for the first time since March 2020, I was able to get off the aircraft, clear customs and immigration and take a cab home. What a relief that was.

"Due to Hong Kong's quarantine restrictions, FairBreak had to shift the Invitational to Dubai at very short notice. Shaun visited Dubai for the first time in his life on the 4th of January 2022, when he and I flew there from Sydney. In December 2021 we pulled the plug on Hong Kong. We had been in discussions with Cricket Hong Kong who had been working with the Hong Kong government to try to get quarantine exemptions for the players and officials.

"We had set a cut-off date, the 15th of December, to make a decision. Unfortunately, the 15th of December arrived and the quarantine exemptions remained the same. The Hong Kong government was not in a position to guarantee anything and we could not run the risk of the tournament being affected due to COVID-19. We had invested too much already to not hold the tournament at all. So, we had to make another plan.

"On the 22nd of December, a week after we pulled the pin on Hong Kong, I flew down to Sydney and sat with the FairBreak management team to discuss alternative arrangements. In the meantime, I had spoken to the United Arab Emirates Cricket Board and told them that FairBreak would like to host a women's cricket tournament in Dubai. They were receptive to that.

"Shaun and I flew to Dubai from Sydney in early January 2022 to start discussions and make arrangements. In May 2022 we held the tournament. Within three months of visiting Dubai and concluding negotiations with UAE Cricket. It was an incredibly fast turnaround.

"At that point, Australia still had COVID-19 testing requirements also. When I flew into Sydney, I had to test on arrival and then I had to stay in my hotel until I got a negative result. On the day I was leaving I had to go to a public testing facility. I went to The Prince of Wales Hospital in Sydney, near Coogee, and stood in line, in the rain, from 9:30am to 4:30pm waiting to get tested. On arrival in Dubai, I had to do another COVID-19 test and again on departure from Dubai.

"We started discussions with the United Arab Emirates Cricket Board and permission had to be obtained from the UAE government. We also had to apply to the Dubai government to develop a set of COVID-19 protocols. These had to detail how we would test the players when they arrived, what would be the arrangements if anybody tested positive, and the isolation planning we would put in place so that each team stayed on separate floors in the hotel. Therefore, if a player, or a few players from a team got infected, their isolation on a particular floor of the hotel could be guaranteed.

"We had to make arrangements with the hotel to have all of these protocols documented. Then we had to present all of this planning to the UAE Cricket Board, who then presented it to the UAE government. Thankfully, in March, Dubai took away all these quarantine requirements, and we all breathed a sigh of relief. This is just a sample of the logistical planning we went through when we changed cities for the tournament.

"The sponsors we had signed up for the tournament in Hong Kong are based here in Hong Kong, and many of them were not willing to stay on board for a Dubai tournament. Consequently, we had to find a whole new set of sponsors so that the tournament could happen in Dubai. We also had to make different broadcasting arrangements.

"We then had a further set back because one of the biggest draw cards of the tournament didn't come about. We had contracted six of the top Indian women players to come and play at the FairBreak Invitational. Unfortunately, at the last moment, the Board of Control for Cricket in India, the BCCI, refused to allow the Indian women players to attend. The BCCI would not issue them with NOCs [No Objection Certificates] because the FairBreak Invitational overlapped with their Indian domestic T20 tournament and the girls had just come back from the World Cup.

"When we lost those Indian players, we also lost some of the broadcasting deals and sponsors who had signed up for the FairBreak Invitational based on the fact that the Indian players have substantial numbers of social media followers and the vast size of the Indian cricket-watching audience.

"We went through so many challenges, and still made it happen. Even though we had the tournament running in Dubai International Stadium, we were not in a position to sell corporate boxes, because to allow spectators into the stands and corporate boxes, we had to make security arrangements with the government, with the police, traffic control, everything. There was just no time for that.

"Even though Dubai had relaxed some of their rules, they were still being strict on COVID-19 and they were not prepared to give public gathering permissions. And it was much too complicated for us to get around it all.

"Every day, we took the hurdles as they came. We dealt with the issues right in front of us. We didn't bother too much about what had happened yesterday or what could happen tomorrow. We just kept moving forward."

Moving the FairBreak Invitational 2022 to Dubai was inspired. Was it your idea?

"When we were looking at alternatives for Hong Kong, I knew that Dubai Stadium was an ideal place and that they'd be receptive. Even in the midst of COVID-19, they had run the India Premier League and the World Cup, so they had experience of handling events. Plus, Cricket Hong Kong and UAE Cricket have a good relationship. The current director of UAE Cricket was very helpful. He is the former national coach of Hong Kong.

"And the women's coach of the UAE national team is the former women's coach of Hong Kong. So, we had solid Hong Kong connections in UAE. Both boards have a good relationship, and with the International Cricket Council headquartered in Dubai, it made working through the hierarchy and getting the sanctions much easier operationally.

"Large numbers of ICC and Asian Cricket Council staff attended the tournament and watched the women's cricket. They were very appreciative and supportive of what we had achieved. When they saw and understood what was happening in the cricketing world for the first time, they were quite impressed. They could see that the quality of the play was good, and they could see first-hand the way we conducted the tournament was excellent with outstanding officiating and anti-corruption measures in place.

"FairBreak's anti-corruption measures in Dubai were crucially important because match fixing is the bane of any sport. Unfortunately, match fixing situations are increasingly coming to light in men's cricket, and because Dubai is a centre for these activities, we wanted to be extremely careful. Our female players were coming from thirty-five different countries. And when you have naive women coming from Africa, Latin America and some of the poorer Asian countries, the glitz and glamour of Dubai would be an eye-opener for them. We did not want them targeted by match fixers looking to influencing betting."

How do you see FairBreak in the pantheon of world cricket?

"FairBreak has broken the mould when it comes to women's cricket in terms of being the first tournament to mix Associate players with Full Member Nation players. Taking them on tours and playing the matches that were arranged in 2018, 2019 and 2020. Bringing emerging female cricketers from different parts of the world, bringing in the superstars from different parts of the world, getting them all to mix together, stay together, play together, and then expanding that concept into a world first tournament. Six teams, ninety players, with over fifty women from Associate Nations and thirty seven women from Test playing nations, playing in what was the first ever women's T20 international tournament. And not following the usual nation versus nation format.

"We brought in players from thirty-five different countries. Not many people know that cricket is played in thirty-five different countries. If you look at men's cricket, it focuses on the top ten, not even the top twelve cricket playing countries. Maybe eleven and twelve get a sneak in here and there. And out of the top ten countries, the top three or four are the ones who get the most exposure.

"With FairBreak, suddenly the world is seeing somebody from Rwanda, somebody from Tanzania, somebody from Sweden. Women from Brazil and Argentina coming and playing cricket. And women players from places like Nepal, Bhutan, and Hong Kong.

"When you think of Hong Kong, you think of a trading, foreign exchange, finance, shipping and port city. Not a cricket city! In a place where real estate is like gold. Hong Kong has only three turf pitches. But players still come out to play cricket. And they're eager to show what they can do. That was an eye opener for the ICC, ACC and the cricketing world. As well as the cricketers of Test playing nations. They were all stunned. They never thought something like this could happen. They said, "We thought you guys were just talking about it, but you actually made it happen in the thick and thin of COVID-19.""

Did any Dubai locals attend the matches in the stadium?

"Although the FairBreak Invitational was publicised on local radio in Dubai and the UAE, attendance was minimal. We finally got permission for one section of the stadium, one quadrant, to permit the entry of spectators, but they came in free because there was no ticketing. There was no time to arrange security, barcodes on tickets, scanning of tickets and so on.

"We used two or three of the corporate boxes for invited guests and VIPs. Commercially, the stadium has twenty four corporate boxes to sell. If it had been a normal tournament situation, where spectators are allowed in and corporate boxes could be sold, we would have sold those boxes and we could have generated ticket revenue from paying spectators. But all that was lost. It was March by the time the UAE government removed some of the restrictions. And in April and May, there were still various COVID-19 restrictions in place. Even today [October 2022] there are still COVID-19 restrictions in Dubai. They are slowly being removed just like other nations worldwide are removing their restrictions."

Lengthy cricket tours and tournaments take their toll on players. How has FairBreak addressed this?

"Everybody has been talking about the FairBreak Invitational since May. All the Test playing nations' cricketers who played in Dubai are calling us and saying they want to play again. The tournament was the most fun they ever had. Because at the end of the day, they got to meet people and players from so many different countries. That has never happened before. Normally, when they play at an international level, they're in a circle, in a bubble. If they go to a Big Bash League or an India Premier League, they only meet four or five international players, while all the rest are locals.

"And then there are restrictions in terms of the bubble. Where they can go, where they can't go. In the last couple of years, players have spent a lot of time in their hotel rooms. We allowed our players to wander around freely, mix with everybody, have breakfast with everybody, go to the swimming pool, go on desert safaris, and have fun in Dubai. They enjoyed it immensely and the players bonded very well.

"Some of the Test playing nation girls told me that when they are stuck together in a team, and they're playing in a tournament for two months straight, or they're on the road for two or three months, they go down to breakfast every day and look at the same faces. It gets a bit stale. Also, players have huge pressure on them mentally and physically when they are away at tournaments; because they're away from home, their partner, their parents, their pets. It's a big thing.

"FairBreak have looked at all that. We have consulted at length with all these women who have been playing this format of cricket, especially the ones from the Test playing nations, and we have asked them what they would like a tournament to look like. The overwhelming answer we got, after collecting everybody's answers, was something like Grand Slam tennis. One city. One venue. One stadium. Fifteen days. Finished. Come in, play, and have fun. Go home. Play high quality games. Have the ability to bring parents or partners. Not having to leave a pet dog or cat at home for two months. They'd prefer to leave a pet for two weeks with a sister, brother or neighbour and then go home. Believe me, so many female players said that they don't like being on tour for long periods of time because they don't want to leave their pets alone!

"We started to realise that we needed to treat the players not just as cricketers, but as human beings; to ask them what they want and give them what they want. They want to play cricket, but they also want to live the life of an ordinary human being. So that's what we gave them in Dubai and that's what made the whole experience a breath of fresh air. And everybody loved it.

"In Dubai, the Associate players could walk around the hotel, talk to Heather Knight, Stafanie Taylor, Laura Wolvaardt or Marizanne Kapp across the table, ask for advice and get it. Then share a cup of tea, go swimming together or shopping and sightseeing. Nothing builds bonding better than that. Today, all these girls talk to each other, support and congratulate each other on social media.

"When a FairBreak player from the West Indies watches an Associate cricketer doing well in an African or Asian regional tournament, they are now reaching out and saying, "Hey! I saw your scores, you did well. Come on, smash it". There's nothing better than getting encouragement from a mentor.

It's like Roger Federer calling up a grade two tennis player and saying, "I watched your scores. You did well".

"That's what is happening today. The FairBreak camaraderie uplifts the spirit of all the women players out there. Normal international cricket doesn't facilitate those opportunities. Traditionally, what we see is England versus India or Australia versus England. Players see the opposition as the enemy and they don't mix with them. At the FairBreak Invitational, everybody was free to mix. Nobody felt that any player was a threat or an adversary and they all mingled with each other. They played in the right spirit and it was good fun."

How did FairBreak empower women across the whole tournament?

"For the seventh team, the tournament officials, we brought in seven female umpires. It was the first time ever in an international tournament that there have been seven women umpires. Four of them had come straight from the Cricket World Cup. And they told us that they found the atmosphere and learning at the FairBreak tournament better than the Cricket World Cup. Many women's tournaments over the last couple of months have featured more women umpires. We set the tone for that. Before FairBreak, women's tournaments were umpired by men. We brought in seven women. We had eleven officials, out of which seven were women. We had two match referees, and one was a woman. So, we had an eight woman to five man split amongst the thirteen officials. And that has never happened before.

"For the six teams, we had twelve coaches and assistant coaches. Ten of them were women. All the managers of the teams with women. All the liaison officers of all the teams were women. So, it was complete empowerment of women in sport that happened out there. On a scale that has never been done before.

"The traditional cricket establishment has been running tournaments for years. We are the new kid on the block. We are the newcomer that has come in, and during our very first tournament, we have set standards and markers which, we believe, will soon become industry standards."

Was there a particular part of the FairBreak Invitational 2022 that resonated deeply with you?

"Dubai's opening ceremony, when all the teams stood side by side, sparked particular joy for me. The messaging of the opening ceremony, "We are our own leaders, we have our own minds, we will chart our own paths", was awesome. There was not a dry eye in the whole stadium. It was quite emotional. The opening ceremony was the culmination of everything that FairBreak has been striving for after years of talk and hard work. It was also rewarding because three months earlier, we didn't even know if we could get a stadium for the tournament to be held in.

"Pakistan's Zeb Bangash delivered a two-song set for the opening ceremony that began with the popular title track of the Pakistani drama series, 'Sinf-e-Ahan' and finished with an English, Hindi and Urdu rendition of Lesley Gore's feminist anthem, *You Don't Own Me*.

"Shaun had discussed the theme of FairBreak and the tournament with Bangash in advance. He wanted her performance to reflect the fact that FairBreak is a gender equality movement and the female players taking part in the tournament are from many nations.

"The song *You Don't Own Me* was considered outrageous in 1963 for its anti-patriarchal stance, and the lyrics are about a woman denying the wishes of a man. Since then, the song has been claimed as a feminist anthem and has been covered by many famous female artists such as Dusty Springfield. Undeniably, the song's message underscored FairBreak's drive to lift female cricketers and let them shine. Also, "Don't tell me what to do…" has become a mantra for Shaun and some of our players!

"Zeb Bangash paid homage to empowered women across the globe. The cricketers of FairBreak's six teams flanked her to the right and left during the performance. Bangash said she was immensely proud to be a part of the tournament, and praised the achievements of her Pakistan countrywomen, Sana Mir, Bismah Maroof, Aliya Riaz, Diana Baig, and Sana Fatima.

"Bangash also spoke about the importance of such a tournament for empowering women: "Ladies, today I dedicate to you a poem in my native

Urdu celebrating you and women everywhere. Each of you 'Women of Steel' inspires me and countless others with your passion and commitment. May there never be any looking back – onward and upward."

"Dressed in a cobalt blue suit, Bangash wore a necklace that had been strung especially for the opening ceremony and that honoured the diversity of our ninety women from thirty five countries."

There were twelve Hong Kong women playing in the FairBreak Invitational in Dubai. How do you think they performed and what did they take home?

"Dubai was a fantastic learning experience for the Hong Kong players. They took away so much from it. A couple of them did very well. The rest of them gained invaluable experience, not just playing, but in terms of staying together in the same hotel with the superstars who are their idols. They now understand that these women are ordinary individuals who are willing to share their knowledge and encourage younger players, and who are willing to mentor them during training and playing. The learning experience they got during those two weeks was incredible and all of them are eternally grateful.

"Not only the women from Hong Kong benefited. All the women learned so much – it was a gold mine. It's one thing having a skill set, training in the nets, and playing in your local league. But to learn the finer points of the game, and to see what separates the great players from the less experienced players. This gives everyone a target and a pathway.

"The game of cricket, at the highest level, is played in the mind. It's about toughening up the mindset. Believing in self, improving playing skills and the tricks of the trade. That's what separates a star player from an ordinary player. Every player lifted their performance during the tournament. It was incredible."

How involved do you get with sponsorship and broadcasting for FairBreak?

"We all have our hands on the tiller looking for sponsorship deals. Shaun, myself, and a few of the commercial people in FairBreak. We have a bunch of people who believe in and are passionate about the movement and we are all working on seeking sponsorship.

"The FairBreak Invitational was challenging because by the time we had travelled to the UAE, got all the agreements signed, and transferred the tournament from Hong Kong to Dubai, it was already the end of February 2022. With only three months, we had so many arrangements to make as well as contacting potential sponsors and having discussions. For the FairBreak Invitational 2023 in Hong Kong, we will have more time. We have a structure already in place, we have commercial and marketing people on it, and we are working with the exciting city of Hong Kong.

"Hong Kong has successfully run multiple international sports tournaments and brings a wealth of experience and knowledge. The city's contacts in the sponsorship space are invaluable. Plus, we have loyal sponsors from the past tournament. And we are working as a team with Cricket Hong Kong. In 2023, we will have many more irons in the fire compared to the short period we had to seek sponsorship for Dubai.

"Personally, I have two or three hats on at any one time. I am a sponsor of FairBreak. I am one of the equity holders of FairBreak. I am the second largest equity holder in FairBreak after Shaun. And I am a Cricket Hong Kong official.

"We broadcast the Dubai Tournament in 142 countries and we didn't pay a single penny for the broadcasting, in fact we received broadcast revenue. For 2023, we are targeting long-term broadcasting commitments. Having secure broadcast revenue will make a serious difference to the bottom line. If you look at most of the T20 Men's Cricket series worldwide, whether it's Big Bash League, India Premier League or The Hundred, the majority of their earnings come from broadcast revenue.

"We are taking a new product and its content into the broadcasting marketplace. This is not just about women's cricket, it's also about Associate women's cricket. We are combining and offering a unique product that nobody else in the cricket broadcasting market is offering. And we've set the standard by showing how we can run an engaging and massively successful global tournament."

How operationally involved do you get with FairBreak?

"I will always make time for FairBreak. I will always be fully behind it. Even when I'm travelling every day, I keep track of what's happening in FairBreak and I get involved. I split and manage my time so that I can follow my passion and support women's cricket.

"As a business owner of Gencor, I don't have to do everything myself. I have a great team of people working for me. Most of the time I am busy with my role as a scientist. I work on clinical research, product development, and strategic partners for the long term. My business involvement at Gencor is a long-term approach; what I do on a daily basis involves building for tomorrow. I have a management team in the business who take care of the deliverables.

"In a similar way at FairBreak, we are developing a management team to whom we give guidance and they follow up on operational issues. We use our business connections to develop commercial relationships, we talk to companies and people, and constantly spread the FairBreak message. We look for like-minded organisations to support us."

How is FairBreak fundamentally different to other cricket tournaments?

"FairBreak practices clean sport. We have a clean sport philosophy which means that FairBreak does not solicit or accept any sponsorship or funding from alcohol, cigarettes, gambling or betting related organisations. These are the most common causes of domestic violence and family breakdown, and they are a waste of money. We don't want to be associated with those things.

"Neither do we want to run FairBreak like a franchise model, the way the men's tournaments are run. In the India Premier League, players are auctioned and each franchise decides how much salary they will pay each player. They decide who they will bring into the team and who they will buy and sell at auction. That's what is happening. FairBreak does not believe that the auctioning of women is an appropriate way to run a cricket tournament.

"At FairBreak we have a standard pay structure. We have graded players A,B,C and D and for each grade the pay scale is the same. Each team is balanced not only in terms of the number of Test playing nation or Full Member Nation cricketers it contains, but also the number of Associate Nation cricketers it contains.

"Also, the teams are evenly organised in terms of opening batters, wicketkeepers, fast bowlers, spinners, and all-rounders. We organise that balance very carefully. Every team is balanced to have the same salary caps so that there are no disparities. We make it as fair as possible in every area, so that for every team there is the same salary cap, the same A,B,C and D gradings and the same player makeup.

"We have a management team who are all experienced professional cricketers like Geoff Lawson, Alex Blackwell, Sana Mir, and others. Shaun and I also contribute. We blend all that input and experience together so that each team is fairly structured and evenly balanced.

"FairBreak owns all the teams in the tournament. Similar to the Big Bash League and the Women's Big Bash League, Cricket Australia owns all the teams in those competitions and they give one to Perth, two to Melbourne, two to Sydney, one to Brisbane, and one to Hobart. In the UK with The Hundred, the England & Wales Cricket Board owns the eight teams in that league. They give some to the North, some to the South, two to London, one to Birmingham and so on.

"At FairBreak, we call for expressions of interest and players approach us requesting to play. Players also contact FairBreak selectors directly and our selection committee puts together the teams, a salary structure, the skill mix and a reserve list. The sponsors get only the brand rights for a particular team. They don't get to own the team, but they get fifteen brand ambassadors from fifteen different countries. They get brand exposure in those countries and they can use those players for brand promotion.

"If sponsors want to do individual marketing, endorsements, social media endorsements or to get commercial revenue, we tell them to make a deal with the player. Pay the player to be their commercial revenue generator, and FairBreak will not take a penny. FairBreak will help the players to make revenue if that's what the brand wants. If the brand wants to send their commercial message into Argentina, Brazil, Uganda, Tanzania, or into Namibia, use the cricketer. She can be their brand ambassador, but they make a separate deal with her.

"It's similar to how it works in the Tour de France. The cyclists in a TDF team ride for a brand or multiple brands. They are brand ambassadors. And when they go beyond being just brand ambassadors and do commercial promotions, they make their own deals. That's the distinct difference.

"This removes the ability of Team A or Team B or Team C having more sponsorship money than another team and being able to spend more money at a player auction to "buy" higher ranked players, skew the skill levels in the teams and increase the probability of winning. Not having an auction system removes that advantage.

"Of course, it has taken FairBreak time to convince many brands that this format is a sound idea. Male marketing managers think very traditionally. They want to apply the same format and terms to women's cricket as those that are used on the men's T20 circuit. They just could not understand it. They wanted to own the female teams and they wanted to auction, buy, and sell players, and to apply the same rules as they do in men's cricket. But FairBreak has continually refused to conform with this. A few of them, men of course, were pushing back hard saying, "Why? Please explain to us why you think our model won't work in women's cricket like it does in the men's?"

"FairBreak's answer is simple. If we are running a tournament, our first duty of care is to protect the girls. Nobody, under our remit, is going to buy, sell, own, or auction a woman. It's morally incorrect."

How will Hong Kong shine during the 2023 FairBreak Invitational?

"In April 2023, we are hoping for a packed out Kowloon Cricket Club. We are quite used to conducting these cricket tournaments in Hong Kong. We've done the Sixes for thirty years now, we also run the T20 Blitz and multiple international sporting tournaments.

"Hong Kong is well set up to handle these events and Kowloon Cricket Club can seat up to 4,000 people. Plus, we have corporate boxes and we always sell out the tickets and the boxes during tournaments. And the atmosphere of Kowloon Cricket Club, a small club in the centre of the city surrounded by high-rise buildings, gives us a unique charm. The ground is walking distance from the hotels and the waterfront. Everybody can go out to the bars and restaurants after the matches and enjoy themselves. Kowloon Cricket Club is located in Jordan, a shopping and sightseeing centre. It's always buzzing.

"The ground at Kowloon is much smaller than Dubai International Stadium, so filling it will be much easier and the atmosphere will be excellent. It'll be fun to see the girls hitting sixes into the stands and the crowd ducking! Kowloon Cricket Club is a famous place. Massive stars like Shane Warne, Glenn McGrath, Brian Lara, Mohammad Sami and Wasim Akram have played there. It has serious history! Hong Kong cannot wait to host the FairBreak Invitational in 2023."

Can FairBreak stand-alone financially?

"We are expecting FairBreak to stand financially on its own feet from Hong Kong 2023 onwards. We are expecting to cover all the costs of that tournament and even make a small profit. We have all hands-on-deck and we've secured quite a few sponsors already.

"We had a target for the last tournament about how much we would invest and how much we expected to come from sponsorship revenue. And we met that target. We knew that in the first year, we could not meet 100% of our expenses from sponsorship revenue. It was not fully funded from my side or from Gencor, we had brand sponsors investing money."

Where is FairBreak headed in the long-term?

"Now, as well as in the medium to long term, we are looking for FairBreak to be seen as an organisation cutting across borders and providing equal opportunities to all, irrespective of country and culture. In the women's cricket arena, whatever happens is very country specific. We break borders. We are about helping women to develop, and we don't stop at just cricket. We give the girls career and education advice; we help with sponsorship. We are here for women from all nations. That's why we are called FairBreak Global. We look globally at the development of women and the development of women's cricket. Wherever there's an opportunity to provide chances, we will provide them.

"In today's world, many consumers want the products they use, for example tea and coffee, to have been produced sustainably and ethically. Organisations are choosing to ensure that their resources are sustainably sourced and a fair price is paid to growers. We follow a similar philosophy; we believe in fair pay and opportunity for everybody across the globe irrespective of gender, country, or race."

Finally, who were your cricket heroes when you were growing up?

"I had two Indian cricket heroes when I was a young boy: the opening batsman, Sunil Gavaskar, and Kapil Dev the fast bowling all-rounder. Outside of India, Richard Hadlee from New Zealand, and Viv Richards from the West Indies. The first live cricket game I went to was in 1975, India versus West Indies at Chepauk Stadium in Chennai. Clive Lloyd was the West Indies Captain. It was a debut series for Viv Richards and Gordon Greenidge of the West Indies. I remember every bit of it. I remember India winning, so it was even more fun!

"Coincidentally, Shaun's cricket heroes were also West Indies players. Everybody loved their carefree, calypso style of batting, bowling, and having fun. They never took anything seriously. And they always had a laugh and a good time."

"I'd love to be part of FairBreak again if the opportunity arises as I had an incredible time in Dubai and love what it all stands for. Thank you for inviting me last time!"

Sarah Bryce, Scotland

The Bradman XI v FairBreak XI at Bowral in February 2020

It was decided that FairBreak needed to play some cricket in Australia. They needed to demonstrate what they could deliver. Not just in England, but at home in the cricketing nation where the movement had first started.

Shaun Martyn had grown up in Bowral in the Southern Highlands and had a close association with the renowned Bradman Oval. He had frequented this historical oval since first having been coached there as a small boy of seven years of age and having played in the historic game against Australia to relaunch the ground.

On 4 September 1976, improvements to the grounds were officially recognised with the re-dedication of Bradman Oval featuring a cricket match between a local team and a Jack Chegwyn XI led by Australian Captain, Doug Walters. Sir Donald Bradman and Bill O'Reilly both attended the celebrations as special guests. The match was commenced with O'Reilly ceremonially bowling the first ball to Bradman. A seventeen-year-old Shaun Martyn opened the bowling. He was the youngest member of the "local" team featuring emerging young Australian cricketers and local players. He opened the bowling against the then Australia XI including Rick McCosker and Alan Turner.

Martyn has had a long affinity and excellent working relationship with Rina Hore who was the executive director of the Bradman Museum and Bradman Foundation for many years. The Bradman Foundation had never fielded a Women's XI, so Martyn met with Hore, and suggested that they create a Bradman Foundation Women's XI to play a FairBreak XI in an exhibition match. The very first Bradman XI v FairBreak Global XI (dubbed the FairBreak Smash) duly took place on the afternoon of 22nd February 2022.

Alex Blackwell, former Women's Captain of Australia, skippered the inaugural Bradman Women's XI. As a former Bradman Scholar, and most importantly the first female Bradman Scholar, Blackwell received much needed financial support from the Bradman Foundation during her years at the University of New South Wales where she studied medicine while playing professional cricket.

Interviewed on the day by corporate sponsor Andrew Wildblood of Vocus Communications, Blackwell said, "The FairBreak initiative is all about creating equal opportunities for women from all around the world to reach their potential, and in particular through the sport of cricket...I have had a wonderful time playing for my country, for New South Wales, for many other teams...it's all about promoting opportunities for the next generation, not just for women in Australia, but for women all around the world and that's why I am so proud to be a part of FairBreak."

In addition, a preliminary match was played by the FairBreak II squad against Sydney Cricket Club before lunch, and a High Tea with Ann Sherry AO, was hosted indoors at the Bradman Museum.

Sherry, Chairwoman of UNICEF Global in Australia, an organisation delivering aid to children in many difficult to access, under-developed nations of the world, remarked on the day, "Sport is really important for all kids, it's great for health and it's a great place to come together and learn amazing things from each other. In the development context, girls are often excluded from lots of things, and in many of the countries we work, there are no options for girls. Sport gets girls out of the home and into environments where we can talk to them...and the power of sport is that you suddenly open up global opportunity.

"If we ever want to have proper equality, we need to have men and women equally participating in sport. It's real-life examples of the sense of possibility that comes from an event like this...the participation of these women from countries where they are not that valued on a day-to-day basis...and sport gives them value. Coming together to learn from each other across national boundaries, language boundaries, racial boundaries. All those things that we say we want for a better world. Sport does that. That's the reason why all the elite sporting codes are opening their doors properly to women. They now understand the power of that as well, and we are all going to push into that harder."

Also interviewed on the day, FairBreak XI skipper, Sana Mir, the former Captain of Pakistan, acknowledged, "FairBreak means a lot to me...growing up in Pakistan...there were no pathways for girls in Pakistan...we didn't have mentors with us at the beginning of our careers. FairBreak offered me an opportunity to be a mentor to women players in the Associate Nations…and I took it with both hands…it's wonderful to be there for people and it helps us pass the knowledge of cricket to people who we might never meet. And they get a mentor in us and they learn the game quicker than if we were not together.

"Any cricket that comes home to Pakistan, we feel very proud…the nation is crazy about cricket, we are cricket fanatics….We are very grateful to all the countries who have visited in the past to play the men's and women's teams…and now that Test cricket is being played that is exciting for us. The infrastructure of cricket in Pakistan is growing…it doesn't have as many layers to it as we can see in Australia, England, or India. If I compare from 2005 to now it's growing slowly. The game has changed for women over the last 15 years…the skills, the competition, and the financial aspects of the game…and the engagement we can now enjoy is remarkable."

The Bowral match generated unexpected publicity when the Home Affairs office of the Australian government initially denied the Botswanan player Shameelah Mosweu a visa to enter the country and play in the FairBreak XI on the basis that she was a "flight risk". Mosweu received a notice from the Australian government reading: "I am not satisfied that you genuinely intend to stay temporarily in Australia."

Shameelah Mosweu is currently one of the best female cricketers in Botswana, and in 2020 had represented Botswana in nine T20 Internationals, taking five wickets. "It is absurd she is being considered a security risk," Martyn said in a statement at the time. "The denial of this opportunity goes against everything that Australia aspires to in proclaiming a 'fair go' for all. Shameelah is a great example for the young men and women of Botswana and every country where opportunities to perform on a world stage are limited. She deserves, as does everyone, the right to accept opportunities to showcase talent and continue to grow as a person and inspire".

He described the decision to deny Mosweu a visa as "incredibly un-Australian". He continued, "It's not what we are about at all. We invited the Botswana Cricket Association to recommend a couple of players to our program…we were so impressed with Shameelah from a cricketing perspective and as a person that we decided to invite her to this program in Australia."

Martyn also said it was "ridiculous" that the visa was denied on the basis that "she wasn't going to go home" when FairBreak had paid for her return tickets. "She was booked to fly here on the 17th of February, and fly out on the 23rd," Martyn continued. "She is an elite player, if she was living in Australia, she'd be playing WBBL cricket, she's not someone mucking around at cricket."

At the time, former Australian Test bowler and FairBreak head coach Geoff Lawson also described the decision as "mindless" and described the trip as "life-altering" for her. He stated, "Mosweu is a seriously good player, it affects the team, and it also affects her progression and development. The best players in the world are here now for the 2020 Women's World Cup. It's a once in a lifetime opportunity. It's the mindless actions of bureaucracy. It's someone sitting at a desk going tick cross, so that's disappointing when an individual's circumstances aren't really considered."

Former NSW Premier Kristina Keneally echoed the condemnation, tweeting on social media:

> "Curious. The Morrison Govt turns a blind eye to 100,000 airplane asylum arrivals (many being trafficked here to work in exploited conditions). Says 'not a problem'. But then it blocks one elite female cricket player invited here to play in a tournament"
> Kristina Keneally (@KKeneally) February 19, 2020

Mosweu's absence would have seriously impacted the FairBreak squad if she had been denied entry to Australia. Fortunately, the public and media backlash caused the government's decision to be quickly reversed in time for Mosweu to travel to Bowral and open the batting for the FairBreak Global XI.

Rina Hore
Executive Director of the Bradman Foundation

Rina Hore is the former executive director of the Bradman Foundation in Bowral. Now retired and living on a farm outside Braidwood in NSW, she first met Shaun Martyn when he hired the Bradman Oval for one of his corporate networking cricket matches. At the time, he was Lisa Sthalekar's manager. He introduced Hore to the FairBreak Global movement a few years later.

Hore had been aware of WICL and the gender equality cause through the women's cricket network. She also knew Lisa Sthalekar as a young player coming up through the ranks. And Alex Blackwell had been supported by the Foundation as a Bradman Scholar. Hore was also a former team manager at Cricket NSW and had managed these young women when they played state cricket.

With the successful FairBreak XI tours to England in 2018 and 2019 as proof of what could be done, Martyn approached Hore about getting a FairBreak XI match on the ground in Australia. He had collateral from the matches in England and was able to show her photographs and testimonials.

Happy to assist, a date was set for the 22nd of February 2020, and Hore made the historic Bradman Oval in Bowral available to FairBreak. Her motivation was not only her support of Martyn, but because she felt it was time to drive change for female players who did not get enough match play opportunity.

Martyn was presenting a chance to provide an extra match to a range of young players who would probably never get to play with notable cricketers, so a mix of juniors and internationals really appealed to her. Hore then set about helping Martyn turn it into a landmark event while Martyn worked on assembling the players and organising the games. The day allowed for two matches which enabled them to field the Sydney Cricket Ground Women's XI who were trying to get themselves established. They played the team named FairBreak II in the morning, before lunch. The day would be an excellent opportunity to provide many young women with a quality game of cricket against international competition on the historic Bradman Oval.

Hore's involvement was project managing the venue. She is extremely proud that they were able to field two matches on the day. Not only was it a wonderful opportunity to launch FairBreak in Australia, but it was also significant for the establishment of the SCG Women's XI who were getting to play against quality opposition.

Hore hosted a High Tea in the Bradman Museum. Anne Sherry, the head of UNICEF Global was the guest speaker. In addition, up on stage for a Q&A, was an impressive panel consisting of Australian coach Julia Price, Sana Mir the former Captain of Pakistan's national team and Australia's former Women's Captain Alex Blackwell. All spoke articulately to the assembled audience.

Both matches were well attended by Southern Highlands locals and the followers of the players who came from the Sydney Cricket Club, as well as the younger and lower grade teams. All drawn to the famous Bradman Oval to mix with captivating international players.

The members of the Bradman Museum were all invited to the High Tea. As were Bowral locals, a few players not involved in the matches due to injury, local dignitaries, and the mayor of Wingecarribee Shire. A few cricket dignitaries from Cricket NSW also attended plus the tournament's sponsors.

Hore secured sponsorship for The Bradman XI team, captained by Alex Blackwell, from a telecommunications company called Vocus Communications who were already a partner of the Bradman Foundation. On the day, they filmed interviews between the CEO of Vocus and the players and captured excellent content. A short promotional video of Vocus supporting FairBreak was produced afterwards. The Vocus Communications CEO was thrilled with the amount of exposure that FairBreak gave his company because the matches and most of the day's events were live streamed.

Hore recalls the day with elation, she said, "Andrew Wildblood was able to interview the head of UNICEF Global, as well as the two captains, Sana Mir, and Alex Blackwell. There are some fabulous photos of the two teams and the trophy. The Vocus marketing team edited all the content and put it up on the company's website and social media. Vocus Communications got great value out of it. The CEO respected the FairBreak cause and the effort we put into the organisation of the day.

"One of the drawcards to get Vocus sponsorship was exclusive access to the international players and the ability to interview them. Vocus were seeking a new international audience and the significant social media following of some of the players promised to deliver that. Gencor and TechnologyOne were FairBreak's sponsors on the day.

"The Bradman Foundation members were ecstatic with the whole event. It was a very successful day for us in terms of the quality of the players, the coverage of international players was exceptional. It was incredibly special. It was a marquee match and was well received by everyone locally and all the dignitaries. Everyone likes to see a marquee match like that. And the weather was glorious. We had fantastic sponsors and it got global coverage. Shaun delivered global streaming of both matches and most of the day's other events."

The 2020 event was so successful, Hore and Martyn decided to repeat the event towards the end of the season in March/April 2021 when COVID-19 restrictions eased and cricket was allowed to be played. Junior, local and a couple of international players who live in Australia were assembled at the Southern Highlands ground the day before, but heavy rain on the Saturday morning cancelled play completely and caused widespread disappointment. Fortunately, no accompanying social event had been organised due to the prevailing COVID-19 restrictions around hosting indoor events at that time.

Hore admitted she was saddened about the switch of cities from Hong Kong to Dubai as she was planning to attend the tournament at Kowloon Cricket Ground. Despite that she followed it on screen at home. She stated, "The live streaming of FairBreak's matches has been crucial. Many of my friends watched Dubai and they all raved about how good the tournament was. The coverage was just outstanding. I think Shaun has built a solid following on the excellence of his media people who have been instrumental in getting it out there globally."

Hore drew upon her years of cricket experience and reflected on why FairBreak is so significant for women's cricket. She said, "Shaun does it because of his passion for the players. He is giving female cricketers valuable opportunities to play and to be involved. He is offering the next level of play, which is missing in women's cricket.

"The ICC are starting to build the U/19s now, but they have not yet hosted the inaugural U/19s Women's Tournament. That's scheduled for early 2023. Girls have been playing U/19s and U/15s competitions in their own countries for the last twenty years. But there has been nothing offered to them internationally at the next level. Shaun is filling a gap there, and he's brought in the Associate Nations as well, which has never happened before."

I asked Hore how this compares with the opportunities to play internationally that are offered to the U/19 boys. She informed me, "Well, the girls are thirty years behind the boys. Boys have been playing in ICC Boys Under19 international tournaments for thirty years. The first Girls U/19s tournament isn't scheduled until February 2023.

"If you look at the Australian Men's team, indeed every international men's team, most certainly in the Test nations and ODIs, you can track all of the players who have come through the U/19s international pathway. All our Australian players will have played the ICC International U/19 Boys tournaments. Whereas the inaugural ICC International U/19 Girls Tournament is thirty years behind and hasn't even happened yet. Admittedly, it's twelve months delayed due to the COVID-19 pandemic, but it's still thirty years longer that the boys have had this pathway in place.

"The chances for girls to get to play at a level with international exposure have been very sparse. There has been no structured competition. Furthermore, most of the money that has been made available annually to foster women's cricket, and is now quite substantial, goes to the top tier teams.

"Shaun is giving girls from Associate countries the opportunity to play with ladies in the top tier nations and that's true progress. Those girls will learn skills they can take home to their own countries and it will speed up the development of emerging players in those Associate Nations.

"The boys have always had that type of system. The girls haven't quite got it yet, so Shaun is filling an obvious gap, and at a time when we need more content and the girls want more opportunity. I reckon he is still pulling teeth. Because that's how women's cricket works. There has to be people prepared to fight the battles to win the war, and that war in women's cricket and female sport is ongoing. Shaun is right in the middle of it.

"He has really nailed the global exposure. It has made sports viewers start a conversation and ask about this organisation that is helping grow women's cricket. They are asking, "Is it a threat? Is it like the IPL? Is it going to take away from the women's game?"

"That's how cricket works. The cricket boards are paranoid. Which is why the Women's IPL has taken so long to get going. They are afraid that growing the women's game will detract from or take away from the men's game. But it's a totally different product.

"The individuals in the countries that have quietly and tirelessly promoted women's cricket over the last ten to fifteen years are now getting some real cut through, and Shaun has been able to expose a gap in the global development of women's cricket. It will be interesting to see how many players who play in the ICC's U/19 Girls tournament in January 2023 have already played for FairBreak. As the young girls in Associate Nations move up, we will be able to pin it back, historically, to the significance of FairBreak.

"Watch the performances of the players in Hong Kong in 2023, and I bet each and every one of them will hold their own. We will be able to trace that confidence back to the opportunity that was provided to them in Dubai, at the Bradman Oval in 2020 and the England tours back in 2018 and 2019. Invaluable exposure and experience for young players is crucial. The girls pick it up very quickly and they get accustomed to it and they collaborate with each other.

"Today, men's and boy's cricket are cut-throat. Everyone wants to be a professional cricketer and they are walking all over each other to hustle for the opportunities. Whereas the girls are still wanting to help each other. There is a healthy mindset in the women's game around helping each other.

"The girls, and I have said this throughout the forty years I've been involved in women's cricket, the girls HAVE to enjoy playing. If it becomes a chore, they move on and retire. The girls enjoy the experience of playing together. They have just as good a time off the field as they do on it. They don't have a vindictive streak in any of them. They're competitive, yes, they want to perform, but they're not openly destructive to other players.

"Girls want everyone to succeed. At the moment, the current cohort of players are excellent at fostering younger players. They just need the opportunity to be with those younger players. And there's no pathway there internationally other than with FairBreak. So that's why it isn't surprising that this concept is successful. Shaun has a unique formula and he had a window of opportunity."

Hore knows, from experience, that it takes an enormous amount of time and effort to pull any sporting tournament together. During our interview, I shared with her some of the behind-the-scenes dramas in Dubai that she would not have been aware of. Despite there being a carefully picked team of dedicated staff, the event experienced several issues that were outside of their control; for example, trying to get the uniforms out of customs, businesses shutting down for Ramadan and the Emirati head of state dying and throwing the region into forty days of official mourning.

"Such drama gives the story even more flavour", she laughed enthusiastically, "and shows the fortitude it takes to put an event of this size together when you don't have a massive paid workforce to do it. That's why I was in awe of the success of it. For someone looking on from the sidelines, it appeared seamless. Many of my friends are golfers. They don't talk about cricket to me, but for the first time in a long time they were talking energetically about the cricket.

"They were fully invested in the Dubai Tournament because they had come along to the High Tea and the FairBreak XI matches in Bowral, and they had met some of the international players and watched the younger players. They had become avid followers because they got to meet some of these cricketers.

"I look forward to reading the FairBreak book and learning about what went on behind the scenes because I know, from personal experience, how hard it is to put on a cricket match for women in a world where everything is still very much governed by the man's dollar. Men still control the dollars in global sport."

Jaimie Fuller
SKINS Founder and Social Activist

"A man is known by the company he keeps..."

Aesop

Jaimie Fuller has built a successful business career around his greatest passion, sport. He was the Chief Executive Officer of the international compression apparel brand SKINS from 1998 to 2019. He is now the Chair and co-founder of eo, an Australian-based sports technology company utilising world-class sports scientists and engineers to help elite athletes redefine their limits. eo is developing a range of products designed to improve performance, accelerate recovery and adaptation, prevent injury, and aid rehabilitation.

Fuller is also a prominent sports activist, initiating campaigns and speaking out against cheating, systemic corruption, and human rights abuses at the highest levels of several international sports including cycling, football, and the Olympics. He has led campaigns against homophobia in sport and he is a regular commentator and contributor for public forums and conferences around the world on the role sport can play in helping to change society for the better.

It was extremely important to interview Jaimie Fuller for this book. I wanted to capture his perspectives on FairBreak and the organisation's journey. He also spoke to me at length about the far-reaching effects of his social activism. I hope the readers of this book will find what Fuller had to say informative about what goes on in that space. He is a passionate advocate of FairBreak's mission and has been an empathetic sounding board for Shaun Martyn for many years.

"I have used my business brand, SKINS, as a platform for social activism. My first crack at that was back in 2012, in the wake of the Lance Armstrong saga. In 2014, Shaun and I first started talking about trying to use sport as a lens for social programs and so we looked at prejudice across three areas: gender, race, and sexual choice. We started articulating around these topics and started pushing out campaigns and generating publicity. This was before FairBreak. This was when the organisation was still known as the Women's International Cricket League.

"Shaun and I got talking and collaborating and I helped him however I could with whatever intellectual property I could bring to the table. And it's built from there. Obviously, I am a huge fan of FairBreak and what they are doing around resolving injustice.

"FairBreak is a business and I am a businessperson who understands the realities of life and the fact that there are people in positions of power within sports governance who suppress the things that we want to see changed. Probably because they're old. It's true! Go down an age group or two, and you get far more open minds. My kids are far more accepting of difference. People in positions of power are older than me and many of them are dinosaurs who don't care about the issues. All they are interested in is money. Quite often they're interested in money for themselves, and that's when corruption plays a role.

"I'm not saying that's the case with the ICC. But I have had plenty of contact with individuals in world sports governance who have been corrupt. Football is a perfect example. FIFA is riddled with corruption. Guys, in power, raking in millions at the expense of the game and at the expense of people playing the game, the fans, the grassroots and the facilities.

"When you get individuals, like Shaun, who have the right intentions, who are wanting to move the needle and use sport to progress society, or even just to push for progress within sport itself, there is an element of needing to be realistic.

"For example, take the gender situation in cricket. The harsh reality is that when you look at the money that is generated in the sport through broadcasting and ticket sales, the majority of it is coming from the men's game as opposed to the women's game. To sit there and say that the Australian Women's Captain should be paid as much as the Australian Men's Captain, I don't agree with that. But what should happen is Cricket Australia should be investing in the women's game and closing the gap. And there has been some progress made on that level, but not enough progress, and not fast enough.

"We are seeing now, particularly in the women's game, much more interest from cricket viewers. That was evident years ago. But there are old men who sit at the top of the tree who are uncreative, and have a cookie cutter, formulaic mindset. You have to go out and prove to them what can be done before they'll believe it. As opposed to a mindset that facilitates getting in there early, starting the ball rolling, building momentum, and then watching it grow earlier and quicker. And that is what FairBreak butts up against.

"The role that I can play for Shaun is to come at this from a commercial perspective. There are a couple of things I can do for him. Firstly, I can offer my platform. Unfortunately, I lost my platform back in 2019 when the whole SKINS thing imploded. So, I have spent the last three years getting my new business, eo, to where it is now. When we have a platform again, FairBreak will be one of the organisations I will work with to champion the causes we all believe in.

"Secondly, I have a lot of experience in the governance space in terms of my activism and making change happen. Just because you want to make an impact doesn't mean it's going to happen. You've got to be strategic. And the fact is I've done it, and I've gone the hard yards. And once you've done it, you then get ticks in the credibility box.

"When you sit down with the media, everybody has an opinion and everybody wants their opinion heard. But the media don't print everybody's opinion. They print the opinions of those they call "subject matter experts". And through the work that I have done, there's a lot of media who look at me as a "subject matter expert" on issues to do with integrity and sport and issues to do with eradicating prejudice in sport. So, I can bring that expertise to the table for FairBreak.

"Shaun has been absolutely driven by all the right sentiments. And he's delivered the first tournament, which is a big thing. But there are always going to be cynics who will look at what he's done and say, "Well, this is just a money play". And I know this because I've had the same accusations made about me. But Shaun has to go through that journey and it costs a lot of time, money and sweat to achieve things. And Shaun has achieved that with the FairBreak Invitational in Dubai. That is a big tick in the credibility box.

"I can bring not only strategic experience and knowledge, but hopefully, my attachment will bring endorsement, credibility, and authenticity. I have been involved with several campaigns in cricket [Fuller is referring here to *The Change Cricket* campaign for the redistribution of resources from richer cricketing nations to poorer ones]. Back in the day, I took on the English, Australian and Indian Cricket Boards. The three countries who plundered world cricket for their own benefit. The three most powerful cricket nations who put their heads together and conspired to take the lion share of funding from the ICC. Which meant that funding was taken away from poorer nations who really needed it.

"From memory, there were ten Test playing, Full Member Nations who all shared equally in 75% of ICC funds. They each got 7.5%. And then all the Associate Nations like the Netherlands and Ireland shared the other 25% of the money available. Australia, England, and India conspired with each other and pushed through a change to the funding distribution whereby they alone took 52% of the money between them. India alone took 32%. England took 12% and Australia took 8%. Each of those countries enriched themselves, voted together, and used their collaborative power to get the decision passed through the ICC that they could take most of the funding. At that stage, India had $2 to $3 billion in reserves. India didn't even need the money. And when they did that, they deprived countries like Pakistan, South Africa, New Zealand, and the West Indies. It was a short-term money grab, which was not technically corrupt. But it was morally and ethically wrong to divest the smaller nations who really needed it.

"In 2015, an award winning documentary film was made about the subject called *Death of a Gentleman*. I got involved with launching the film and a public awareness campaign in the UK. We published a full-page advertisement in the local newspaper of the chairman of the ECB's village announcing the funeral of Test cricket. We organised a funeral march and a wreath was laid outside The Oval Cricket Ground in London by a Conservative Member of Parliament. We did this to officially proclaim that these three nations were killing cricket for everyone else. This created broader awareness because most people did not know anything about what was going on at the top of world cricket. So, when the scandalous facts emerged everybody said, "That's horrendous. How can they do that?" So, when you orchestrate a campaign like that, suddenly the pressure gets applied and the situation is unwound.

"But the issue for me was why did they do it in the first place? It was obviously ethically and morally bankrupt. You have to understand what the ICC is. The ICC is basically ten representatives from the top ten cricket playing countries. And what happens behind the scenes is India says to South Africa, "If you don't support this decision, we won't tour to South Africa". And if you understand the money trail, all of these cricket nations make their money out of broadcasting rights.

"How much money do you think Cricket Australia gets for the broadcasting rights for a series against Sri Lanka, or against New Zealand, or against Zimbabwe? When Zimbabwe tour Australia, Cricket Australia sells the broadcasting rights and receives revenue from the Zimbabwean Broadcasting Corporation. Imagine how much more revenue Cricket Australia gets for an India tour to Australia? Cricket Australia can sell those broadcasting rights in India where there are a billion people wanting to watch it. Those media rights are worth a vast amount of money.

"So what happened was the three powerhouses of England, India and Australia went to Sri Lanka, West Indies, New Zealand, Pakistan, and South Africa and said, "If you guys don't support us to push this funding decision through, we are not going to tour and play in your countries and you won't get the money from the broadcasting revenue from our tours". It was horrendously successful and horrendously cynical.

"This gives you an insight into the way minds work in sports governance, and when I said to you at the beginning of this interview that this is all about money. This is REALLY all about money! This isn't about how do we promote a game and get girls into it and help break this awful dynamic of a pay gap between the men and the women. This isn't about how do we bust all that open so that my daughter has the same potential rights as my son.

"It's technically not corrupt. It's morally corrupt, it's ethically corrupt, but it's technically not corrupt. Take the instance of when Sepp Blatter sold the broadcasting rights for the Caribbean for two Football World Cups to a guy named Jack Warner for US$600,000. And Jack Warner on sold those rights for US$20million. Sepp Blatter did a sweetheart deal because he wanted Jack Warner's continuing support so that he could stay on as FIFA president.

"There is no evidence that Sepp Blatter got a piece of that $19.4million windfall. I believe he gave that financial windfall to Jack Warner. But he got Jack Warner's networking votes when it came to the next FIFA presidential election. Blatter was earning three million Swiss Francs every year. He never put his hand in his pocket for anything. Private jets, 5-star hotels, he was treated like a head of state everywhere he went, and that's what turned him on. Whereas Jack Warner wanted the cash. When you sell broadcasting rights like that for $600,000, when you're deliberately and knowingly undervaluing them and selling them, that is technically corrupt. Whereas all that cricket funding stuff with Australia, India, and England, that was only ethically corrupt.

"Most people need to understand that FIFA does not own world football. The ICC doesn't own world cricket. We, the people, own cricket, and we own football. It's ours. And people like Sepp Blatter, when he was president of FIFA, refused to reveal his salary. And the perverse thing is, we own FIFA, it's owned by everybody. We employed Sepp Blatter. Yet he would not tell us how much we were paying him. To add insult to injury, FIFA has got a special designation in the Swiss legal system as a charity, and the reason that FIFA is registered as a charity is so it doesn't have to pay tax.

"FIFA enjoys tax free status in Switzerland. As opposed to ordinary businesses that pay tax. So, when you think about it, not only are we not allowed to know how much Sepp Blatter was paid, but the organisation is also a charity. So, you've got opaqueness within a charity, the running of that charity and the decisions that it makes about finances. It makes no sense. If an entity is registered as a charity, then it should be a transparent entity, because we want to make sure that the maximum amount of money goes to where it needs to go.

"FIFA uses the money they distribute like a carrot. They have funding they send to countries and they basically say, "If you want this money, you'd better vote for me", and whoever is the incumbent in a position gets to…manipulate it. And that's why sports governance bodies are open to being bastardised and corrupted, and cricket, quite frankly, is no different.

"When I talk about being realistic and practical, it must be about more than just motherhood statements. When we believe in these wonderful values, the desire to achieve them has to be underpinned with realism and practicality. And you've got to understand the structure, the levers, and the motivations in order to navigate the system.

"For example, in 2015, we ran a social activism campaign on the FIFA World Cup. We realised that we needed to humanise the victims of the corruption within FIFA. And the best way that we could expose that was by looking at the labour abuses going on in Qatar for the construction for the 2022 World Cup.

"Qatar has a population of 2.3 million people. Of those 2.3 million people, only 350,000 are Qatari nationals. Just under two million people are migrant workers. Two million workers come from impoverished South Asia nations like Nepal and Bangladesh and work in Qatar. And the laws in Qatar are such that when those workers go there for a job, the first thing they have to do, once they arrive, is hand over their passport to their employer. They are in Qatar for a two-year contract and they cannot leave and they cannot change jobs. They are housed in appalling living conditions. They work six days per week, twelve hours per day. Very often they are paid, if they are ever paid, very late. I am talking six months, nine months, twelve months without being paid.

"We realised in early 2015 that we needed to put a human face on all of this because most people are not aware of or don't really care about corruption. What really drove it home was a conversation I had with a journalist in the UK, and me saying to him, "I need to work out how to get through to people that this corruption is happening", and he said to me, "I would suggest you think about the Milly Dowler Effect".

"Milly Dowler was a fourteen-year-old schoolgirl who disappeared one day in the UK. The police searched for her and eventually her body was found. She had been murdered. It was a shocking tragedy. But why this became such a big issue was because her parents kept calling her mobile phone and leaving messages, and the police were able to trace, through the telecommunications company, that messages were being cleared from her voicemail. So, they believed that she was still alive because she was clearing her messages.

"It turned out that it wasn't Milly who was clearing the messages. It was revealed that *The News of the World* newspaper had hacked her phone and they were clearing her messages. And this is what blew up into The Leveson Inquiry in the UK. This is what led to Rupert Murdoch sitting in front of a House of Commons Committee, apologising and admitting that it was the most humbling day of his life. Milly Dowler's murder exposed the phone hacking that these newspapers had been doing for years.

"The reason I bring this up is because phone hacking by newspapers was not a priority before the Milly Dowler case came to light. Nobody was that bothered about Hugh Grant and Sienna Miller complaining about it. The moment that Milly Dowler's phone was revealed to have been hacked, and the tragedy of a murdered schoolgirl and what her parents went through emerged, that collapsed the whole tabloid media sector in the United Kingdom for a period of time. And ended up with Rupert Murdoch going through the most humiliating of investigations. And it fractured politics in the UK.

"I needed to find the Milly Dowler Effect. I needed to put a human face on the corruption. Many Nepalese workers, at this time, were dying in Qatar on construction sites. Dying of heat exhaustion, dying due to poor work safety standards. I flew to Qatar and was introduced to a person who was, literally, a fixer, by the head of sport at the BBC and I was smuggled into labour camps. I took hidden camera footage, and I interviewed workers, and I took it all back to London and we made a short film called *The Hypocrisy World Cup*. Then we took that human tragedy film, and we targeted Coca-Cola, Visa and McDonalds who were FIFA's sponsors and we went after them.

"We showed them *The Hypocrisy World Cup* and we said, "You are hypocrites, you signed up to the United Nation's Charter of Human Rights. You sponsor this organisation, FIFA, which suppresses human rights by awarding the World Cup to Qatar, which has a kafala labour system, which not only takes away the rights of workers but kills them in their thousands." At that stage, it was estimated 6,000 migrant workers had died in Qatar. Thousands of people were dying in the construction of the infrastructure for the FIFA World Cup!

"That led to Coca-Cola, Visa and McDonalds condemning FIFA and demanding that Sepp Blatter step down. That had never happened before. No sponsor had ever demanded the resignation of the president of an organisation on the scale of FIFA. So, after telling you all this, the point I want to make is that there are things that can be done. And that sometimes you've got to take the gloves off and you've got to fight dirty to get a crucial message across.

"When the FIFA issue blew up, Coca Cola, Visa and McDonalds put out press releases saying, "We expect our partners to perform at the highest levels and we look forward to FIFA embracing these values." It's not until you shine a light on an important issue and personalise it that people take notice and say enough is enough.

"There are all sorts of things that can be done, but they need to be done well. Just sitting there saying fluffy stuff doesn't cut it. I can tell you most business owners in my shoes would never have done what I did because it's risky and you're going to upset people and rock boats. But I was very clear at the time that it was a business strategy. It was a way of not only leading change, but also having my brand out there and it being synonymous with this social activism and the media writing about it. It's press and PR and doing television interviews. And with each of those, the message goes out that Jaimie Fuller is chairman of SKINS or eo, and that works for me."

[Further Reading contains an article from *The Guardian* dated 1st March 2016 by Ali Martin titled "ECB Chief, Giles Clarke to explain role in ICC Takeover to MPs"]

"FairBreak is a platform for us semi-athletes in Associate countries to feel equal and an opportunity to feel like we belong in the world of professional sport. Dubai FB122 was one such experience that assured me that I belong with the best legends of the game. It has been game-changing in taking my cricket to the next level."

Sindhu Sriharsha, USA

Meet The Lawyers

Charles Cowper and Kym Livesley

Charles Cowper was at Gadens law firm in March 2016 when he first met Shaun Martyn at their central Sydney office. A female lawyer from Gadens had attended a sports forum, been impressed with what Martyn was doing and had arranged an introductory meeting for him at Gaden's offices where he met with Cowper who offered him pro bono advisory assistance. The deal being that once FairBreak was sanctioned by the ICC it would then become a normal commercial relationship.

What reservations did you have about Shaun Martyn and his venture?

"This business goes back a long time, surprisingly, so I take my hat off to him. I respect his resilience because when he first started this journey EVERYTHING was against him. The cricket authorities worldwide were against it. He told me, "I don't have approval from the ICC. I don't have approval from Cricket Australia. I don't have approval of the Indian Cricket Board or the English Cricket Board".

"And I thought to myself, "Well, these are very powerful organisations. Good luck!" At the back of my mind, I kept feeling, "the chances of this flying are…yeah, good luck to him". But he stuck to it, and all sorts of things were thrown at him. COVID-19 and then Hong Kong. All sorts of issues. Just when he thought he'd got there, something else would blow up.

"One day, when Shaun was particularly frustrated and disheartened, I asked him, "When is enough enough Shaun?" He believes I posed that question as a test to determine how long he was going to be in the fight. Whether he would see it out, and what it would take for him to give up and walk away.

"Shaun's tenacity was just amazing, and as lawyers we just ran with it. Then finally all the dominoes started to fall and he got ICC approval. I think he may have had somebody on side at the ICC or the ECB who championed his cause, and then Cricket Australia fell into line.

"There were times when I thought it would all end up in court. I could see someone at the ICC challenging his ability to run a women's cricket competition. That it would end up in some court somewhere, at great expense to him, where they would just blow him out of the water."

How did Dentons (although you were a senior partner at Gadens when you first met) provide legal assistance?

"Shaun had an Information Memorandum which needed some work. We got approval for the firm to do some work for him on a pro bono basis. Acknowledging that if this thing flew, it was going to get big and, at some point, he would need some capital funds to pay advisors. He would need the best accounting advice, tax advice, legal advice, and advice to secure his intellectual property. That was going to cost money.

"Documents such as an Information Memorandum when you're trying to put an organisation like this together are significant. Shaun's IM, at the start, was very light on detail and he was proposing to use it to help raise finance and find a partner to get some money and backing. He didn't have his background documents and instructions thought through. So that was the advice we were giving him at the time. He needed to turn his mind to the detail of the structuring. All that got properly detailed and documented when Kym Livesley and his team at Dentons got involved with shareholder agreements, etc.

"It was a softly, softly, slowly, slowly approach. I was concerned. This was an international venture and he was going to need to work out where would be the best place in the world to set up. Where best to structure it all from a corporate tax point of view. How to protect the intellectual property.

"At that stage, FairBreak wasn't on the agenda, it was still Women's International Cricket League. Then over the course of the next eighteen months or so, the FairBreak brand started to emerge. I was concerned that he needed to protect his intellectual property, in such a fashion as to not have the day-to-day operations put any intellectual property at risk.

"Early on, I was introducing him to people around Sydney who could give him some tax and structuring advice. And to help register trademarks. Dealings with Shaun were such that he'd go away for a long period of time, disappear, and then pop up in India or England. We'd hear nothing for months and then suddenly he'd be back saying we need to do this, this, and this.

"I always wanted to know where he'd got to and what he'd done with the advice I'd given him. I was concerned that, perhaps, he wasn't dotting the i's and crossing the t's. I'm a typical lawyer! Obviously, he was trying to, strategically, get the whole concept approved at a higher level, and get financing in place with his partner from India at Gencor, Mr. Venkatesh.

"I was concerned sometimes that he wasn't giving it the detailed attention it deserved, but I think that was all swept up at the end once he understood what he was doing. He had a partner, he knew that money was coming in, and he had defined how it was going to work. Because it was a bit of a journey, and it was developing both in his mind and as he spoke to people and received feedback. The concept changed a bit along the way. So, it was probably just as well we didn't get into too much detail in the very early days.

"When he started to put meat on the bones, so to speak, Kym Livesley took over and he did all the heavy lifting on drafting the documentation and the negotiations."

Tell me about how you and Dentons have connected with FairBreak's Corporate Social Responsibility program

"During the years we have had some fun. Dentons supported a function of Shaun's at the Sofitel Hotel in Sydney. We took a table at a sports focus function he ran with the fellow from Solar Buddy, Simon Doble.

"Then we had a Solar Buddy evening in the Sydney office of Dentons on a Friday night where we got lots of people in, had a few drinks, and we all sat around the table and assembled all the Solar Buddy lights. We had them branded with the Dentons logo.

"I was keen to explore opportunities in our PNG office. I wanted to roll out those lights in the villages of Papua New Guinea where security for women particularly is a major concern, and for the kids to be able to do their homework and go to the bathroom at night. So we sent several boxes of the Solar Buddy lights up to our PNG office and we got them distributed up there."

How did you get involved with the match in Bowral, FairBreak's first game on the ground in Australia?

"We started to get some buy-in from the Dentons office around what FairBreak was trying to achieve. In the week before the FairBreak XI game in Bowral in February 2020, just before the world went crazy with COVID-19, we had a function in the Sydney office and we invited Alex Blackwell, Mariko Hill and the Captain of the USA national team, Sindhu Sriharsha. There was a Q&A, and we had a partner from our Brisbane office, Kirsten Pike fly down to join us. I didn't know it at the time, but Kirsten used to play cricket for Australia. She flew down for the evening and we had a great function in the office in the run up to the game at Bowral.

"My wife and I travelled to the Southern Highlands for the weekend, and we went to the cricket in Bowral. The weather was absolutely freezing. It was still supposed to be summer. It was just after the bushfires, but the weather was starting to change. It was also just before COVID-19 and, of course, a week or two later, Shaun wouldn't have been able to do any of it because people couldn't enter Australia from other parts of the world. There was also the problem of getting a visa for the player from Botswana, Shameelah Mosweu. Fortunately, that turned out well and he got some publicity out of it."

How did Dentons get involved with what happened next?

"From my point of view, the whole tournament thing went on the back burner during the pandemic. Everybody stayed home and worked from home for two years. The whole issue about launching the tournament, I think he was talking about Singapore to start with, and then Hong Kong. I'm not sure of the extent to which all those democracy demonstrations and the crackdown in Hong

Kong affected the plans. Hong Kong might have become difficult for him. And of course, there was Hong Kong's twenty one days quarantine situation. So he ended up launching, spectacularly, this year in Dubai.

"I stepped back from the FairBreak work a few years ago when I stepped back as a partner of Dentons. Shaun needed more hands-on help with shareholder agreements, player contracts and team contracts. So, Kym Livesley took over and he went to the tournament in Dubai where Dentons sponsored the stumps and we put the firm's logo on the sleeves of the umpires' shirts.

"There's nothing quite like testing it and seeing the success of it. Perhaps we can leverage more involvement from the firm as a sponsor next year when we can see what we got from it. I'd like to go to one of these tournaments, myself, at some stage. I'll probably go next year, in 2023, to Hong Kong.

"I was really pleased that the firm had stepped up to it and seen the value in it. Particularly as Dentons like to make a bit of noise about diversity and inclusion. This became much more than just a cricket competition. It became more about raising up opportunity for women in emerging countries. It got some buy-in with the firm. I tried to get the London office interested at one stage in the games that Shaun was having in England, at Wormsley, but it was all too hard for them."

Did you watch the FairBreak Tournament in Dubai?

"I engaged with the Dubai tournament through social media. Every LinkedIn post I saw seemed to be about the FairBreak tournament. He's nailed that well. I think the members of his digital marketing team are doing a great job. Even between tournaments when there's downtime in activity, they keep the message out there."

How do you reflect on the part you and Dentons have played in FairBreak's journey?

"I have to say FairBreak is a relationship that I am very happy and proud to be involved in. It's good at any stage in one's career to be part of something that is going to make a difference. I am really glad that Dentons engaged with it and we were able to help deliver the Dubai Tournament with some acknowledgement of what FairBreak is doing. Because the firm as a whole, internationally, has diversity and inclusion as one of their main drivers, so it was a no brainer. It did take me some time to convince both our women's group in the Sydney office and, more broadly, some of the internationals, to come on board.

"Now they've seen there's been success, we can circle around next time and keep promoting it. Especially as there are a few FairBreak players who work in the legal world, Yasmin Daswani, the Hong Kong player, is a lawyer in London for example. There are some very impressive young women involved with FairBreak and it's a really good story. So, I'm glad it's being told. Shaun needs to be acknowledged.

"I watch the Australian cricket teams, male and female, whenever they play. I'm a great cricket fan and I was aware of the emerging women's cricket competitions nationally. I'm not sure when the WBBL started but I think it might have been a Cricket Australia response to some of the things that Shaun was doing.

"FairBreak has brought a new dimension to it all though. Shaun doesn't just pick the elite national players. He'd come into the Dentons office and tell me about a girl in Vanuatu who bowls faster than whoever. Or a girl from the Netherlands who hits the ball out of the ground. He was always talking about these non-traditional cricket nations with all this talent. So, I'm glad that we have been able to make a small contribution to it all."

Kym Livesley is a partner in the Sydney office of Dentons, the world's largest law firm. He manages an international and gender diverse team of managing associates and oversees all the legal advice work for FairBreak.

From a personal perspective, Livesley enjoys watching cricket and numerous sports. He attended high school in Adelaide where Ian, Greg and Trevor Chapell were ahead of him at school and the standard of cricket was exceptionally high.

FairBreak resonates for him because of the mission. He said, "To be inclusive with these young female cricketers all around the world. We've got our domestic T20 and we have the Australian national team, but it's the opportunities being given to the girls in the Associate countries that really matter. Countries where some of them don't even have kit, they don't even have a bat or gloves. Dentons were delighted to be able to assist. It is an honour to be associated with such a cause.

"I've always been interested in women's cricket, but this is a unique construct. I've found FairBreak to be more egalitarian and more inclusive of the range of young women from underdeveloped nations who have never had opportunity before. Our little group in Dentons is quite diverse which I really like.

"I get exposed to various issues that women, especially in sport, are facing. Sport is not as inclusive as it might appear. My team helps with the sports law issues. The fact that it sits perfectly with our diversity and inclusion group is purely coincidental. The sports law background that I have has probably helped in terms of assisting Shaun and Geoff.

"The biggest roadblock for FairBreak was the ICC and getting approval from them. That's taken many years. Everybody has their fiefdom and everybody wants to protect their patch. Anybody coming in, suggesting something new, tends to shift the balance. Some people get concerned about their own position and their organisation's position. When someone comes up with a good idea, it's human nature that others want to put it down because they wish they'd thought of it first. I think all those reactions were at play from a political and human point of view.

"What Shaun and FairBreak have done is open the eyes of the ICC to a distinct tournament format that can be more inclusive. I hope FairBreak prompts the ICC and other associations around the world to look at their own backyard in terms of how they approach women's cricket.

"I personally would like to see FairBreak become a permanent fixture on the international cricketing calendar because it offers something that's unique. It's a combination of women from thirty five countries, where most of them would never have got the chance to play with the major cricketing nations like Australia, India, England, and South Africa. There is a place for it in my view, and I'd like to see it continue. I don't see why it shouldn't continue, and in fact, evolve and become stronger.

"Of course, there were all the other challenges. The management and administrative challenges in the last eighteen months. COVID-19 being a giant challenge. Not going to Hong Kong, which was terribly disappointing and having to relocate from Hong Kong to Dubai. Extraordinarily challenging in terms of the logistics required."

Dentons sponsored the umpires and stumps at the FairBreak Invitational in Dubai, and Livesley flew into the United Arab Emirates enroute to a partners' meeting to watch the tournament from Days 3 to 5. While on the ground, he was brought up to date with some of the trials and tribulations Martyn and the FairBreak team were dealing with behind the scenes.

"One of the administrative headaches was the money cards for the per diem [daily allowance for meals and incidental expenses] payments to the players. We are still negotiating with AirWallex to get back the actual outlay that was required to get another company to do what they should have. AirWallex spruiked that their product could do all these things, and the fact is they could not. It was a complete revelation to them. They knew exactly what the international tournament was all about. They knew what was required and their product just did not deliver."

Livesley was impressed with everything else at the FairBreak Invitational, he said, "Dubai was curious because, obviously, there was no crowd. It was slightly bizarre because it was an empty stadium. Nevertheless, everything else about it was very much a professional T20 type approach. The broadcasting was exceptional, very impressive. The media room, the interviews with the players after the game, the quality of the broadcasters. The commentators who described the games were second to none. It was excellent, and I think it probably shocked some broadcasters when they rebroadcast it.

"Dentons really had only a small part to play in the whole thing. But we were blessed and honoured to be associated with it, to be able to help and contribute. It was an absolute pleasure to be able to get there for a couple of days. I did a Player of the Match presentation to the Japanese player, Shizuka Miyaji. She was delightful.

"In the VIP box you could sit at the various tables and speak to the broadcasters, journalists, the players, and the families who were just gobsmacked at what was being provided. That their daughters were playing with all these women from all over the world. And the concept of having their country's flag on the back of their shirts was a stroke of genius by Shaun."

"I think FairBreak is a unique tournament, as we get to take the field with girls and women across the world. I have hardly played cricket against the Associate Nations. I never thought I would play with them in the same team. I was pleasantly surprised by some of the talent on show and I have never even heard of some of the countries the players are from. It was a special experience and I think the FairBreak Tournament has got massive potential and will grow the women's game."

Marizanne Kapp, South Africa

What is a #fairbreaker?

Shaun Martyn tells the quirky story surrounding the term #fairbreaker: *"When FairBreak first began producing cricket bats for female players, we also needed bat stickers. Our good friend and gear supplier from NAS in Mumbai, Eruch Patel, had been producing excellent bats, gloves, and caps for FairBreak as well as some of the playing and training kit.*

"Eruch did a terrific job working with me on designing the bat stickers. We waited, with great anticipation, for the first bats to arrive in Australia with our new sticker design on them. Imagine my shock when I pulled the first bat out of its cover and the sticker said 'fairbreaker' not 'FairBreak'. I was mortified as we wanted to immediately send these bats out to players who had little or no gear.

"Henry [Geoff Lawson] was fantastic. While I was losing the plot, he saw an opportunity. Being the social media gurus that we are (not), we stuck # in front of the word and suddenly we had a brand-new gender-neutral term. Next, we started talking about and using the term #fairbreaker.

"And the question was asked, "What's a #fairbreaker?" The answer was immediately obvious: a person who believes in diversity, inclusion, opportunity, and equality is a #fairbreaker. We suddenly had an inclusive term that encapsulated everything about us. I can't thank the person who stuffed up the typesetting of the stickers enough. They gave us more than we could have ever asked for".

"I was thrilled to contribute strongly with the gloves, opening with the bat and winning many Tour accolades. It was a privilege and honour to captain the FairBreak XI twice against the Netherlands, leading us to two victories and securing our first FairBreak International Series win....and being positive ambassadors for the principles of FairBreak - values that resonate strongly for myself...Such an incredibly positive, affirming experience for all involved. Thank you."

Ariana Dowse, England

2ND INNINGS
THE #FBI22 IN DUBAI

Leadership is the ability to hide your panic from others

Jack Gibson

Shaun Martyn Describes Dubai

The main reason that Cricket Hong Kong and I decided to move the May 2022 FairBreak Invitational from Hong Kong to Dubai five months before the event's first coin toss, was due to the twenty-one days of compulsory hotel quarantine introduced by the Hong Kong government during the pandemic. FairBreak could not afford to quarantine ninety cricketers for twenty-one days. Nor did we want to subject invited players to three weeks of isolation when many of them had just emerged from quarantine situations at tournaments or representative games leading up to our event.

Hosting the FairBreak Invitational in Dubai was the only practical option we had available at short notice. While the management team briefly considered Thailand, it was felt, on reflection, that the Dubai International Stadium was our best option.

The tournament achieved everything I hoped it might, except the financial returns. While playing in the United Arab Emirates' national stadium, which seats 25,000 people, was an incredible experience for the players, it did not allow FairBreak to have the spectators, nor sell the revenue-generating corporate boxes we had planned for the Hong Kong event. Crowd engagement would not be as good in Dubai as the much smaller Kowloon Cricket Ground. The extreme heat and Ramadan did not help matters. But we needed the calibre of venue that Dubai's International Stadium provides. Furthermore, we needed a choice of five-star hotels that could cope with COVID-19 situations if necessary, and of course, security.

On arrival in Dubai, we encountered several significant problems. The stadium had failed to mention that they did not have a sound system and I, assuming they had one, had not asked. Hiring a sound system at the last minute held up planning and impacted the budget by US$50,000.

The logistics and arrangements continued to be problematic. Performers were late for the rehearsals of the opening ceremony. Branding was still being sorted out and the players' cricket uniforms arrived late having been stuck in customs. They were finally tracked down in a warehouse due to incorrectly attributed import codes. When the boxes were opened, the shirts did not have the players' names printed on the back as had been arranged, at length, with the supplier. Elle Williams had only forty-eight hours, thanks to the holidays and business hours associated with Ramadan, to arrange for ninety names to be printed onto the correct shirts ready for the first game.

"Elle Williams is a diamond. Diamonds polish other diamonds.
Elle was the main diamond polishing everybody.
Tell her that. In Dubai, she was running all over the place.
God bless her, she's got energy"

Vidya Rao

At one point, I was questioning my idea about the flags on the backs of the players' shirts because it was proving so difficult to get everything arranged. Elle Williams and Renee Montgomery were amazing in the way they handled all of that. We had to bring additional people in to re-sort all the playing kits. Everyone went above and beyond to make it happen.

People kept asking me how I felt now that the tournament was finally happening after such a long and arduous journey. The only answer I could muster, while dealing with multiple dramas not of my making, was that I just wanted to get the first ball bowled. I kept thinking that I should be feeling more emotional. But I only felt quiet relief.

Sterre Kalis from the Netherlands, a #fairbreaker for many years, came over and stood with me when that first ball was bowled, and it wasn't until later that I fully appreciated just how much that gesture meant for us both. Her show of support for me and FairBreak is something I will never forget. This was also a dream come true for her and all the Associate Nation players. They could finally be seen as equals on a global stage. It was a surreal experience because what I had been picturing in my head for a decade was unfolding before my eyes. Yet none of it seemed surprising to me. It was if I had seen it all before.

I found the lead-up to Dubai excruciatingly difficult. There was the weight of expectation after such a long time and the added pressure of having to move the event from Hong Kong because of the city's COVID-19 quarantine restrictions. The sentiment was that if we did not take the window the ICC had offered us, we might not get it again. It was crucial to play the tournament no matter what. To demonstrate what our vision was in a real sense.

Financially, we knew that it was not going to be what we had hoped for, but we took the longer-term view that if we could get the broadcast reach we wanted, good quality production and top-notch cricket, then financially, we could recoup our losses in future tournaments.

Simultaneously, I was going through several personal challenges in my life that were impacting my energy and wellbeing. I had also contracted COVID-19 in January and recovery had been slow. It was almost a perfect storm.

Thankfully, I had been supported by Verona Kite for some time. Verona has always looked after my travel arrangements, but she had taken on a much more significant role in my life. Her care, affirmation and counsel around everything I was doing with FairBreak was invaluable. Always pushing me to be better and supporting me in every way, especially in some very dark moments. I am forever in her debt.

Roy Burton and I developed bronchitis during the tournament. Essentially from the constant changes in temperature between the hotel and the stadium and the exhaustingly long days. With double headers (two games per day), none of us were getting to bed before 1:00am or 2:00am every night. We would collapse, try to get a few hours of sleep and then be back on deck again the next morning.

There would be informal meetings over breakfast then a management team briefing at 10:00am and then we'd all go to work again. The resilience and unshakable commitment demonstrated by everyone meant we just had to turn up and do our jobs, regardless. Nobody wanted to let anyone down.

Having Paul Burnham, the founder of The Barmy Army, in Dubai was invaluable. He assisted us in so many ways. Paul worked extremely hard helping with sponsorship and connections. It was incredible to have such an iconic cricket brand involved in the tournament.

It was also very special to bring Mrs. Vidya Rao out from India and have her there as part of the tournament and working with us. Vidya has been an exceptional part of FairBreak since 2013.

During the tournament we had the assistance of Lindsay and Lyn Brown from Narooma, the NSW South Coast town where I live, and their good friend Chris Heazlewood. Lindsay had already done a fabulous job in securing Jennifer Westacott as our Patron. He oversaw the trophy design, medallions and presentations. Lindsay continues to be a key part of the team, and recently managed the FairBreak XI Tour to England, Scotland and the Netherlands.

There were issues with the AirWallex money card system we had organised to pay the per diems to players and staff, but due to the excellent relationship we had with all the players we found a way around that financial issue.

We had also set up, with Cricket Hong Kong and the ICC, a system where all players' and officials' payments were deposited into a central bank account prior to the tournament. An official from Cricket Hong Kong had visibility on that account throughout so there could be no concerns regarding fees not being paid to players or officials. This is an issue that has plagued T20 leagues around the world for years. Personally, I am still owed money from an IPL franchise I worked for years ago. I have given up hope of ever receiving that money.

Lisa Sthalekar and I insisted, back in 2013, that players' and officials' payments should be held in a bank account prior to the start of any tournament. We wrote to FICA about this arrangement around that time and FICA's CEO, Paul Marsh, agreed that it was a policy that needed to be introduced. No arrangement like it was in place back then. Today, it is an official FICA and ICC policy. Yet again, we were ahead of our time.

In Dubai, we had in our favour an amazing television team in WildTrack Productions and Azhar Habib, with superb commentary led by Adam Collins. I was also able to rely on consummate professionals Geoff Lawson, Simon Taufel, Colin Tennant, Anoop Gidwani, Manvi Dhodi, Sam Charnley and Roy Burton. Additionally, we had players, coaches, managers and a FairBreak team all on the same page and totally committed. Whatever anyone was going to throw at us, we could handle it and find a way to shine.

Our media team of Claudia Lamb, Georgie Heath, Annesha Ghosh, Ebba Qureshi and Roshni Krishnan did an outstanding job from the outset. Press conferences ran seamlessly, and I lost count of the number of hours Claudia Lamb put in on all our graphics, branding, interviews, and socials.

Working with WildTrack Productions was an excellent experience. They delivered the best images any of us had ever seen in cricket. I made the conscious decision to let them direct the production. The only requirement Geoff Lawson and I asked of them was that they concentrate on the players. They captured the emotion of the players, and the effort, determination and joy they exhibited. Combined with Claudia Lamb on the graphics, they created a sensational package.

We did not want the broadcast to be overloaded with technical cricket commentary. There is far too much of that now in my opinion. Our commentary team did an outstanding job telling the players' back stories and highlighting the incredible diversity on show.

Adam Collins produced an enormous body of preparatory work, researching players and leading the commentary team. [Further Reading contains a sample of Adam Collins' commentary dossier] Despite several members of the commentary team being given their first opportunity to have a go, it resulted in exactly what we had hoped for: fresh, enthusiastic commentating with plenty of cricket smarts behind it, but not self-indulgent. The commentary team perfectly matched the philosophies of diversity and opportunity which are so important to FairBreak.

As for the players, managers, and coaches, they were outstanding in every way. Their commitment never wavered. Prior to the first game I had a private meeting with all the captains and Minx [Mignon du Preez] in the boardroom of the Intercontinental Hotel. Minx was about to be announced as our Head of Marketing from January 2023, so it was important to have her in the room for that meeting. It was a highly productive gathering, aligning all the team captains with the key principles of FairBreak and answering any questions they had leading into the tournament.

I am a firm believer in speaking to players and asking them how we can make life easier for them. It has been our modus operandi from the start, and it will continue. Too often, assumptions are made about players and what they need. Having open communication and trying to put in place what they want, as much as possible, means they are more invested in the process. If you want to get the best outcomes and the best performance, it's as much about the messaging as it is about the gym or the nets or any number of training drills.

At an international level, the skill sets, and the physiology of the players are all quite similar, so the easiest way to improve performance is through good, open communication.

One of the really touching moments in the tournament was when Katey Martin, the formidable New Zealand wicketkeeper, came up to me and confided that she was going to retire from her professional playing career, and it was significant to her that she announced her retirement at the close of the FairBreak tournament. Read on for Katey's perspectives on this decision and her insights into playing for the Tornadoes, the tournament's winning team.

A highlight for everyone was Shoaib Malik's guest appearance at the tournament to meet players and officials. I had gotten to know Shoaib during his time in Australia with the Hobart Hurricanes, and, of course, when he was the Pakistan captain when Geoff Lawson was Pakistan's coach. Ebba Qureshi and her family are also great friends of his. Shoaib always promised he would show up if a FairBreak tournament ever went ahead, and true to his word he did. Shoaib has been a loyal advocate of women's cricket and his appearance in Dubai, interviews and comment added further endorsement to our movement.

I have alluded to just how difficult delivering the Dubai event was. Everyone worked tirelessly and by the time we got to the semi-finals, we knew that we had successfully delivered a quality event. Everyone was looking forward to enjoying the finals weekend. How wrong we were about that! We had not accounted for the President of the United Arab Emirates, Sheikh Khalifa bin Zayed Al Nahyan passing away on the 13th of May.

We were informed that this meant that the city and country would immediately enter a forty-day period of mourning, and all activities, sport included, would be stopped. Only a few members of the FairBreak team were aware of this information and we certainly did not publicise it to the players or coaches. We all took a deep breath and thought through what our options might be. We waited nervously for a government official to turn up to tell us to abandon play.

I could not believe that this was happening. It had been such an odyssey to get to this point. The culmination of everything we had worked for and the close of the tournament were in sight. And now there was a final twist. I can remember just sitting quietly and thinking, "Someone really does not want us to get this done".

I never divulged to anyone just how challenging it was for me to sit and wait for the inevitable shutdown to occur. It was like waiting for a train wreck. Fortunately, no officials arrived to shut us down. We were finally informed that we could continue the tournament without public announcements, music, cheering or applause. The remaining games had to be played in a respectful silence.

FairBreak complied with these requirements, but we still managed to revel in the final days of play. It was disappointing that the spectators and families who were in the stadium couldn't celebrate, but we were immensely grateful that the outcome was not much worse. The final was a wonderful conclusion to the tournament.

The players thoroughly enjoyed the FairBreak format. One city. One venue. Playing every day for several days then a free day, and then more back-to-back games. Staying in the one hotel, just moving to training and then the games meant that they could relax between games, rest and recover without having to constantly pack and move. It also meant that some players could have their family or partners with them. This is a fundamental format shift that should be adopted in all T20 tournaments. There is no reason why players cannot play every day for three to four days, then take a break and repeat.

We believe our format is the way forward in an increasingly busy playing schedule. Shorten the time away so that balance can be restored with family, rest, and recovery. Increasingly, we are seeing players across many sports taking extended breaks for personal reasons. It is no coincidence that these breaks are directly linked to workload and burnout.

Following the FairBreak Invitational, it has been fascinating to see how many players loyally identified with their team over a short period of time in Dubai. At the recent Asian Cup qualifiers there were several social media posts by FairBreak players from different countries reuniting as '#Falcons' or '#Tornadoes'.

In the years leading up to the tournament, a recurring censure from sponsorship agencies has revolved around how players and fans would identify with teams that were not geographically based. I reminded them of the Tour de France, where participants ride for a brand, as an example of how this can work. Fans and viewers identify with players and teams as much as they identify with a region or a brand.

If you build the profile of a player and the brand sponsor engages with their fan base, it's easy to build a following. Putting the flags on the back of the players' shirts also means that countries can identify and engage with their players. Watching the SDG FairBreak Invitational became a geography lesson for many viewers around the world.

Moving forward into the planning for Hong Kong 2023 and beyond, FairBreak has learnt many lessons and will continue to practice 'clean sport'. We will continue highlighting the players and the countries they represent. FairBreak uniforms and playing kit will always be made from sustainable fabrics, and we will never take money from betting agencies or alcohol.

We believe in repurposing and reusing signage where possible. We have already shipped some branding from Dubai to Hong Kong to reuse, and we will then send it on to the USA to be made into carry bags and pencil cases for disadvantaged children.

We surveyed all players and officials after the Dubai tournament, and we will continue to ask for feedback so that we can best engage with them for their benefit. The work we started with Associate Professor Deirdre McGhee and Breast Research Australia will continue and evolve as we look to innovate and drive research into best practice health and wellness for all female cricketers.

It's a constant effort to progress the FairBreak movement, to secure funding, to educate people around the value of women in sport, to celebrate diversity and to create opportunity.

Although we are mentioned in dispatches as 'disruptors', it's not how we feel. FairBreak are agents of change, innovators, supporters, and advocates. We are here only and always for the good of the game, and for the myriad of people from all countries and persuasions who come together to play and watch cricket.

There now follows several interviews with a diverse range of professional individuals who were part of the delivery of the SDG FairBreak Invitational in various capacities. I hope you enjoy reading their perspectives. In addition, Further Reading contains a number of media articles discussing the success of the SDG FairBreak Invitational in Dubai.

"It was an amazing experience to be able to play with our idols. I played alongside Heather Knight, Laura Wolvaardt, Deandra Dottin and learnt so much from them. And it was important to see that our love for the game is global and to develop friendships with players from all those countries. It was one of the best weeks of our lives. Opportunities opened after the tour as more people found out about Cricket Brazil and were interested in the work done over here. In Brazil and abroad, we had a chance to show what we currently do! Another good point was that due to the accessible broadcast, Brazilians could watch the games, and they were fascinated by the whole structure and want to keep evolving to reach tours like that too!"

Roberta Moretti Avery, Brazil

Anti-Corruption Officials

Anoop Gidwani and Colin Tennant

Corruption in sport, specifically cricket, is not restricted to men. The women's game is now a legitimate target for match fixing and bribery. To this end, Colin Tennant and Anoop Gidwani were employed as integrity and anti-corruption officials at the SDG FairBreak Tournament in Dubai in May 2022.

Anoop Gidwani is a chartered accountant by profession and has been working with Hong Kong's ICAC (anti-corruption agency) as a forensic accountant for thirty six years. He used to be an ICC cricket umpire and retired after umpiring five hundred matches both locally and internationally. He is also a Director on the Board of Cricket Hong Kong, overseeing all their integrity matters.

Gidwani described the SDG FairBreak Tournament as a unique experience for several reasons, most notably because Dubai is the betting capital of the world. In terms of the risk element, the location was extreme.

Generally, the cricketers of Test playing nations are paid handsomely enough that the temptation to make extra cash on the side for passing on information, throwing a game or following the instructions of dishonest bookmakers is now rare. Those players have too much to lose if they are caught. However, players coming from Associate Nations who are not from affluent backgrounds are now considered legitimate targets. And it is not only the players who are at risk. Their coaches, managers and physiotherapists are too. Anyone who is closely involved with the women's game is now a target for match-fixing and bribery.

There were many low paid players from Associate Nations participating in the Dubai tournament. For example, two women, representing the Philippines, are domestic workers in Hong Kong. The salaries they receive, stipulated by the Hong Kong government (not their employers), are less than HK$5,000 per month (equivalent to less than $1,000 Australian Dollars). Bookies know that the potential for players on low incomes from developing countries succumbing to temptation is real, and so they target them. The opportunity to make relatively small amounts of cash could quite easily be a motivation to fix a match when you have nothing much to lose.

The Associate players are naïve about the various methods employed by bookmakers and their agents to recruit them into illegal activities. Therefore, Gidwani and Tennant's challenge was multifold; to spread knowledge amongst the players; to make them aware of the risks, and to reinforce the absolute requirement to report anything suspicious. If the women were approached or contacted by suspicious persons, they needed to immediately report this to the tournament's integrity officers.

Several reported incidents occurred, indicating that the players fully comprehended what they needed to do. Not reporting an incident is considered an infringement. Players do not necessarily have to physically take money or do something to influence the outcome of the game, but if they are approached and do not report it, they are committing an offence.

Education, enforcement and the risky environment made Dubai a challenge. The process of educating the players commenced about a month before the tournament. FairBreak's integrity officers contacted all the players and set them online Anti-Corruption Code education tasks, divided into four modules of about 15-20 minutes each, with questions at the end they had to answer. Their responses were recorded. Before the start of the tournament, Gidwani and Tennant gathered the players, into small groups, in a room, for face-to-face briefings. Attendance was compulsory, and if the online education had not been completed properly the women were told they would not be allowed to play.

The questions in the online education modules are based on the ICC's Anti-Corruption Code. The players' answers were assessed for an indication of which elements of the Anti-Corruption Code they did not understand. Those elements were then clarified and reinforced during the briefings. The consequences of players not reporting an approach, and the significance of taking a bribe had to be clearly understood by everyone.

Every player's login to the online modules was registered and tracked. Gidwani was able to detect how much time each player spent on the tasks. It is a sophisticated model, such that fast forwarding through it was obvious and he knew immediately which players had done so. While not naming and embarrassing specific players in the meetings, he hinted that he knew exactly who had not completed the modules fully and suggested that they go back and complete them or the opportunity to play in the tournament would be withdrawn.

Requiring the women to complete the online education made them aware of the pitfalls, the consequences, and the types of approach they could expect. What may seem like an extremely innocent approach generally is not so, and just such an approach did arise during the tournament.

A suspicious character was seen at the travel desk of FairBreak's hotel, leafing through logistical information, bus timetables, player assembly times, etc. He was seen loitering around the travel desk area for over three hours. He was covertly observed and photographed by the integrity officers. On the day of the semi-finals, he was spotted in the stadium's VIP Lounge. The only people allowed to issue passes for the VIP Lounge were the FairBreak management staff, the captains or managers of each team, and Cricket Hong Kong, the tournament's hosts.

Gidwani approached the man in the VIP Lounge, took him aside and enquired how he had accessed the area and who had given him an invitation. With consent, a copy of his passport and UAE residency identification was taken, and a background check conducted with the Emirati police.

Enquiries revealed that the man had approached one of the Pakistan players in the hotel lobby, saying he was a fellow Pakistani and a cricket enthusiast who had been a photographer at past tournaments. He requested a pass to the VIP area. Without knowing him, she issued him with a pass. Investigations suggested that he was an extremely undesirable character. He was immediately evicted from the stadium and blacklisted from future ICC Tournaments.

Even though this character did not offer anything to anyone, this is generally how the process starts. They befriend players, get close to them, try to win or build their trust. No offers are made immediately, it is a gradual process.

Approaches were also made to the female players via Instagram Messenger by so-called overseas "player managers" representing famous international players and expressing a desire to manage them for no fee or promises of an introduction to teams where they could earn substantial incomes playing cricket. Again, these online parties were fully investigated and found to be undesirable. No money was offered, but approaches were made.

The integrity officers' objectives were fully served. All the players responsibly reported the approaches. They understood what they had to do and complied with what was expected of them. The anti-corruption officials dealt with the advances by blacklisting or ensuring the perpetrators were prevented from further involvement in cricket.

Even if a player is not instructed to fix a match but is told to arrange an incident in a match this is also considered an offence. For example, bowling two wide balls may not change the outcome of a match, but it is enough for punters to bet that a bowler might concede two wide balls in a particular over. Punters will put a wager on whether the event happens or not, and so the involved player is assisting the bookmaker to earn money. This is called "spot fixing" as opposed to fixing the outcome of an entire match. Spot fixing is where somebody tries to manipulate a game by underperforming and that is an offence.

Accepting a gift, however innocent, and not reporting that gift is also an offence if the player does not get clearance for it. For example, if a player performs well in a match, and a spectator approaches them afterwards saying, "I'm a great fan of you and your team, here is an expensive watch as your reward for playing well", that individual has not asked the player to do anything. They have given the player a gift as a token of appreciation for excellent performance.

Integrity officials do not prevent the player from accepting the gift. But the gift should be reported and the player should seek permission before accepting it. Integrity officers can conduct background checks to see if the person who is giving the gift is legitimate or not, and whether there is likely to be a hidden agenda.

Accepting a gift with a monetary value of US$750 or below does not have to be reported. Above that amount, the player needs to report it. Generally, they are allowed to accept it. Anti-corruption officers are not there to stop players from receiving rewards for great performance. Their objectives are to protect the player from compromise and to maintain the integrity of the game. If the benefactor is clean and bestowing a gift born out of genuine love for cricket and their admiration of the cricketer, the player will be allowed to accept it.

Furthermore, a cricketer, during their career, and for two years after having played their last game, is not allowed to bet on any cricket match, whether they are participating in it or not.

The online education for the FairBreak Tournament was a unique experiment because of the disparity in experience of the ninety players involved. Generally anti-corruption officials conduct group briefings with players just before a tournament starts. Highly experienced cricketers who regularly play at an international level engage with this material so often they do not need a two-hour briefing. Many of the FairBreak players had limited or no experience of an international tournament and needed to complete the education. The language barrier was another reason they conducted the training online. Some of the FairBreak players have limited English.

The FairBreak officials sent the online modules to all players a month in advance so that anyone requiring help or translation into their own language could arrange it before arrival. As an observer, I question why the ICC does not use a portion of its vast financial resources to have its Anti-Corruption Code and any associated training translated into all the languages of Full Member and Associate Nations. And uploaded into an app that cricketers can download onto their smartphones or devices for easy reference.

Gidwani explained the significance of FairBreak's integrity training. He said, "This was the first time we have put the Anti-Corruption Code information in an online format. Another benefit of this format was that the players could revisit it several times if they needed to. If they had only attended a face-to-face presentation, they may not have understood everything. Our online training also facilitated the players seeking clarification from us by email if they needed to. We reached out about five days before the tournament, for this very purpose. On arrival in Dubai, we had meetings to build the trust of players so that they felt comfortable talking to us. We did not want them to regard us as high-handed or officious. We wanted them to see us as friends and protectors. We did not want them to get into trouble.

"Another important aspect the players required training about was the sharing of information, both verbally and online. Again, this is an activity that players could do completely innocently, but by doing so they can unwittingly provide information to bookmakers. If they reveal that a particular player is not going to play tomorrow because they have COVID-19 for example. They are not supposed to reveal that information to any outsider, because that information can be used by betting circles.

"Any information that is not available to the public or to the media, that is known only to the players, whether that be player injury, team selection, who is going to bat first if they win the toss, the batting or bowling order. This type of information is "team talk", it is privileged, and players should not be revealing it to anyone.

"Suppose, for example, a player makes an innocent phone call to their parent and says, "I've got a hamstring issue and I don't think I can play tomorrow." They do not know who their parent might tell. They may completely trust their parent, but that parent may innocently tell another party who may pass the information to somebody else who provides it to a betting circle. And if it is traced back that the player revealed the injury information and it manipulated the gambling on a match that player can get into serious trouble.

"Sanctions range from a minimum of six months to a maximum lifetime ban, depending on the severity and the seriousness of the offence. If you Google match-fixing in cricket, look at the names of the players who have been banned over the years, the countries they played for, what they did and how long they were banned for. It makes for interesting reading. Years ago, match fixing and the revealing of information was not such an issue and players escaped lightly, but today with the prevalence of online gambling and the huge sums of money involved, any type of match fixing is severely sanctioned and players risk never being allowed to play for their country again."

There were six teams in the SDG FairBreak Invitational. On any given day, four teams were playing on the field. Two teams played a match in the stadium at 4pm, another two teams had a match at 8pm, and the two teams not playing were back at the hotel. Tennant and Gidwani split their duties such that one of them was always in the hotel and the other in transit to or at the stadium. They were always available to the players in case any incident occurred.

"Both the stadium and the hotel are risky. In fact, the hotel is riskier than the stadium because the players are relaxed. They may be hanging out in the lobby, beside the pool, having a meal in the bar or whatever. They can be approached by anyone.

"We patrolled around constantly, keeping our eyes and ears open.... going into the restaurants and bars where the players were gathering and keeping a look out for unusual individuals approaching the players. There is nothing wrong with them having a chat with a stranger, but if they seemed suspicious or if their conduct or the context of their talk with the players was something to be concerned about, then we would intervene.

"I think the players were quite guarded, and rarely was a player on her own. They always moved as a group, which is what we advised them to do. Because when you're in a group it is difficult for someone to penetrate and pick off an individual."

Women are now a greater target for corruption because the men get more games and earn more match fees. In India for example, the national players are treated as demi-gods, so they also receive advertising and endorsement revenue. They are so rich it is pointless them being tempted by bribery.

Opportunities to corrupt the women exist, however, because they are paid so little. Players from cricket's Associate Nations are paid nothing to play for their country. They may get free flights, free accommodation, and a small daily allowance, but they sacrifice their personal and employment time to play and practice for no remuneration. An offer of, say, US$20,000 is more than they could ever make in a lifetime of playing cricket.

Now that FairBreak has launched these women on to the international stage and more matches are being played, the opportunity for these bookmakers and match fixers to target the women will rise rapidly.

"No bookmaker reveals who or what they are," said Gidwani. "They introduce themselves as people from the media, or as player agents so that they have a cover for their activities. One of the bookies who tried to establish contact with a FairBreak player through Instagram said he was a player agent and had a sports equipment company. When we checked him out it was a bogus company. They always have a cover for their real activities.

"Dubai has developed into a centre for corruption due to its wealth and a national obsession for betting and gambling. They bet on camel races, horse races, anything that moves. When a cricket ball is thrown, they will bet on that too. Dubai has very lax enforcement in terms of anti-corruption, there is no ICAC, and there are no currency restrictions. If a player is given US$100,000 in cash, he can put it in his bag and fly out of the airport and nobody will stop him. Dubai is the sort of place where if you do not make a nuisance of yourself, you can do anything.

"Cricket as a sport is still under the radar for the Chinese, who are also big gamblers. Therefore, the FairBreak Invitational in Hong Kong in 2023 will also be a major concern in terms of corruption risk."

Colin Tennant was also an Anti-Corruption and integrity officer at the FairBreak Tournament in Dubai. He has worked in senior Anti-Corruption roles for the International Cricket Council (ICC) and in the British Police Force. Tennant and Gidwani worked collaboratively to monitor the tournament for corrupt activity in order to protect the integrity of the game.

"I've worked for the ICC in an Anti-Corruption capacity," said Tennant, "and I have attended many franchise tournaments, ICC tournaments and bilaterals. The FairBreak tournament was very good. It set the right standard. The main issue with franchised tournaments for competitors and staff is payment. Very often, the players just don't get paid. So big cricket tournaments like the Caribbean Premier League and the Bangladesh Premier League, and even smaller ones like the Canadian Premier League, have a notorious history of not fulfilling their contractual obligations.

"This generally happens in the men's tournaments. The tournament organisers pay an amount at the beginning and then another payment halfway through, and then the final settlement at the end of the tournament. The biggest problem is where they pay the first installment to the staff and players, but they don't pay the rest. And these players have to keep going back to these tournaments because they need the money.

"For many of the men's tournaments, they'll attract a lot of big names, and they will, very often, pay most of the money to the big-name players. But the other guys, who really need the money to make up their salaries because they don't earn a great deal, just don't get paid. And that leads to the enormous problem of corruption. Because it gives a "way in" to the corruptors to come in and entice these unpaid players with, in effect, guaranteed money. FairBreak did not do that. FairBreak paid everything that they said they were going to pay, on time. FairBreak completely broke the mould.

"There were a couple of issues with sorting out banks and how the transfers would go across, because the Australian AirWallex cards FairBreak set up for the per diem payments didn't work outside of Australia. But FairBreak staff kept everybody informed about what was going wrong. In the end, it didn't actually matter. The communication was very good and FairBreak resolved it.

"ICC tournaments are national events and they pay up, but even IPL can have issues. I talked about Bangladesh before. Backtrack to the Bangladesh Premier League in 2013 and there are players who didn't get paid. They didn't get paid in 2014, they didn't get paid in 2015, and they still haven't been paid. But they are enticed back year after year because these cricketers need the money. They keep going back knowing that they are owed money in the hope that they might eventually get it. From a corruptor's perspective, they've immediately got a perfect "way in" because they know that some players haven't received their money from years before.

"FairBreak broke that mould. As a franchise tournament, the main interest for players is, I'm afraid, the money. It's their salary. FairBreak broke the mould with how they dealt with that, how they kept everyone informed and how they resolved the issues. It was excellent.

"Most tournaments work on three payments. A player signs a contract and gets one third of their contracted salary. Halfway through the tournament they will get another third, and on the last day of the tournament, they'll get the final payment plus any win bonuses due to them. Invariably, they are always paid the first installment. Then they're committed. They go to the tournament and start playing. They are expecting the second payment, but that, very often, doesn't arrive. So then they are in a situation. What do they do? Do they strike, or do they keep hoping they will get paid?

"For example, at the Sri Lankan Premier League in 2020, three of the teams threatened to walk out because they hadn't received their money halfway through. A Masters tournament for older players in Dubai was called a money laundering exercise; the whole tournament was funded by drug money and the players threatened to get on a plane and leave because they hadn't been paid. So, the organisers brought in cash for them. This type of nefarious activity undermines a tournament.

"FairBreak didn't operate like that. FairBreak paid what they said they would pay to the players. And when they couldn't pay because of the issue with the per diem cards, they didn't deceive players at any stage. They said, "This is the problem, this is what we're doing to resolve it". And they did resolve it, pretty quickly. The whole thing was well organised and, I think, most people watching it were quietly surprised about how well it went."

Colin Tennant believes the online ICC Anti-Corruption Code online training needs modifying, such that all the players need to have completed it before they get to the tournament. He admitted, "While the concept is a good one, the training is broken up into four or five sections and the further the players got into the event, the less involved with the process they became, because they were so absorbed in the tournament. And we had trouble enforcing the rule that if they didn't complete the whole training package they couldn't play.

"The players had to complete stage one before the tournament started, and there was a second stage two or three days after arrival in Dubai. Then after another three or four days, there was a third stage, and then a final stage.

"We lost control of it. The further it went on, we lost control because, not unreasonably, as the women got deeper into the tournament, they became more distracted. The online idea together with the face-to-face training was excellent in theory. The online package was very good. It's the best one that I've seen. Much better than the ICC's.

"I did have concerns about how it would come across at the start, but those fears were unfounded. It was a good package. But in hindsight, I would require players to have at least two sections completed before they turn up to the tournament. Then have a refresher in the middle. Don't have a rule that you cannot enforce. And the rule was, unless you finish each module, you cannot play. We lost control of it because we couldn't tell a team we were dropping players out because not everyone was completing their online training!

"The further we got into the tournament the more players were not completing it. Not for any corrupt reason, but because they had become so engrossed in the tournament. Let's not forget, this was intense. They had two days playing, then a day off, then two days playing, then a day off. It was busy. I think the idea that everyone could find ten minutes to do it was good in theory, but in reality, not everyone did find ten minutes to do it. Because the athletes invariably got more involved in their preparations than in doing an Anti-Corruption Code package.

"That said, I don't think we lost anything at all. I thought the anti-corruption side of it went very well. I think I told Shaun it was probably the best response to any tournament I've ever been to. But the training part, I think we just need to move it forward a bit before the tournament starts. It doesn't need to be four modules. They could do it in two. We are not reading a set of rules to them.

"What we're trying to do is to raise awareness and to get them comfortable with speaking to us, on a one-to-one basis, about any issues or concerns they have about corruption. Not only at a FairBreak tournament, but about anything that has happened to them.

"If we can build that relationship, players will tell us about things that have happened under the Anti-Corruption Code, not just at this tournament but elsewhere. Because they need to be compliant before and after. We don't want to scare them off. It's a matter of them being aware of the Anti-Corruption Code they have to follow, by us saying, "Here's a couple of examples to raise your awareness about how shady people might approach you. How you have to be careful about what you say, or what you do, or how you have to be suspicious of somebody, out of the blue, wanting to sponsor you". We raise awareness that they can come and speak to us at any time. I would suggest condensing the modules into two 15-minute segments which they need to finish before they turn up at the tournament.

"As a concept, the online training was definitely worth doing, but I don't think it worked properly. You have to remember that some of these girls had never ever come across the Anti-Corruption Code process before. The England girls and the Australian girls would have done so at the ICC tournaments. But the Brazilians, the Namibians, never ever. They didn't even appreciate there was a corruption problem.

"If I was a corruptor, I might be interested in the England Captain because of where she's going to be playing, but my easy short term profit is in targeting the girl from Brazil, for example, who doesn't get paid by her country and is coming across to play because someone sponsored her. As a corruptor, if I can give the Brazilian US$2,000, the impact of US$2,000 on her family life is disproportionate to giving US$2,000 to the England Captain."

As an objective bystander, I believe it is a flawed system to be sending a global governing body's Anti-Corruption Code in an online training format to players with limited English. And expecting those individuals to seek help reading it or getting it translated so that they can comply with it.

I put this argument to Tennant and he said, "The FairBreak online training was good because it was fairly simple. But if English isn't your first language, it does make it more difficult. The cost of doing language specific training is prohibitive. We told the players that if they had any serious issues with the language, we had two days before the tournament started for them to approach us for help.

"Anoop [Gidwani] has a couple of languages other than English. He was happy to sit down with an individual and somebody who speaks their language plus English and go through it with them. Within the budget, that's the only way we can do it in this type of tournament. Yes, it is an issue, and in an ideal world, we would give them the Anti-Corruption Code training in their mother tongue.

"It would be a great conversation starter with the ICC. All they've done at tournaments within the last few years is to have an Anti-Corruption Code manager giving the presentation in a language of the region, like Hindi for example. But not everyone in an Indian or Bangladeshi team has Hindi or Bengali as their first language. It may be Gujarati or something else. It's just not as simple as you might think.

"When you dig deep down it's a complicated issue. FairBreak dealt with it in a reasonable way which was, "You must complete this online training by the tournament start date. If you're having issues with the language, we can address that a couple of days before. It should take about half an hour to sit down and go through it with you". It was just to give them an awareness of the corruption issues so we can tick a box and say, "You've been given the heads up about what can happen, the onus is now on you to tell us about things you're suspicious of." And the message that we tried to get across was, "We are not the police. We are not trying to catch you."

"The ICC are definitely still stuck in a mindset that they are the policeman and it's their job to catch people. And when they catch people it's a deterrent to others. Whereas the reality is, and you can ask David Warner, or Colin de Grandhomme, or Joe Root, for example, it absolutely turns them off. We've got to build relationships with players and prevent things happening in the first place rather than trying to catch people.

"I think we achieved the right message at FairBreak because the girls really did report everything. 99% of it was rubbish, but it was exactly the response we wanted. We warned them that social media is the number-one way that match fixers will contact players. Anything that they were concerned about they could speak to us. And the response from the women was absolutely fantastic.

"I think we reported three matters to the ICC during the FairBreak Tournament, and they took on "disruption" on all three issues, which involves getting in touch with the individuals and telling them the ICC is aware of what they are up to and they are not to do it again. When we can't necessarily nail down exactly what they're doing, just making them aware that we are interested in what they might be doing very often puts them off enough to disappear.

"We made it very clear to the guy who turned up in the VIP Lounge at the stadium and two of the online fake profiles, that we had informed the ICC they had made approaches, and that they were now being investigated by the ICC and to desist from whatever they were doing.

"At future tournaments, as part of the briefing, we will need to give all the FairBreak staff a more formalised briefing of the risks of handing out tickets and information to outsiders. Because FairBreak staff fall under the Anti-Corruption Code as well. Tournament staff have access to substantial amounts of inside information about the teams and what is happening, and they could inadvertently pass that intelligence on. Our original plan included giving a quick briefing to everybody, but that fell through the cracks in Dubai. Logistics just got in the way. For future tournaments we need to make sure that we dedicate thirty minutes to everybody being aware of their obligations under the Anti-Corruption Code.

"I think one of the players might have known the Pakistani and given him tickets, whereas if we had have known earlier that he was hanging around and the questions he was asking, we could have suitably briefed the players. Preventing corruption is an ongoing process throughout a tournament. We could have said, "This guy's been hanging around. If anyone sees him or has contact with him, please tell us", and raised awareness of it that way.

"We didn't have that knowledge until after it happened. And that was not through anything corrupt, it was just out of widespread ignorance of the techniques of match fixers. I'm pretty sure that he was sent there to contact players. Which is their first line of attack. The contact may not have been for that tournament. But it might be for the next one. To start building a bit of trust with the players.

"You must give them credit. These match fixers are very professional at what they do. I used to be involved in the recruitment of police informants. We became very good at recruiting informants over time by changing the way we did things. Bookies basically use the same techniques to recruit match fixers.

"At future tournaments, as part of the briefing, we will need to give all the FairBreak staff a more formalised briefing of the risks of handing out tickets and information to outsiders. Because FairBreak staff fall under the Anti-Corruption Code as well. Tournament staff have access to substantial amounts of inside information about the teams and what is happening, and they could inadvertently pass that intelligence on. Our original plan included giving a quick briefing to everybody, but that fell through the cracks in Dubai. Logistics just got in the way. For future tournaments we need to make sure that we dedicate thirty minutes to everybody being aware of their obligations under the Anti-Corruption Code.

"The tournament ran without a hitch. I'm not exaggerating in any way. I've seen bigger tournaments, with much more money thrown at them, organised less professionally. FairBreak was very good. The women competing were probably the most cautious and the most receptive to the Anti-Corruption Code message than anyone I have dealt with before. Even at a Women's World Cup. This bunch of players at FairBreak were the best of the lot. They took the whole thing on board, they were proud to be there, they were respectful of being there, they were grateful to be there. They demonstrated all that in the way they behaved and carried themselves. It was excellent.

"It was a very good tournament overall, and if I was Shaun, I'd be taking this to America. This is a product that the Americans will absolutely latch onto. I think the product is such that FairBreak could take it to the West Coast of America, to Los Angeles. Or to Chicago or New York where there is an enormous Indian community. They will embrace this tournament straight away because Indians absolutely adore cricket, and if it's their daughter playing, they'll love it even more."

Umpires and Referees

Simon Taufel

Simon Taufel is an Australian and one of the world's most experienced and decorated international cricket umpires. He is also a highly sought after corporate trainer specialising in leadership, conflict management and resolution, goal setting, continuous improvement and personal development.

Throughout his thirteen-year career, Taufel officiated 74 Test matches, 174 ODIs, two T20 World Cup Finals, seven IPL finals, and the 2004 Champions Trophy final. As a member of the ICC's Elite Umpire Panel, he won five consecutive ICC Umpire of the Year awards between 2004 and 2008. During this time, he was considered to be the best umpire in the world. Taufel is also the youngest person to have received the ICC's Bronze Bails Award for umpiring 100 ODIs.

Taufel led a combination of young and experienced umpires and referees at the FairBreak Invitational. Named "the seventh team", the officials were required to perform and be just as successful as the six playing teams: Tornadoes, Spirit, Warriors, Barmy Army, Sapphires and Falcons.

To open our interview, Taufel told me his reasons for heading up the seventh team in Dubai. He said, "Officiating traditionally gets a bit of a raw deal when it comes to cricket tournaments and cricket administration. I'm always very passionate about looking after what's known as "the third team" out on the field. You need three teams to have a good game of cricket. Normally the third team gets left behind a bit. I'm passionate about supporting the officials who need to be focused and accountable. I want to understand what that extra team needs to look like, and to get all the little things right. Apart from the playing conditions, rules and regulations, who's going to be an advocate for them? Who's going to be representing them and having a seat at the table when it comes to all those matters that need addressing?

"The other reason I wanted to participate was FairBreak itself. Having seen some FairBreak cricket matches when I lived in Bowral, I could just tell that it was a movement and an element of the game that is going places and has a role to play. And I'm always excited to go places, as an individual, where we haven't been before.

"I bought into Shaun, Venkatesh and Geoff's vision around what they were trying to do with female cricket and female sport. Equity, equality and all those sorts of things that are missing in today's modern world a little bit. I was very happy to offer them my expertise, support and collaboration in what I think is a really good project.

"I lived in the Southern Highlands for thirteen years, and in the last four or five years of that, I was involved with the Highlands District Cricket Association. Plus, I had also done some ad hoc work for the Bradman Foundation. You can't live in that backyard and not get involved. I had already officiated a couple of matches for Shaun to add profile, significance and integrity to what FairBreak was doing.

"FairBreak is filling a gap, filling a void. It's doing some things that the governance of the boards and the cricket authorities really haven't taken up. It's a very good project in that way.

"Venkatesh and I had an opportunity to put a team of umpires and referees together. He already had some ideas about what he wanted to do with the composition of the officiating team. It was important because for a tournament like this, even though it was being run by a domestic organisation like Cricket Hong Kong, it was really an international event, and with that comes plenty of opportunity for the growth and development of people; to show what they can do on a global stage with lots of TV cameras and lots of international people around like players, coaches and administrators. We knew that if we combined international standard officiating and offered opportunities to match officials who had not been in that space before, then we could exponentially grow their development.

"Let me give you some examples. There were three umpires at the Invitational who had never been involved in International third umpire duties before. For them, it was a real opportunity to get thrown in the deep end and to get some training and development on the job. And to get some instant feedback and feedforward to help them develop faster as match officials.

Take someone like Shandre Fritz, for instance, who is a match referee from South Africa. She has been with the ICC for several years. She told me, "I've learned more in the last two weeks than I've learned in the last three years".

"That happened simply by having some international standard officials around her and giving her access to more tools and resources. She spent time around me and others, and she was brought to the floor. Therein lies the opportunity. It's not about whether a person is male or female. It's about the role. It's about what they add to cricket. This is not about where you come from. It's about your cricketing skills and abilities being given the chance to grow and develop and to show the world what you can do.

"Our challenge was this melting pot of nine different countries, from an officiating perspective, coming together. I really didn't care about whether they [the officials] were male or female. It was important to bring together nine different officiating standards and to get them to gel as a team.

"Luckily, with the support of Venkatesh, we had a tournament preparation day with all the teams before the event started in Dubai. On that training day, we tried to do a number of things. We conducted team building activities; we played games and exercises where we got to know everyone; we worked out what pushes everyone's buttons; what they were expecting from the rest of the group; and how we were all going to perform as the seventh team in the competition.

"When you bring those things together, there's a range of dynamics. You've got the fundamentals of the roles of being an on-field umpire, the TV umpire, the fourth umpire, and the match referee. It's how we combine as a team for success. It's how we work together both on and off the field.

"One of the great things I think we achieved as a group was the camaraderie and team spirit we developed. That aligned well with the FairBreak experience. From a playing perspective, we could see at the welcome drinks at the hotel before the competition started, that there was a palpable sense of spirit within the room. We could see that this wasn't going to be about who was going to win and who was going to lose. It was about this tournament being an opportunity and an achievement in itself. That we were all there to help each other, to celebrate, and to improve as people and as cricketers.

"During the tournament, we had some challenging conversations between the more experienced and the less experienced individuals in the match officials' team. It was very difficult to leave three umpires out of the finals based on performance. But when we are signed up for meritocracy and team success, we needed to deliver. Even though those three people were disappointed, they still turned up to the finals to support, observe and continue learning and growing. That was a tremendous attitude.

"As a team of officials, we were focused on adding value to the event. We were supporting the tournament's objectives and keeping the focus on the cricket so our mistakes had to be minimal. Our performances as officials were very good overall. There was a lot happening behind the scenes that no one else saw, and we were fixing or addressing that on the fly. Which is where our value as officials comes in.

"It was challenging, it was exciting, and it was rewarding. Everyone walked away having learnt something new. Everyone walked away with fond memories and as better officials. That is always my objective whenever I work with other umpires. How do we make this game our best game? And more importantly, how do we leave an event or a season being an improved match official compared to when we started?

"We ticked a lot of boxes in that space. Those things happen due to a tremendous amount of preparation and hard work. And a cooperative attitude and collaborative spirit that everyone plays their part in. When I work with a group of people from an international level and below, I call them "the chasers". Because they are the people who want things that others already have. The chasers always have a great attitude and work ethic and they are very easy to work with.

"Match officials often get given a raw deal when it comes to support and resources. For the FairBreak Tournament, I was responsible for nine umpires and two referees. One of my challenges was to appoint them to the matches in the various four umpiring roles and the referee role. Therefore, for any match, we needed five officials in each officiating team.

"When leading an officiating team, I always try to allocate the officials a variety of playing teams. And grounds. Although that was not applicable in this case because we were in one venue. By doing this, officials don't end up watching the same team all the time. Neither do they want to be umpiring with the same officials all of the time. They need variety. We also need to have a range of assessors, those who are the match referees. And we want to give them a variety of roles. On-field, third umpire and fourth umpire. We need to be equitable and to share the love amongst all these variables."

In the lead up to the FairBreak Invitational, I was tasked with writing some of the media releases. One of those media releases announced that the tournament's officiating team would be supported in their objectives by a technology platform called refbook, offering high levels of feedback, real time information and customised tools. FairBreak and refbook were partnering in a trial and development opportunity for the betterment of the game and officiating. Alongside Simon Taufel as officiating director, the pilot would be the first time an ICC-sanctioned event had implemented a dedicated technology for managing tournament umpires and match referees.

It was also announced that refbook would be used as the umpire management and allocation platform. It promised to provide new levels of professionalism, automation and analytics for the tournament's officials. The platform also guaranteed real-time data insights to facilitate the allocation of on-field umpire, TV umpire, and match referee crews to the most appropriate games and to deliver a seamless experience for the overall officiating function.

In the light of this pilot, I questioned Taufel about refbook and he explained, "What refbook does for us is to assist in the appointment process. refbook does what's called an auto assign where you can feed in the parameters around what you're looking for in terms of that variety of roles. refbook can do an auto assign in thirty seconds, whereas it can take me between eight and ten hours to assign roles depending upon the number of games and officials involved. refbook removes the heavy lifting from the coordination and appointment of match officials. It also reduces human error and increases the accuracy of the outcomes we are looking for. The platform is still developing the selection and the appointment areas but the allocation part is already done.

"We want to try and improve what we do and to continue to give match officials better support in that area. Performance development is the next step with refbook. It's essentially a platform of management that is specifically focused on match officials and match officiating. As opposed to a company with just a management platform with an add-on for the match officials' management which doesn't really look after all their needs. It just manages their payments, their flights and accommodation, their clothing and personal data. refbook is a platform that is centered around the match officials' needs and it can actually link into everything else."

I speculated whether refbook is similar to the individual who has to draw up a very complicated roster. Taufel agreed and said, "In very simple terms, refbook creates a roster of who is going to be working on any given day in the stadium and what they will be doing. It assigns match officials to cricket matches and coordinates and manages all those assignments to ensure that every match official gets a variety of partners, teams, locations and roles across the duration of the tournament. They also get a variety of assessments and it ensures that their job allocation is in line with what the selectors of the tournament need.

"We had doubleheaders most days. Therefore, we had ten officials involved every day. Because we had two matches daily, I didn't want any of the umpires or referees backing up or doing two games in a row on the same day. Therein lay the challenge; I had to coordinate up to 13 match officials across 34 matches. Make sure none of them were doubling up on the same day. And ensure they were all getting a similar amount of on-field, television, and fourth umpire appointments, and a variety of teams and assessors.

"Each match had five officials: four umpires; two in-field, one third, one fourth and one match referee who was overseeing the match and doing the assessment. Then for the second game we had a different set of five come in. So, on each day we would have three officials that were not working and we carried a couple of extra officials because of COVID-19. In case anyone was unavailable due to illness.

"We left it to the individual officials to decide whether they went back to the hotel or whether they stayed at the stadium. And similarly for the second group. They were welcome to come to the stadium with the first group on the first bus for the first match, or they could come later ahead of their assigned match. Umpiring is mentally taxing so taking a break is important.

"There was a tremendous opportunity to accelerate their learning and development so they could stay on if they wanted. If they did the first game, they could stay on and have the opportunity of seeing the game from inside the production room where the director was and to understand how they operate and what they do. They could go and sit with the third umpire in the match, or the referee at the top of the stand and get more of an insight into how others worked.

"Because match referees work on their own in every game, there's nobody to share or bounce stuff off. Therefore, they could observe what the other referees were doing and the way that they operated. They could learn from other people and not operate in silos all the time. It was a personal choice to be doing this if they were not officially working. We certainly encouraged it, but we didn't say they had to do it because everyone feels differently about how they want to get the best out of themselves.

"There were referrals to the third umpire during every innings in every match. But we didn't have a DRS [Decision Review System]. We had run outs and stumpings and catches that could be referred to the upstairs umpire. In modern day cricket, the role of the third umpire is, in my mind, the hardest job in the team because they get asked to do everything and they are a support mechanism for the team.

"Even though there wasn't DRS, the third umpire still had a massive role to play in officiating the game and supporting the two on-field umpires to have the best game they could have. So, from a performance perspective, we monitored, we assessed and we critiqued all the third umpire performances accordingly. It is a different skill set in that environment where communication and composure are probably the two most important attributes required of the third umpire.

"If I can use an analogy, it's a bit like being an airline pilot where you have hours and hours of observation and a couple of minutes of panic. When somebody draws that box and they send a decision up to you, your heart rate goes from 60-70 beats a minute to more than 160-170 beats per minute. Suddenly you need to have your best pilot at the controls. Someone who's got the ability to remain calm and composed, to review the television pictures and come up with the right decision. Because in that box we have a zero-defect objective. Nobody will forgive a mistake as a third umpire. That's why this was new territory for some of the officials in that environment. And the only way you can get better at it is to keep doing it."

Taufel has spoken freely about umpires needing more support to deal with the stress that comes with the scrutiny and backlash that occurs when working with elite sports in public environments. Naturally, there will always be variations across an umpiring team in terms of the intrinsic resilience of officials and whether they are being provided with support in this space.

He expanded on this and said, "Everybody handles pressure differently. Some people are naturally more composed or able to focus on the present rather than worrying about the past or the future. Or dealing with outside elements. Officiating is a bit like public speaking. The more you do it, the more comfortable you get at it. But it doesn't necessarily make it any easier. You just find a way to deal with it better or to manage it. There will always be a situation, a bad day, a bad game, a comment, or a situation that makes you self-doubt and self-reflect. And that's when you want the strength and support of the officiating team around you.

"There are things you can do before the tournament to prepare your resources strongly enough so that you will be okay. But something can still happen during the tournament. Mistakes are part of umpiring. Things happen. People talk. Commentators say silly things. They judge before they know. Spectators have an opinion. As officials, we've got to be somewhat bulletproof. We have to keep a bubble around us where we can listen to feedback, we can decide whether to take it on board, or we can let it go. That's why we need a lot of experienced people around us. To bring that third person into the room with an objective view. To create a culture of talking about the stresses and pressure about what goes on, and to really debrief and unpack every performance. We need to be able to take the learnings away and not get bogged down in the scrutiny, pressure, or the inappropriate feedback. The psychology of officiating is very important.

"Venkatesh wanted me to do a lot of mentoring around the umpires in this tournament. Having a lot of experience, having made mistakes myself and having gone through the best and the worst that umpiring has to offer, I think that advice, feedback, feed forward, that process of discussion and debriefing gave the officiating team a bit more confidence, resilience and ability to recover quicker from any minor setbacks that may have occurred.

"I was in the stadium for every game and the match referee conducted a debrief on every match. Then I would give my input. I would ask questions like, "If we had today over again what would we do differently? Does anyone want to talk about or raise anything?"

"Like all sporting contests, you learn more about the sport, or cricket umpiring in this case, off the field in the change room, or at the breakfast table, than you do at the game. What I loved to do during the FairBreak tournament was to sit down in the breakfast area at the hotel roughly between 7:00am and 10:00am and be available for any of the officials who wanted to talk about what they saw the night before in their last game and how things were tracking. We had a WhatsApp group in which we shared lots of information about how things were going, anything we needed to address, or any trends we thought were requiring attention.

"I made myself accessible for those corridor conversations and that one-on-one time in a non-threatening environment where any hang ups, concerns, doubts or issues they wanted to get reassurance or clarity on could be had. I was available for those three hours and that worked well."

During the FairBreak tournament, Taufel was interviewed and he reported that some members of the officiating team were getting some "money can't buy experiences". I asked him to expand on what he meant by this and he said, "For example, our officials had the ability to sit with the director in their room while they were watching another game of cricket and to appreciate what being a third umpire is like from the other side. They could see how many people talk to the director. What they need to do. The camera angles. The replays. The timing. Their environment. They could see the game through a different lens.

"Another example was being able to shadow another umpiring team. To shadow another third umpire. To shadow another match referee and to see what they do and to see why they do it that way. To see if their way is a good way. To see if there is a better way.

"Tapping into former elite umpires like myself was another "money can't buy experience" for them. They could shadow me. They could live in my back pocket and they could get me 24/7. They could follow my critique, follow what I did, and see things the way I see them. And then to work out whether that was going to be helpful to them.

"Those are just a few examples around why tapping into what FairBreak has to offer in that space and being exposed to international umpiring for a fortnight was so beneficial. Because some of them hadn't been exposed to that world before. To be able to live and breathe that experience for an extended period was valuable in all sorts of different ways."

Taufel clarified the career pathway for an umpire. He said, "The pathway for umpires is an improvement opportunity for administrators because the pathway isn't clearly identified or communicated. From a domestic or national perspective, an umpire's pathway is very similar to a player's; work your way up through community cricket, through premier cricket, fifth grade, fourth grade, third grade, second grade, first grade. Then, hopefully, you make what's called a State Panel where you come under the auspices or notice of the national selectors for umpires.

"Then you try to work your way up to a national level within your country such as South Africa or Australia. The pathway can become disjointed next, because at what point does the ICC notice you? Do they get involved? Do they appoint you to a tournament and see what you are like? There's a real challenge here around clearly identifying what the pathway is. Then finding the talent. Who are the selectors? Who are the umpiring selectors? And what does the ICC want to see in a cricket umpire?

"There's a lot of work to be done around this. Where can we identify what traits, qualities and abilities the ICC are looking for in an umpire? Who selects umpires? Are we being consistent with the selection policy? Currently, I can't find an ICC selection policy. I can't find an ICC pathway articulated anywhere, which is interesting and problematic. And that reflects on what the national bodies and domestic countries do to be consistent. So it's a bit hit and miss in that respect.

"There are eleven ICC Elite Panel umpires now. Normally there's twelve. But currently, there's eleven. Every Full Member country, of which there's twelve, would have three or four umpires on the International Panel. Based on those mathematics, there are about sixty people eligible to officiate International cricket. We had an accreditation program in place between 2013 and 2016 where we were looking to benchmark and accredit umpires based on their abilities and meritocracy. But I think that system has fallen away slightly over the last three or four years with COVID-19 and various other things.

"There's definitely an opportunity for the ICC to look at this and say, "Is there a better way? How do we make sure that we've got the right umpires coming through and the right umpires staying?"

"We don't have a pathway for the cricket umpires of Associate Nations to get to a World Cup, or to achieve an international standard. Fortunately, FairBreak offered the opportunity to take some umpires from different levels of the game and put them together to accelerate their development. But in terms of Associate Nation match officials, those organisations and governing bodies have limited resources and access to what's required.

"Hopefully, I can jump in with FairBreak and bridge some of those gaps and try to address some of these issues. But it's a short-term Band-Aid type solution. Fundamentally the system needs to be structured in a way where we've got umpire coaches, umpire selectors and match referees who are accredited and trained. And we've got accreditation programs for umpires to ensure that they've got every opportunity of being successful so that we give the game the best officials we can."

Broadcasting

Adam Collins – Commentator

Adam Collins is an Australian cricket journalist and broadcaster living in London. His impressive resumé is detailed on his professional website, https://adamcollins.com.au and states that his "career started with a decade of advising Australian politicians, including a Prime Minister, before he followed his first love. His writing appears around the cricket world, mostly for *The Guardian*, and he is the Australian correspondent for *Wisden Cricket Monthly*. He commentates on radio and television and has been travelling the world calling the game since 2015. He is a member of various commentary teams including Sky Cricket and the BBC's Test Match Special in the UK and for SEN Test Cricket in Australia and New Zealand. He has worked on two ICC World Cups, calling the closing stages of the tied 2019 decider at Lord's. In April 2021, he was named the Christopher Martin-Jenkins Broadcaster of the Year."

Adam Collins has long been a passionate advocate of women's cricket, and with a formidable reputation for ball-by-ball commentating, Shaun Martyn invited him to lead the broadcasting team at the FairBreak Tournament in Dubai. I interviewed Adam in his London home over Zoom and he spoke comprehensively and fervently about the whole event.

"It was a positive broadcasting experience for everyone involved. I was one of the only people in the team who had any meaningful commentary experience, so that meant I felt a certain amount of responsibility, day-to-day, to make sure everyone stepped up. A few were learning on the job. They hadn't done much at all of anything like this, ever. But they were commendable in the way they took to that task. I was mindful of that and treated it with the utmost respect.

"I did gargantuan amounts of homework [a sample of Adam Collins' daily dossier for the TV commentary for the FairBreak Invitational can be found in Further Reading]. I always apply that level of preparation when I'm commentating on radio or television. But I thought it was even more important with this competition because there were so many women playing that no one had heard of before, and it was their first opportunity to play with that kind of coverage, that kind of scrutiny. I owed it to them, their stories, and their families to, not just get the pronunciation of their names right, but to have a really good sense of how they had arrived in Dubai that week and the journey they had been on to get there. I found that really quite nourishing from a broadcasting perspective.

"Because we were all co-located, we were able to see the players around the hotel, at breakfast or by the pool. I was there with my partner Rachel, and my daughter Wini, who had just turned two. My Wini had never met another Wini before. When Winifred Duraisingam got Player of the Match, she had never met another Winifred either, so we were able to get the two of them together for a couple of lovely photos. Malaysia's Winifred is an absolute delight. I really enjoyed getting to know her.

"Andrea Mae Zepeda who is a doctor from Austria. I was so chuffed when she got the opportunity to take the field. The Argentinian bowler, Mariana Martinez, who I'd spoken to at the cocktail function. She was so desperate to get a bowl. And when she finally did, we were so invested in it! And the Brazilian teenager…Laura Cardosa…you sense these cricketers who are so young…and are professionals…some of them are just hoping to get on this journey, on this circuit, on the roller coaster. They want to buy a ticket to the roller coaster of professional cricket!

"It's just that their countries aren't quite there yet, so they see FairBreak as something that bridges the gap, and I think that's part of the mission statement, to give women a "fair break" in the game, and Shaun is big on that. Whether you're from a Full Member Nation like Australia or England, countries that dominate women's cricket, or if you're from an Associate likeArgentina, you should still be provided with a fair go to let your skills do the talking, and that's what FairBreak delivered this year.

"Compared with tournaments in other parts of the world, male or female, there was a real startup vibe, and I mean that positively, not pejoratively. Shaun was hands-on to the extent that the day before the first game, he was personally organising volunteers from the UAE crew who would be able to retrieve balls. When there were problems with the PA, Shaun was there on the tools. The boss of the whole operation was getting things sorted out.

"It did feel like a startup with all hands-on-deck. Even though it was a private equity tournament and carried the impression of being big money because of the wages that were paid out to the players, it still had that energy associated with, "We're all mucking in together". You wouldn't get that at an ICC event, which I've done in the past. Or if you're working for Sky Cricket where there are people, upon people, upon people and every possible thing is accounted for. Shaun was doing it with a small team of staff. So much of it was around what he was able to do inside each twenty four hour period which reflects the decade of work that he had put into it before. So that was really cool.

"From the moment we arrived, we were all mucking in together, we were all part of it. I wouldn't say we were activists for FairBreak necessarily. But I do feel as though we felt like we had a job to do as ambassadors for FairBreak, be it on the broadcasting, on social media, and with the interviews of the players we were doing.

"We sensed that there were some slightly chaotic scenes in the background, but it didn't feel problematic. It felt reflective of that startup energy I mentioned before. I've been involved in things like this before. I'm an entrepreneur in different parts of my life, and I know that when you are working furiously to get something new off the ground, you need to accept the fact that not everything will be perfect. Despite your best intentions, something crazy will happen at the last possible moment. And you must accept that people have faith in you, and that they believe in you, and they've got your back. And everyone had Shaun's back.

"Shaun was serene. I guess it's the analogy of the duck that is furiously paddling away beneath the surface but looks calm above the water. Shaun had that energy about him. A lot of work was being done behind the scenes, and Elle [Williams] was working around the clock, as well as Henry [Geoff Lawson] and all the guys who've been with FairBreak for a long time. And the social media team who were brought in and doing a lot of work round the clock too.

"I knew that there had been some hiccups with the shirts. Some of the player's shirts had the wrong flag printed on the back. For example, Hayley Matthews had the wrong Caribbean flag printed on the back of her shirt. But Shaun's team sorted it. And I have to say, printing the players' flags and names on the back of the shirts was quite an effective device rather than numbers.

"There was no one out there undermining or questioning what was going on in the days leading up to the competition, even when the per diems didn't work. My impression was that people were cool about it. They probably provided Shaun and his team more leeway on that than they would have provided to, say, a major broadcaster. Elle made it very clear to all of the players, if they were experiencing hardship, they could get money from FairBreak at a moment's notice. There was never any problem around people having money to spend as they required in an expensive city like Dubai.

"The death of the United Arab Emirates President [Sheikh Khalifa bin Zayed Al Nahyan] on the 13th of May prevented celebrations towards the end of the tournament but didn't have a big effect. Let's be blunt, there were no crowds anyway. There was a natural atmosphere and the players were adding to that with their own style of celebration. This tournament didn't really need the players sprinting onto the pitch going wild when they won. The product spoke for itself.

"The fact that it was serious cricket was clear to anyone who was watching it. Even though it was an exhibition tournament, the players treated it seriously. I think it might have been a tiny concern of mine going in. I might have said to people, off-handedly, "These might need to be slightly organised games." By organised games what I mean by that is that the captains might have to engineer it that the good batters, the experienced Full Member Nation batters, bowl and bat against each other in the first part of the innings, and the less experienced batters and bowlers duke it out in the second half of the innings.

"Anyone who plays cricket knows...or has played Sunday afternoon, jazz hack beer games...social games... where you've got three or four really good players and the rest are...not making up the numbers...but the quality drops off quite quickly...I thought that might happen. But that fear was quickly allayed. The Associate Nation players were able to compete with the Full Member players, especially when it was Associate Nation bowlers bowling to

Full Member batters.

"I didn't think the gap there was problematic. Indeed, there were several games that were won by the Associate bowlers being very effective. Shizuka Miyaji, who won a game with the ball, and I mentioned Winifred Duraisingam before. They are cricketers who, pound for pound, don't have anything remotely like the experience of their teammates and their opposition, yet they were good enough to win the game with the ball.

"The other side of it was starker when you saw Full Member bowlers, who are full professional cricketers, bowling against Associate batters who didn't have quite the same experience. There was a noticeable gap there. But they weren't confected or contrived games. Remember that semifinal where the Barmy Army lost narrowly to the Tornadoes? That was the closest game of the tournament! That was absolutely fair dinkum, and the Barmy Army were gutted when they lost. I was gratified by that as a commentator, as an observer of the game, and as someone who has been an activist for women's cricket in my career outside of this.

"I've been covering women's cricket for years. I was covering women's cricket back when no one was really talking about women's cricket, outside of a handful of people. When there were really no women's cricket journalists, and I had to go out there and beat the drum, tell the story and be evangelical about why women's cricket mattered. Why it was on the rise and why people should get on the bandwagon. Remembering all of those early days, it felt like this tournament was in keeping with that rise of women's cricket, and that the cricket was serious as a result.

"It was a quirky team. Izzy Duncan had done county cricket, BBC Radio, but nothing for TV. Mark Farmer was going to be doing occasional guest spots. His title is something like Head of High Performance for Cricket Hong Kong. He was going to provide special commentary on the Hong Kong players because there was a dozen of them playing, and on Cricket Hong Kong as the host. In the end, the scarcity of experienced commentators meant that it became apparent, almost immediately, that he was able to upskill quite quickly. He's done some commentary before on streams. By the end of the tournament, in fact quite quickly, he fell straight into the groove. He worked it out, he understood it, he got it and he was excellent.

"Izzy [Duncan] did colour the whole way through. On TV you have a lead who's steering the ship and doing the ball-by-ball commentary, and the colour commentator jumps in with whatever they see that might be interesting to add to the story. Georgie Heath, basically a work experience student was also doing colour. This was probably the first time she ever earned money from journalism and was able to draw upon her well documented health troubles. She's had this quite extraordinary story really, where she nearly died and a few years on from that she decided to become a sports journalist. She did some retraining and ended up doing social media. And because she's an industrious, confident, capable communicator, she pretty much blagged her way onto the television coverage, bless her, and did colour the whole way through and acquitted herself really well on zero experience. I can't tell you how little experience Georgie has, but she stepped up. In the context of what we were doing it was fine, and it worked out really well.

"Melinda Farrell who is battle hardened. Mel's been around the traps for twenty plus years in the media and has done a lot of commentary as well, so having Mel there was good. And of course, Geoff Lawson, who's been doing bits and pieces of commentary and lots of radio especially as a summariser. Because he'd done so much of it, he was able to become one of the lead callers as well without too much difficulty. With him being a man of such vast experience and integrity around the world achieved across more than four decades in the professional game.

"I think the tournament should have a place in the calendar each year because, simply put, FairBreak is paying the players better than a lot of other competitions and domestic cricket. When you consider the number of Associate players…the money they can earn across a fortnight…I don't think it's exaggerating to say…this is life changing for them…in terms of how much money they might earn in a calendar year, this will be a significant chunk of it. So that's really important.

"Players like Heather Knight, Shabnim Ismail, Grace Harris, Sophia Dunkley, Sophie Eccleston, they're all doing well money-wise now. They're on professional full-time contracts. They aren't earning what the men are, but they're earning good cash. So this competition is designed to bring those two worlds together, and that's good and positive.

"Where that balance lies in the future, time will tell, as in how many Full Member players will be there along with Associate players, I think that's contested space. That's a good thing. There will be debates around the composition of the tournament in years to come. It's a good problem to have that the India Premier League is starting up for women next year, so the dates that we announced on finals day for 2023 will no longer happen…we've seen the announcement that FairBreak has been pushed back to April 2023.

"But you know that's good. It's a positive thing that the women who are on the circuit can go to the Big Bash. They can go into the PSL in Pakistan, which will probably start next February or January. They can go to the women's IPL. They can go to the FairBreak tournament. They don't have to go to all of them. They can be selective about what they choose to play in. They can earn money on the circuit. None of these competitions are cannibalising each other yet, which is what I've been vocal about on my platform and podcast.

"Let's make sure that women's international and domestic cricket don't make the same mistakes as the men's scheduling. That they don't have cricket tournaments overlapping all the time. That they have a really clear ambition about what parts of the twelve month cycle are devoted to international fayre, and what parts of the international cycle are devoted to T20 competitions, or The Hundred in England. There's the Big Bash League, The Hundred, potentially the PSL. There's the IPL starting up. The Caribbean Women's League. Competitions popping up everywhere and that is tremendous. We should embrace that and we should provide almost first-mover advantage for those who were there at the start, like the Big Bash.

"And FairBreak sits slightly separate to that. It's not being run by a Full Member country, it's being hosted by Cricket Hong Kong, who are just as entitled to have a productive, profitable women's tournament as any other nation is. So to that end, the fact that they've been one of the first movers, they've moved ahead of India and ahead of Pakistan, that should provide them a slightly more privileged position when it comes to scheduling.

"And the fact is, we're only talking about ten or twelve days, roughly a fortnight. If you said to the boards around the world, a fortnight of the year, at a time when there's not a lot of international cricket being played in April, is going to be devoted to FairBreak, I doubt there'd be that much resistance. And the ICC have, helpfully, made positive noises about this.

"The truth is, the ICC should have done something like this before. They should have seen an opportunity to provide a similar kind of tournament involving Associate players with Full Member Nations a decade ago. Well, at least five years ago. FairBreak has bridged the gap beautifully, and now the ICC are quite supportive, which is great news. Because there were issues with the boards like Australia and England, who dominate the ICC. It's good now that they're all on board and seeing it for what it is, contributing to the women's game.

"I'm not ruling out a major board killing FairBreak, that could happen, we shouldn't be naive about that. If the BCCI, Cricket Australia, and the ECB wanted to kill FairBreak, they'd find a way of doing it. I don't think they will though. We've passed that point. They found a way of suppressing the movement when it was seen as a rebel league more than it is now.

"Regarding India not releasing their players this year, let's be blunt, England could have easily done the same, as could have Australia. I don't think that will kill the competition, but those boards control the ICC when you boil it down. World cricket is controlled by India, with support from Australia and England.

"There are some structural challenges around Hong Kong in 2023. The Men's UAE T20 legs starting in January permit nine foreign players in each starting XI and that's slightly outrageous. It's going to completely tip the balance in Men's T20 cricket. It's going to create a climate where it becomes a bit of a global All Stars League. Now FairBreak was that too. You could have only a couple of Hong Kong players in each team. In theory, the ICC could crack down on the number of foreign players in T20 domestic competitions, which could provide a challenge but I don't think they would do it. They wouldn't do it to the women's game. They might do it to the men.

"So, there are some threats, potentially, or some hurdles to clear or to navigate down the track. But as it stands right now, I don't sense that. I sense that Cricket Australia happily released their players, albeit not their best players. But they let players go. The ECB let some of their very, very best players go. Heather Knight, Sophie Ecclestone, Sophia Dunkley, Danni Wyatt.

And they all want to come back, by the way! I know those girls quite well and they loved it. They had a great time. They all made $20,000 in two weeks, let's be blunt! Some of them made $25,000. Like Heather Knight. And that's crazy money for two weeks work as a women's cricketer. The topflight cricketers got US$20,000 for two weeks work which I believe in the women's cricket world is incredible! Compare that to The Hundred where the very top banner players are getting £32,000 for a four to five weeks work. FairBreak, pro rata, is as good as it gets. So why would they not want to be part of this? They're all great ambassadors for it.

"What will happen in 2023 regarding India? I don't expect India will supply players because they've got the IPL immediately before it. But they might. Player power might win out. The Indian women may say, "We want in on this as well." Pakistan gave some of their best players. The fact that Sana Mir is very involved is very helpful, as is Bismah Maroof. Likewise, New Zealand had their best players out there, and they are poorly paid. New Zealand notoriously, do not pay their women well, not enough of them anyway, so they're always on the circuit.

"Likewise South Africa who have considerable problems in keeping up with pay rates, in that arms race of wages. That's why the South African women are in every single domestic competition, because they get more money from that than they do from playing for their country. Lizelle Lee literally just retired from the South African national team, in no small part, because she can earn just as much money on the circuit. The economics of it suit FairBreak well.

"It was admirable things came together production wise, and there is still room for growth in that space. Remember, that's the shop window, the television. The world doesn't care about who Shaun Martyn is, they don't care about any of that, they care about when they click on the television. Is the cricket any good? Are they finding the experience a good one? I think we could do more on the broadcasting side to improve that into the future. And I say that because FairBreak is super important to me.

"Preparing for a tournament like this as a broadcaster and a commentator is significant. I spent an enormous amount of time talking to people and researching every single thing I could find online about all these players. Some of them I know, they're friends of mine, the international senior players. But some of them I couldn't pick out of a police lineup. So I had to really go the extra mile to learn about all the cricketers. And I'm proud of that.

"I updated the commentary prep every day so that all of their stats were carefully listed. I updated things meticulously because I was quite obsessed, and I shared that document with my commentary colleagues every day. Even though I was doing it, I was willing to share it. I felt it was important that they could all speak with some authority about every player. I was really keen for the broadcasting to be good and that people had a reference that was being updated and circulated on the morning of each day of the tournament."

Lesego Pooe – TV Anchor

Lesego Pooe was the TV anchor host for the broadcasting of the nineteen T20 matches during the FairBreak Tournament in Dubai. She is a young cricket broadcaster from Johannesburg in South Africa. She has worked as a broadcaster and brand ambassador for Lions Cricket TV on SuperSports, a venue media manager for an U/19 ICC World Cup event, and as Cricket South Africa's media liaison and formal spokesperson for the Protea Women's series in India.

Lesego Pooe spoke passionately to me about the FairBreak Tournament. She enthused, "Such an exciting time. It was an amazing opportunity for me to go to Dubai. It was the first event of its kind, so already, my spirits were high. I was so looking forward to it."

Lesego Pooe's average day in Dubai started at 7:30am with a gym session followed by breakfast. Then she went through her preparations for the two games taking place that day. She said, "I'd go through the teams, look at the previous games the teams had played in. Look at the standout players from the previous games. Look at the stats of the bowlers. Weigh it all against the pitch and how the pitch might be playing and see who might be able to play better on that pitch depending on whether it will be a bowling wicket or a batting wicket, to see which bowlers are going to be potentially good at that wicket. Maybe we'll be able to see which spinners or which fast bowlers might be coming in. My predictions for that game. If I see it being a high scoring game or a low scoring game. Who should bat first and how many runs they should be scoring on that day for it to be a competitive score.

"And then I'd set questions for the people I will be interviewing: for the pre-match and the post-match interviews. So, if I am sitting with Georgie Heath, I'd set a couple of questions, and outline the kind of conversation I want to be having with her.

"Then I'd get ready, choose an outfit, and do my makeup. Unfortunately, the makeup artist at the stadium didn't have makeup to suit my complexion, the tones of my skin, so I did my own makeup. We needed to be ready down at reception by 11:00–11:30am, depending on what time they were calling us.

And then we'd go to the stadium where I'd have my lunch and then sit down and go through some more questions because I would get instructions from the producer around how he'd like us to go about covering the day's games.

"Then we'd start the broadcast and I'd do the work, have my opening link, have our pre-match conversations. Then I'd link to the game itself, match number one, and then after that we'd have a break, and then we'd go into match number two because most of the games were double headers. After match two we'd have dinner, call it a night, get back on the bus, go back to the hotel. I'd take a shower, go through some of the things I wanted to wrap my head around before the next day. Bedtime would be around 1:30am. After going live, you're still buzzing. I found it quite difficult to sleep immediately after I got back to the hotel.

"My role as the tournament host involves being at the studio in the stadium. The minute we go live, I am the first point of contact, I welcome everybody. I welcome the entire world to the tournament, and I talk about the matches that will be taking place. After that, I link to Melinda Farrell, one of the broadcasting team who is out on the field with microphone in hand. Her role is to do the coin toss before every single match. Melinda would be standing next to the two captains and the match official, and she'd announce the coin toss between, say, the Tornadoes and the Warriors. They'd do the coin toss and whoever wins the toss will then have a conversation with Melinda around what they are going to do first. Maybe the captain will say they are going into bat first and then Melinda will have a conversation with the captain around why she is choosing to do that. What starting XI is she bringing in? What is she looking to see happen on the field today as far as her team is concerned?

"After the coin toss, then there is the pitch report. They'll come back to me in the studio and I will link back to the pitch report. FairBreak decided to do something new. It's never been done before. They brought in certain players to do the pitch inspection. A player will be in the middle of the pitch, and the camera would be there and they will talk about, "OK today's pitch is a bit slow…the batters who come into bat first, maybe they'll be able to put in a competitive score…or maybe this is a pitch where bowlers can come in and be able to get early wickets". FairBreak brought in some of the players to do the pitch inspection instead of having, as the ICC or other tournaments do, an infield presenter to be the analyst who does the pitch inspection. FairBreak decided to include the players in the broadcasting side of things and that was refreshing.

"After the pitch inspection, they link back to me and then we start looking at the teams. For example, who have the Warriors or Tornadoes decided to bring in? I then have a discussion with my analyst, who is in the studio, about the starting XI of each team. Who are we expecting to be a stand-out player in this game? Are we expecting to see someone get a lot of wickets in comparison to the previous games? I'll start having those sort of diverse conversations around what we're expecting in the next game.

"Then I link it to our commentators. These are the guys who are behind the microphone throughout the entire game. Adam [Collins], Izzy [Isabelle Duncan], Georgie [Heath]. And FairBreak also brought in some of the coaches to share their perspectives on different teams.

"During the commentary, I am sitting inside the studio or by the holding area where I am watching the game because I need to start analysing and taking in all the information needed for me to be able to hold post-match conversations in the studio. I must be engaged throughout the entire game and not miss any action whatsoever. After that, we wrap up the game and I tell my audience that we will be back in a bit for the second game and so the process starts all over again. Depending on which country the broadcast is going out to, the broadcaster will fill that gap between games with news or advertising or something. There was a 35-to-40-minute break between the games.

"Before the very first game, there was an opening ceremony that featured Zeb Bangash, a female singer-songwriter from Pakistan who choreographed the players coming in and turning around so we could see the flags on their backs. FairBreak decided not to have numbers on the player's shirts but have, instead, their names and the flags of the countries they are from. And that was a beautiful thing. I have that vividly in my mind, the players turning their backs, and the camera just panning through all the players showing all the names and flags."

Lesego Pooe echoed the emotional feelings of many at the FairBreak Invitational final by saying, "I haven't been to a lot of tournaments. This was my first experience of being a host and part of the action, and for me I just remember FairBreak having a sense of belonging. There was a feeling of so much gratitude to be part of something so big that was changing the narrative on women's cricket and changing the narrative between cricket's Full Member and Associate Nations. We have never had a tournament in the past that brings both those worlds together, and for them to collide in such a beautiful way was so amazing to witness and to be part of. It was magnificent.

"Melinda, the in-field presenter, was supposed to do the trophy ceremony, but because she fell ill with COVID-19 a couple of days before the final, Shaun came to me and said "Lesego, you're the one who's doing the final, as soon as you're done in your studio, you need to come down and do this trophy ceremony".

"For me it was so scary, but exciting at the same time. I remember being part of that special moment, announcing the winners of FairBreak. As the Tornadoes walked up, the winners of the entire tournament, it was exciting to see the smiling excitement on the players' faces. And giving out the cheques and having all the staff members and the players gathered together in that moment.

"It came together so well. It was a dream finish. I've been in broadcasting before and I know when something works beautifully. To see the way that it turned out was incredible. To see the ladies supporting each other the way they did and seeing Shaun so happy that we have come to the end of a tournament that has been such a tremendous success. It was a breath-taking, emotional moment. I wouldn't change that for anything."

I asked Lesego Pooe about her cricketing background and she described it by saying, "I love telling my cricket story because I'm the only girl and three boys. My brothers and I would always play backyard cricket when we were growing up. There was a pipeline cricket program in South Africa called Mini Cricket that I was part of from the age of seven years old. There was a time when I stopped playing because I was the only girl in a boys' team and for me it felt so awkward. I remember my school principal coming to me and saying, "Lesego, you really need to start playing cricket again, being the only girl cannot be an excuse. You really need to come back because you are good".

And that motivated me. Luckily, my high school had girls' cricket, and that gave me an opportunity to really get to know the game and not just be playing for fun. To really understand the game, from bowler to batter and really get a rhythm within the game.

"My father, Peter Pooe, also greatly influenced my love of cricket and my knowledge of the game. When I was growing up, he would watch Test cricket all day on the television and talk to me about it. Sadly, I lost him to lung cancer when I was a teenager. I am so grateful for the legacy he left me and the positive impact it has had on my career.

"I remember taking cricket seriously in high school. We used to compete with a lot of surrounding schools and I ended up playing provincial cricket for the U/19 Girls' team. Every year for four years I'd always go to an U/19 tournament with Cricket South Africa. We'd travel to different provinces in South Africa, and I got to see how competitive this game really is. But I wasn't good enough to make it a career and play at a national level. I've got a background in media studies so I decided to stay connected to cricket on the media side of things. I've worked with the national woman's team, the Proteas, as a media manager, and then the broadcasting bug bit me around 2018. So that's how I started standing in front of a camera with microphone in hand and talking cricket.

"My love for the game stretches back to when I was seven years old. All that knowledge I built up over the years playing in the backyard and at school has served a purpose. I can speak confidently and articulately about the game. But there is so much more to keep learning, so that one does not become obsolete. We must all have an attitude where we keep learning and growing. FairBreak gave me that opportunity to grow, even when I had never done a tournament of that kind before. Shaun said, "Just come as you are. We see potential in you". And I think that is the beauty about being part of FairBreak, you're given a fair break to show what you can offer and the skills that you have.

"A colleague from Cricket South Africa, the logistics manager for the women's national team, told me about the FairBreak opportunity. He had me in mind and said, "Check this out Lesego. Here's something to sink your teeth into". So, I went online, sent through my application about why I was motivated to be part of the tournament. I just hoped and prayed for the best, and literally a couple of weeks later I got an email from Elle [Williams] wanting to set up an interview between Shaun, Geoff, Elle, and myself. It was such a short meeting, not more than 15-20 minutes. Shaun asked me a simple question, "Lesego, what would you like from FairBreak? What is it that you'd like from us?" I was expecting, "What can you offer us? What is it that you have? What can you bring?" Those kind of questions. I remember just saying, "I really want to be part of this tournament, in whatever capacity. I am a broadcaster and I'd love to be a part of it". I sent him a link to my previous work, and it was literally twenty four hours later I got an email from Shaun saying, "You are now a #fairbreaker! Congratulations you're going to Dubai". I remember calling my mother and crying over the phone".

As a woman, I was intrigued to know how much packing Lesego had to do for this trip. How many outfits did she take? Did she need to go shopping in Dubai? We both laughed when she told me, "I packed nineteen outfits! I forgot that most of the matches were double headers, so I didn't need a different outfit for each game. In the end, I had ample to choose from every day.

"I was really excited about the opening ceremony and game because I'd brought a Ghanaian inspired outfit. The top was made of fabric from Ghana in West Africa. Even though I am a Tswana woman of South Africa, I really wanted to bring my African culture to the opening ceremony. Wearing that Ghanaian top filled me with so much pride. And that is what I want to bring to the future tournaments, wearing outfits that represent who I am and where I'm from. I got really excited about bringing my identity to the world because it's not often that you see tournament presenters and hosts who are from Africa. And not only from Africa, but black, young, and female.

"It speaks about a new wave that is coming on to the horizon, and I am so happy that I'm one of the chosen to be at the forefront of this. When you get given that sort of opportunity, you really must come as you are, so that young girls from across the world, wherever they are from, especially the ones who are from South Africa and the whole continent of Africa, see themselves in me. They can see that my dreams and theirs are valid, and if they too want to be on a world stage, it is very much possible. They can see a representation in the flesh of someone like themselves. But who looks like me, sounds like me, and acts like me.

"It is important that you come as you are, and that you bring your identity to whatever space you find yourself in. There are eleven official languages in South Africa, and I am Setswana speaking, and I wanted to wear something that represents me as a Tswana woman. But the lady who was making my dress did not finish it on time. So, I wore the Ghanaian outfit. I am not complaining, because as a South African I represent not only South Africa, but Africa as a whole continent. Setswana is my home language, and I did incorporate a bit of my language when I was presenting. Shaun specifically told me to feel free to speak in my own language in places. So, there were moments during the broadcasts, for example during the opening game, where I welcomed the whole world to the tournament and introduced myself in Setswana.

"I don't know the viewing numbers for South Africa, but my circle of family and friends were watching the tournament, supporting it, and sending me many WhatsApp messages. Those moments warmed my heart.

"Before we went away to the tournament, Cricket South Africa issued a press release announcing that Laura Wolvaardt, Mignon du Preez, Marizanne Kapp, Sune Luus, Shabnim Ismail and Ayabonga Khaka would all be representing South Africa at FairBreak, and they mentioned me as the main tournament host. They wished us well and congratulated us for the opportunities we had been granted by FairBreak. It was great to see the mother body of South African cricket endorsing us and encouraging the players to go out and do their best, have fun and represent South Africa. That was sent out to the media at large.

"In the last two years, there has been more exposure of and the televising of international women's cricket in South Africa. They have been broadcasting the games the Momentum Proteas players are having with different nations and there is much better coverage of the women's game than in the past. Domestic cricket is a different story though. We have had a Women's Super League happening for the last two to three years, but unfortunately that is not being broadcast on television. In comparison, the Men's Domestic T20 and One Day games are broadcast. More needs to be done to get the women's games at a domestic level onto the television in South Africa."

Lara Richards
Global Media Rights

Lara Richards is based in Perth, Western Australia. As CEO and co-founder of Marron Media, she leads a progressive sports media agency developing media rights programmes to achieve maximum impact, greater revenue and fan engagement for sporting codes. Her primary role is client acquisition, strategising and building new relationships with content buyers within the industry. She has also worked at Sky Sports and the International Cricket Council where she oversaw media rights management, distribution and sales.

Richards acts as FairBreak's broadcast advisor and global media rights consultant. As Marron Media, she negotiated the televising of the SDG FairBreak Invitational by fourteen broadcasters in over 140 territories around the globe.

I asked her to explain what is involved in putting a sports event like the FairBreak Invitational onto global televisions. She said, "First of all, FairBreak organises the production of the broadcast, getting all the cameras and the commentators in place and creating something called a live feed. That live feed is then handed over to an agency like mine here at Marron Media to distribute around the world to broadcasters.

"What that entails, from the very beginning, is finding out information about the production. What will it look like? Will there be notable commentators? Will the graphics be good? Will the whole broadcast be attractively packaged to create a quality live feed? Then I put these elements together and begin marketing the media rights of everything that comes from the live feed.

"I assemble all the documentation. I explain to broadcasters what they will get. Value-adds are important. For example, the opportunity to visit the ground, to speak to players, to get players on Skype and to do media interviews. I create a whole media rights package. I can also offer alternative media, not just TV rights. For example, audio, so the tournament can be broadcast on radio. Or programming rights if they want to create programming.

"When I have packaged these various media rights from the live feed then I give or sell it to broadcasters… and that entails creating documentation and sending it out to the broadcasters – I targeted forty broadcasters for FairBreak initially – and then speaking with them about the package and whether it fits into their scheduling. If it does, then I talk about the commercials and about delivery of that and how they can access all of the content.

"When the tournament starts, I manage all of the broadcasters who have come on board. I make sure they've got the feed and there are no quality issues. I ensure I'm delivering all the contractual obligations I included in their agreements. Post event, I manage the payments, reconciliation and feedback.

"Broadcasters on the subcontinent will pay for content. Purely, because they've got brands that are actively investing in their channel and buying advertising space. They are receiving money in from brands which they can spend on acquiring content.

"It's different when I go out to the West. In the USA where cricket isn't as popular, they have less money to spend on this kind of content, so they won't pay for it. Distributing the rites to an inaugural tournament…I feel like all the broadcasters are in cahoots a little bit…that they speak to each other and say, "We're not paying for the first edition of the tournament and that's just the way it is. We don't know what the audience is, so how can we possibly value what the content is worth?" I have found that for inaugural tournaments, a lot of broadcasters will carry the content on a free basis only."

For FairBreak's first tournament, Richards got a mix of fee-paying broadcasters and carriage-only broadcasters. Her revenue stream, as a business owner, comes from the commission she charges FairBreak for selling the broadcasting rights to the tournament. She expanded, "If I place content with an Indian broadcaster and they give FairBreak US$30,000, for example, then I take a commission from that. Broadcasters never pay an agency."

I asked Richards how she arrived in such a niche part of sports journalism where she sells the media rights for cricket tournaments. She explained, "I started in journalism, which then got me into TV, on the production side of things, working for Sky. From Sky I made the jump over to sports commercial.

"My job at the International Cricket Council in Dubai involved maximising the distribution of ICC tournaments. There was an agreement in place with a broadcaster called StarSports, a big $2 billion cricket deal, and my job was to push them into sub-licensing the rights to different territories because they had bought global media rights. I ensured that they distributed it to Canada or Australia or wherever the contract said. When I left the ICC, I set up this agency, Marron Media, and I now have direct conversations to multiple broadcasters rather than just StarSports."

She also revealed, "I don't have sporty parents and I never went to the cricket, but every year I was sent to stay at my grandparents' house in the UK, and the only thing to do during the summer holidays was to watch Test cricket which was on the television constantly. So, I watched a lot of cricket while growing up.

"After studying journalism, I wanted to read the news. That was my dream. To be a sports news anchor. When I finally got into TV, I discovered that the route to that wasn't attainable for a decade, so when an ICC job came calling, it was a gift. I loved cricket, I got to live in Dubai and I got to work in an alternate area of sport that let me crossover to the commercial side. It was a good fit.

"Since then, I've become even more cricket obsessed. I have submerged myself into the global world of cricket. Up until then, I was very much England focused. Working for the ICC, they told me quite openly, "You can't support a team, you have to love all cricket". So I got to know about cricket everywhere. Yesterday I was distributing content for the United Arab Emirates cricket team. It's very varied, broad, and interesting.

"With FairBreak, Shaun involves all the Associate Nations, which are ranked according to the ICC, and it's just amazing the breadth of players he has involved. Even with the cricket knowledge I thought I had I didn't recognise some of the players on the list. And they all did such a magnificent job in Dubai. They played so well.

"I distribute quite a lot of men's T20 cricket. Coming into this space, I knew I wasn't going to get the England and Australia international content that the big agencies command. So I tried to carve out a niche in the men's cricket leagues, like the Lanka Premier League, the Abu Dhabi T10 and other leagues that have existed for a while.

"What I found with FairBreak, even though it was the inaugural tournament, the broadcasters loved the content and they were highly engaged with it. Normally what happens is broadcasters sign an agreement, I give them the satellite details, they link into the satellite, take the content and that's it.

"During the FairBreak Invitational, I was hearing from broadcasters every single day. They'd ask, "Can we get access to this player because a media outlet in India would like to interview her?" Or they were looking for press conference content. They were looking for promos. They were really getting involved so that they could better promote the tournament on their channels.

"I loved the enthusiasm. It felt like I was working for the ICC again. I was getting daily broadcaster engagement throughout the tournament. Broadcasters were requesting things which doesn't tend to happen that much in men's cricket nowadays. I felt like the broadcasters really woke up to the FairBreak Tournament and liked it immensely. The footage, the imagery, the celebration, the cultural flavour and points of difference that came across were very appealing. They were very different to men's cricket.

"Even though Shaun had support from Cricket Hong Kong, the fact that he was independent and had a vision he was bringing to life, the broadcasters had a lot of respect for that. They loved the content and they wanted to speak to FairBreak players all the time. And this was during the India Premier League! Our Indian broadcaster, Eurosport, wanted access to players like Sana Mir and Heather Knight…to speak with other publications in India and to create some noise….and I found that interesting in itself…because to be asking for that during the men's IPL….you'd think it would be a pointless activity because it wouldn't cut through the male coverage. But it was completely the opposite. We received excellent feedback from the broadcaster. They kept asking for more FairBreak players as the tournament progressed. It was obviously a worthwhile activity for them to be doing. I thought that was a positive message.

"When a broadcaster asks for access to a player to interview them, they will get a link to a Zoom call, via their manager. There will be a congregation of media who will ask the player questions. That happened quite a few times during the tournament. Interestingly, the Indian media don't normally want to speak with the Pakistani players, because of that political tension between

India and Pakistan. But this time they wanted Sana Mir, Diana Baig, and the full complement of the country's players rather than excluding Pakistan. That was very refreshing."

Richards informed me about how women's cricket has changed in recent years. She said, "Cricket in India is like a religion. While working for the ICC, I worked on the Women's Cricket World Cup in India in 2013. Nobody in India knew who any of the female Indian cricket players were back then. The BCCI put them in a terrible hotel near the cricket ground, and their per diems were a third of what the men were getting. Now there's finally some sort of parity being achieved.

"Women's cricket has so much room for growth, which makes it super exciting to be involved in FairBreak. From 2017, when viewer growth really started to accelerate, it was the ICC's vision that Lords should be sold out for the Women's World Cup final in 2017. When that happened, male fans switched on to the fact that Lords was full. It was a case of, "OMG! Hold on a second, there's women playing?" That whole cliched mindset around women's cricket is rapidly changing because the cricket is getting better, it's much more competitive, and it's also being seen. Before now, it was never getting broadcast.

"Over the next few years, I really hope that women's cricket doesn't start to resemble the men's calendar because that is so congested. There's just too much cricket out there. Broadcasters are finding it difficult to schedule all of it because there's just not enough space. And cricket is a very long format.

"What I hope to see over the next few years is quality women's tournaments being broadcast. I was speaking to an Indian channel recently, and they don't see women's cricket tournaments competing currently. They want a quantum of content. They need to create a portfolio all through the year, so that people are watching, becoming more engaged and realising just how fantastic a product it is.

"That's what I hope will happen. We will have quality cricket. Broadcasters will see it as a package and they need to buy it all so that it's being seen for twelve months of the year. Then, hopefully, values will go up, because right now, it's not a huge money-spinner.

"For the SDG FairBreak Invitational, they went off-air between the two matches, so the broadcaster had a forty-minute slot to fill with whatever content they had available. They have to line up that content in advance. They might have a forty-minute highlights program from a previous tournament or they might fill it with advertising depending on what they have available. Hopefully, in future years, FairBreak will look at filling that gap between the double headers.

"The problem with the first tournament was that FairBreak didn't have any content to be rolling out during that window between the games. What we could do for Hong Kong in 2023 is revisit the 2022 tournament and show a highlights package for thirty minutes. Maybe we could roll that content out ourselves because broadcasters love that sort of thing. They love end-to-end coverage. It's appealing because they don't have to do anything. They call it "plug and play". They just plug it in at the start of the match, play it, and then at the end they go back to their regular programming."

Richards has been tasked with finding a lineup of international broadcasters for the FairBreak Invitational in Hong Kong in April 2023. With improved syndication for the second tournament, FairBreak can further expand the reach of their unique tournament format and increase broadcasting revenues.

Maximising distribution means cricket fans around the world can access the event through live TV, catchup, clips or documentary coverage. She added, "At the moment, I am speaking with broadcasters in India and the USA. I have feelers out in South Africa. I am working on Pakistan. Currently, I have thirty three broadcasters on my list as targets for the tournaments in 2023. New channels emerge while other channels fall away, especially in the digital space.

"If a USA broadcaster, for example, becomes interested in cricket content for the first time. I will jump on a call with them and explain to them what FairBreak is all about. It's ever moving and changing. We've got six months until the 2023 Tournament in Hong Kong starts so I'm constantly pushing people to respond. Closer to the tournament, it will be different. They will all wake up and want this unique content and it will be manic. Cricket doesn't work on big timelines!"

I asked Richards whether they had conducted any analysis around which countries had the most viewers of the SDG FairBreak Invitational. She answered, "We didn't get an official post-event viewership report where an agency like Nielsen pulls all the official broadcast figures. If I had to guess, I reckon the country with the most viewers would be in the subcontinent, India, or Pakistan. Probably Pakistan because it was on PTV, the state broadcaster, which is available in one hundred million homes, essentially 80-90% of Pakistan's population. FairBreak had Sana Mir, Diana Baig, Bismah Maroof, Aliya Riaz and Fatima Sana playing from Pakistan. And Sana Mir is a rock star over there.

"And then India probably. The broadcaster we were working with is a digital platform and they say they've got one hundred million active users each month. So, the potential reach in India was huge as well. It's very difficult to get broadcast figures, especially in this digital world, because each country's viewership bureaus don't collect digital ratings currently. It's just not being measured.

"In Australia it was on beIN SPORTS which is available as part of Fox Sports packages. That's channel 507 on the Fox box. I know because I was watching it! We wanted Fox Sports to take the content, but they declined because we wanted them to pay a rights fee. Although they are quite vocal when it comes to their support of women's sport, they did not want to support this. That was disappointing.

"Economics also plays a massive role when it comes to sports broadcasting. COVID-19 decimated everything because cricket wasn't taking place. And now the feedback from broadcasters is there's a recession on and brands aren't spending. So, I am seeking out those broadcasters who still have dollars to spend. And persuading them to appreciate what the FairBreak content is worth."

"The Breast Health Clinical Trial: Associate Professor Deirdre McGhee and Elyse Potter

Almost 60% per cent of female athletes have experienced a breast injury and yet 90% of them have never reported these injuries to anyone.

"This is a silent women's health problem and a silent sports injury"

During FairBreak's international cricket competition in Dubai, Deirdre McGhee, an Associate Professor from the University of Wollongong (UOW), led a clinical research trial into breast support and injury to boost global awareness of these issues amongst the female athletes and coaches taking part in the tournament. One of McGhee's research students, Elyse Potter, a sports physiotherapist with Cricket Australia, accompanied her to the United Arab Emirates.

The FairBreak tournament presented an ideal opportunity for them to conduct a clinical research trial. They were able to assess ninety women of various skill levels and of different body shapes and sizes from a diverse range of cultural backgrounds, all conveniently gathered together in the one location for two weeks.

Associate Professor McGhee works within UOW's School of Medicine, Indigenous and Health Sciences. She is also the Director of Breast Research Australia where for the past twenty years she has led research and education on breast pain and breast injuries amongst active women and female athletes. During her career she has worked collaboratively with Sports Medicine Australia and the Australian Institute of Sport (AIS), creating sports medicine guidelines on effective breast support during exercise.

She said, "FairBreak was an opportunity to share a global education platform, with free educational resources made available by Breast Research Australia (based at the University of Wollongong) and the Australian Institute of Sport (AIS), Female Performance and Health Initiative. We also wanted to recruit, train and mentor Breast Education Leaders (BELs) from the thirty-five participating countries to take this vital health education back to active women and female athletes in their own countries. We wanted to promote breast health awareness to women all over the world".

McGhee has also developed a world-first Sports Bra app, a free online tool that helps women of all ages, breast sizes and activity levels to independently choose a sports bra design that will fit them correctly. A well-fitted and supportive bra allows women to exercise in greater comfort and reduces exercise-induced pain by up to eighty five per cent.

Elyse Potter wanted to investigate a broad spectrum of factors surrounding breast injury and breast health in the female cricketers as part of her Masters degree. She needed to quantify how many players had experienced a breast injury, how many of them had reported it, how many hadn't reported it and the reasons why. She was also there to investigate bra fit and comfort amongst the players.

As McGhee had no cricket experience, Potter was the ideal candidate to have on board as her apprentice. The data and research McGhee and Potter gathered during the FairBreak Tournament will form a future model of care for physiotherapists and professional female athletes across all sports.

While in Dubai, McGhee and Potter created a private WhatsApp group and invited the ninety players to book in for half hourly consultations with them in a locked and private room at FairBreak's hotel. The researchers introduced themselves to the players as clinicians and assured the women that they were under no obligation to take part in the trial. For cultural reasons, some of the women did not take part; illness and COVID-19 also affected how many players took up the offer of a breast health and sports bra consultation.

They said, "We tried to see as many players as we could. There were two cricket matches on each day, and if players had the afternoon game at 4pm, they had to leave the hotel quite early for the stadium, so we could only see about six to eight players per day."

Fifty four women out of the ninety players were assessed during the consultations. The other thirty six players couldn't be assessed for several reasons, lack of time being the primary one, while illness amongst a few players and cultural sensitivities were the others. They explained, "Lack of time was our biggest problem. By the time we completed the three education sessions, lost time with the opening ceremony, the players' days off and just trying to coordinate getting everyone together. There was just not enough time to see every player."

Prior to the individual assessments McGhee and Potter assembled the players into three group sessions. Two teams of fifteen players each, making thirty women in each session. McGhee led presentations on breast injuries, breast pain and bra comfort in female athletes. She showed the players videos and cross section visuals of breast movement. Cricket is a sport involving a lot of running and upper torso movement. She explained that a correctly fitted sports bra is vital as it greatly improves the posture in the trunk and shoulders.

Potter detailed further, "What really stuck with the players was the fact that in sixty minutes of running around, breasts can bounce over ten thousand times. Often, listening to a presentation involving statistics can be really hard to absorb and people get lost. With this, everyone was engaged because it was so relatable, and the types of slides and visuals Deirdre used to talk about upper torso movement showed how that relates to cricket. And that was the "buy in" for the players to come along to our assessments, "We can look at your bra and we can help you". Lots of the athletes were very keen on having an assessment.

"We did all the assessments in the morning and every half an hour we would have a new player come in. Players would show us their bra, and we assessed how supportive that bra was while they were running on the spot. We asked them to rate the level of comfort in their bra, and how much movement, support, and pain they had. Rate it out of ten. Most athletes rated their bras highly because it was their favorite bra and they'd been wearing it for years.

"The check list for Deirdre's bra test involved a player standing in her sports bra. Deirdre would look at the straps, she would pull on the straps and check how tight they were, or how loose they were. Then she checked the cups to see if there was enough coverage of the breast. She pulled on the front band and checked the elasticity and the thickness of it and did the same at the back. She'd also look at the type of bra the player was wearing. Whether it was an everyday bra or if they were wearing an actual sports bra. Some players from the lower tier cricketing nations had never even had a new bra. Many wore "hand-me-downs".

"Most players' bras were too old and too loosely fitted. Over time bras lose elasticity and so the straps on the back or front of them become slack. Some players weren't even wearing the right sized bra, especially the bigger breasted women. Some needed additional support. Often, bigger breasted women should wear two sports bras when they're playing sport or exercising, and many didn't know that. There was a lot of education. We told them that if they're not feeling supported and they're getting breast pain with just one bra, try using an extra crop top or an extra form of compression on top and see how they feel.

"Then we said to them, "Now we're going to professionally fit you". We used a tape measure, and we had three brands of sports bras in every size and we fitted each player according to her bra size. Once they were fitted with a new sports bra from the range we had been given, we assessed them again, running on the spot, and asked them to rate their level of breast support and breast pain."

McGhee and Potter assessed fifty four out of the ninety women playing in the tournament. Only four women out of the fifty-four who were assessed passed McGhee's special test to determine whether their bra was correctly fitted and whether it was providing them with appropriate breast support.

Potter told me, "The results were quite amazing. Without giving the athletes something different to compare them against, they probably would have carried on thinking their own bra was fine and they would have been quite happy to keep using what they had. But once we put them in a properly fitted sports bra with more support, the responses were fascinating and universally positive about how much more supportive they were."

McGhee confirmed this, "Many of the women were resistant and a bit dubious at first. Many of them told us they were quite happy with the bras they were wearing. However, every player had an "OMG" moment when we put them into a correctly fitted sports bra. Suddenly, they were exclaiming, "Yes please, I want this sports bra!""

Potter explained further, "We measured the players running on the spot and asked them to rate out of ten the comfort and support of their old bras and then compared that to a rating out of ten for their new, expertly fitted sports bra that had better support. I am currently doing some statistical analysis of those numbers.

"We also investigated the use of chest protection. There was a definite reluctance to wear the donated breast guards and breast shields we had available. Although the protection had been designed for contact sports like AFL, Rugby League and fencing, many of the players were reluctant to use them because they had not had a breast injury, they had never thought about it, and never been exposed to it.

"They were happy to try them on though, and to have a feel of them, but only a few players took them away, and they were mainly wicketkeepers. Because if they're standing behind the stumps and there's a fast bowler bowling at 120kmph, and the ball deflects off the bat in an awkward way, they can easily be hit in the breast.

"The more experienced players were more reluctant to try them because they'd got this far in their cricket careers without needing them, so their attitude was why should they start using them now at this stage? Also, as the temperatures in Dubai were uncomfortably high, the players did not want to stand and run around in the heat wearing another layer of material.

"Nevertheless, we wanted them to be aware that breast injuries can occur no matter how experienced an athlete they are, and we wanted to get a guide on what they thought about the breast guards. Would they use them and how did they feel on? The breast shields were quite hard. So, if they were wearing a breast guard, and they took a dive on the field for a catch, many of the players thought that might cause more pain, that it would dig into their skin."

Potter also revealed, "A universal truth emerged that nobody had ever mentioned breast injury or breast support to any of these women, some of whom had been playing cricket at an elite level for over fifteen years.

"Players who had experienced a breast injury while playing cricket didn't do anything about it because they didn't know they could. They just let it go.

So again, it all came back to education. They absolutely do need to report breast injuries to medical staff and a physiotherapist who can give them the right advice about treating the injury, the swelling, the bruising.

"The most common injury is a cricket ball impact to the chest. Non-reporting of breast injury is uniform across all cricket levels, Tiers 1, 2 and 3. Women just put up with injury to the breast, and this has been found to be the case across all sports. So why don't female athletes report breast injury? The most common reason cited was they don't think anyone can help. But a painful, swollen, or bruised breast severely affects a player's performance.

"As physios, we have online management systems, and we have different injury classifications, hamstring strains or quad strains. But breast injury isn't like one of those, and so when it's not an actual injury classification, it affects the number of injuries or breast injuries in the data. Players aren't reporting them because the injury classifications aren't available in the system.

"In the sector of breast injuries, there's still a lot to be done. We need to raise awareness that breast injuries can occur during any sport, and we need to educate athletes to report these injuries so they can be treated," continued Potter.

"At the same time, we have to educate clinicians on treating breast injuries effectively while encouraging sports coaches to create an open and trusting environment, so that active women are not reluctant to talk about breast pain and injuries.

"Our main goal for travelling to Dubai was to educate the global leaders in women's cricket on fundamental female-specific health issues, such as breast pain and breast support, breast injuries and breast protection," added McGhee.

Elyse Potter explained the other reason she was in Dubai, "I also had to go to the cricket games in the afternoons and evening to help out as a sports physiotherapist because I was mentoring all the local UAE physios who weren't used to working in cricket, or weren't used to cricket games at such a high level. I had to show them the ropes, what a medical briefing looks like at the start of a game. I had to get all the umpires together and the physiotherapists and the doctors to brief them about what to do if there was a medical emergency on the field, so that everyone was on the same page. And then I watched the games at the stadium and if there were any injuries and the local physios needed help, they asked me for advice.

"There were plenty of injuries. Lots of soft tissue injuries such as muscle strains, sore knees, and lower backs because the playing surface in Dubai is very hard. If players aren't used to that kind of surface, if they come from a country where there are softer surfaces, or well-manicured fields, their body has to adapt. But also because there were many games in a very short period of time. The tournament was held in the players' off-season and so they were bound to get some injuries. It was just too much load."

At the end of the tournament, McGhee collated ten bags of the unused brand-new sports bras and breast shields and gave a bag each to the players from Associate Nations such as Namibia, Papua New Guinea and Rwanda where it is impossible to access or purchase such items. She encouraged the women to take the sports bras home and to distribute them to other female cricketers or athletes in their country. She also taught them how to use the sports bra app and how to ensure that the bras correctly fit the women they might give them to back in their native countries. All the players at the tournament were also taught how to correctly care for and wash their sports bras to prolong their use.

Potter reported, "Deirdre also recruited a representative from each country to be a breast educator. From countries such as Brazil, Papua New Guinea, and so on. She explained to them what they needed to do, so they could go home to the teams they normally play with and disseminate that information and distribute the sports bras appropriately and to make sure that other female players are fitted properly."

Potter reflected on how she felt about being in Dubai, "The tournament itself was awesome. I work in cricket full time in Queensland and I've been involved in many tournaments at an elite level and overseas, and they're all very different. This one was cool, like we were starting a movement. And that's the difference. This type of tournament was about getting other countries that we never see involved. I was quite surprised. I feel that I'm pretty up-to-date with who's really good in most countries in terms of female athletes and female cricket players. But there were players there I had never seen before, and that's purely because as Australia we play the likes of South Africa and England, but we don't play with countries like Nepal. I was really quite surprised about the amazing talent in these countries considering they really don't have the same resources we do. The general vibe of the whole tournament was pretty cool because often it's very competitive out on the field, and pretty tense between athletes who obviously want to win. But this was different in that it was still very competitive, but it was also that we saw these leaders in cricket helping mentor other players who are young and up and coming. And seeing those players look up to the elite players.

"It was a special tournament. Very different to other cricket tournaments. There was a real sense of community. Rather than just competitive teams playing against each other. There was a common goal of inclusion and promoting women in sport. That was definitely very powerful, even from a physiotherapist's or researcher's perspective. It was like we were part of a movement. Although we were not playing, we were part of getting players out onto the field and promoting the sport and promoting female athlete health. I was totally moved by the whole experience.

"Other international tournaments do not have the same kind of community atmosphere. When you are in your own team, you're there to win, you're there to perform, you're there to showcase your skills. And of course, that was still important in the FairBreak tournament. The players still wanted to win. But aside from winning, and being there to promote cricket, other tournaments do not have those very special components of inclusion and promoting equality that were present at FairBreak.

"I would definitely go to the next FairBreak tournament in Hong Kong and build on the education surrounding breast injuries and bra fit, not only for the cricket players, but for the coaches and the support staff. The more people we can educate about this topic the better, then they can take the knowledge home to their countries and start creating change.

"Deirdre and I recently attended a Women in Sport conference and presented to people from all around the world representing various sports. Our piece on breast health in sport got a fantastic reaction from the audience; that this is a vitally important topic. And is such an easy thing to fix. We can easily teach female athletes how to find and wear the right sports bra. It's something that can change them for the better, not only in their performance, but in their daily lives."

McGhee had similar sentiments and described the FairBreak Tournament as "an incredible moment in time". She called the tournament a "gift to international relations" because she witnessed the women develop bonds, friendships and mentoring partnerships. She will remember forever the tournament's final when all the players came out onto the field in one joyful group. She said, "They were crying, laughing, and singing. I was emotional too and felt immensely proud and grateful to be part of such a worthwhile event. FairBreak's mission and ethos totally aligns with my beliefs and motivations for working in breast health."

Australia is a world leader in breast education. McGhee's body of research is free to access, and evidence based. The educational resources she has developed consist mostly of pictures and videos, with content written for a reading age of fourteen because many of the women they want to reach do not have English as their first language. McGhee's sports bra app is web based and can be accessed on any device. It is free and has been endorsed by the Australian Institute of Sport. She has no conflicts of interest with sports bra manufacturers, and she has made it quite clear that she disassociates herself from all sports bra brands.

When an academic researcher like Associate Professor Deirdre McGhee carries out research, she doesn't just publish her work in peer review journals as this doesn't help the community at large. Her academic role requires her to teach someone else how to conduct research. McGhee deliberately chooses clinicians who work in sport. She says she is training the researchers of the future, akin to an apprenticeship or on the job training.

Deirdre McGhee and Elyse Potter's breast health research is certainly breaking new ground. McGhee laments that women all over the world put up with bad bras. She said, "Most women have a low expectation of their bra. It is a "no brainer" that when playing cricket, or any sport for that matter, a woman should be wearing a properly fitted sports bra with support, so that the risk of developing mastalgia [breast pain] can be lowered.

"Elite athletes are role models for emerging players. When the superstars talk about the benefits of wearing a well-fitted sports bra, the less experienced cricketers listen to them and take note. Behavioural change research nearly always demonstrates that a mentor will influence a person to adapt and modify their actions. It takes small steps to create big change, even when it comes to getting a female athlete to wear a sports bra."

"It is an absolute privilege to be a small part of this organisation. They empower and inspire women to follow their dreams through sport and show the many opportunities out there for female athletes no matter where you come from."

Danni Wyatt, England

" A New Zealand Wicketkeeper Retires
Katey Martin "

Katey Martin is a former New Zealand cricketer who played as a wicketkeeper and right-handed batter. She appeared in one Test match, 103 One Day Internationals and 95 Twenty20 Internationals for New Zealand between 2003 and 2022. She also played domestic cricket for Otago and the Melbourne Stars. Martin was on the winning team, the Tornadoes, at the SDG FairBreak Invitational and elected to announce her retirement from professional cricket the day after the tournament wrapped up. I was keen to get her perspectives on the team, the tournament, her future and why she chose to round off her extensive career in Dubai.

Martin said, "I'd made the decision I was going to retire and that I wanted the FairBreak tournament to be my last one before announcing it publicly. I wanted to be at the FairBreak tournament in my own capacity as an international athlete. I felt that to finish on that kind of tournament was probably more meaningful than, say, the World Cup for me. Not to lessen the World Cup or anything, but it was my opportunity to be able to give back to the Associate countries and those who haven't been in as fortunate a position as I have over however many years I've been involved in international cricket.

"It was important to not announce my retirement until after the tournament so that I could give true respect to the validity of the tournament. I spoke to New Zealand Cricket before I went away and told them that this was going to be my last tournament, but that I wanted to go there and have the attention on the tournament and me playing there.

"Finishing at the FairBreak tournament and giving back to the sport was important. I was fortunate that Sophie [Devine of New Zealand] was presenting me my last shirt, and that our team, the Tornadoes, won the final. It was really special to play in a tournament where I was able to play with athletes I haven't ever played with before. So, I wanted to ensure that nothing was said until after the tournament.

"Before I went away, I wasn't quite sure whether I was going to retire or not. But I think, deep down, I'd had the conversation that I was done, especially at the international stage. Some decisions around the domestic stuff still had to be made. It was an important tournament for me to be at and to have the focus on the cricket aspect of it rather than whether I was retiring or not retiring.

"The Tornadoes, the winning team at the SDG FairBreak Invitational, was an amazing team and we worked really well together. We found our own identity as a team, and that happened naturally. We had some great characters in the team. The Pakistan girls were quite funny and Diana Baig, she's got her own sense of humour. There were many players at the tournament who look up to certain people as great cricketers. Sophie Devine is someone that I would have on my team any day of the week. For a number of those girls to be able to play with someone like Sophie, who they really look up to, and not get overawed by the situation. I think it took them a few days to realise that everybody there was an equal in their own right, and they had as much to give as someone who is well-known, like Sophie Devine or Sophie Ecclestone.

"The team just came together, and we had a couple of sessions where it was more about getting to know each other. Players wrote some facts down about themselves and we had to guess who did what and where they'd come from. I think Diana Baig wanted to do that all day but we had to go and play! So that was a good way of getting to know each other.

"The cool thing was being able to learn about other people's cultures, how they came into cricket and why it's important to them. The thing that resonated with me mostly about our team was that everyone really cared about each other. And it was about helping each other get better. Whether that was supporting each other in the nets, whether it was giving opportunities out in the middle. Winning was, obviously, always important, but it wasn't the most important thing. If you asked every single player at FairBreak, they'd say they learned something new about themselves and something new about their team.

"I've been around cricket a long time but I learned so much about what cricket is like in the Asian countries. Some people don't even know Nepal has a cricket team. But look at Sita [Rana Magar from Nepal] who just absolutely loves cricket. She was beaming from ear to ear. They're all great cricketers in their own rights.

"That's the key thing about FairBreak. It gives everyone equal opportunity to have the exposure and perform, and I can see that those players are going to go away and be better cricketers for it. But also to be able to take back some of the knowledge they've learned to their own domestic teams.

"I enjoyed playing for the love of the game and playing with people where it wasn't about the money. It's never been about the money or the touring life. When you play international cricket for so long, many more pressures come from it. So going back to what I did when I was a youngster and playing with people who just love cricket, that was important. I wanted to play at FairBreak and I wanted to retire there. To finish up, after playing for so many years, in a tournament that took me back to my grass roots and the reason why I actually play the game, that was really special to me."

Asked to name her stand-out moments, on and off the field during the tournament, Martin spoke passionately, "I think the celebrations throughout the whole tournament were right up there. I'll show bias and say the Pushpa celebration of Sita [Rana Magar] and learning about what that hand gesture meant. It just showed the joy that she had in cricket, and then the others copied it and put their own slant on it. We also had Diana's tornado. What stood out most for me was that the players celebrated in their own ways and we were able to learn about their culture and the reasoning behind their style of celebration."

Martin was referring to Nepal's Sita Rana Magar's Pushpa hand gesture which she'd display every time she took a wicket for the Tornadoes. She'd sweep her hand in an upward direction under her chin mimicking the actor Allu Arjun in his 2022 critically acclaimed South India movie *Pushpa: The Rise*. Interviewed after the match in which the Pushpa made its FairBreak debut, Sita explained that the gesture, which had been trending all year in Asia, and had already been used by several male cricketers, has since been adopted into Nepalese culture when celebrating success and enjoyment. It means "I won't bow down, I will stay high", a sentiment appropriate for a nation of people known for their bravery.

Martin continued, "Off the field, it was having the opportunity in the mornings at breakfast to sit with different people and talk to them about cricket and about their life. There were conversations I never thought I'd have with players. Having the chance to talk to players I may never play against or see play and talk to them about their opportunities. I still get messages from a player about her wicketkeeping, and I know that many of the players have continued to reach out to each other. They have kept in touch post the tournament and are supporting each other in various ways.

"Wini [Winifred Duraisingam of Malaysia is pictured on the front cover of this book] and I spent a lot of time together. She'd sit with me most times on the sideline. I don't think she understood a word I said, but she laughed at my jokes. That was a positive. I was able to create quite a cool bond with her. She's the tiniest little human being and she's got the biggest character and she's cheeky as hell. She was able to fit comfortably into the group. She'd sit beside me and yarn away and we'd talk about techniques and how certain players can hit the ball so far.

"One of my favourite moments was when Wini got three wickets, Player of the Match and got given an Apple Watch. She'd got her three wickets and there were only a few overs to go, so we started chanting on the field "Watch for Wini! Watch for Wini!". I was on the sideline with her when Shaun announced " Wini, you've got Player of the Match", and it was like Christmas, she was so stoked and everybody was chanting her name. Apart from winning an Apple watch, which was a bonus, it was the encouragement from us all. The smile on her face, she was so chuffed. Little moments like that happened all the way through the tournament. Wini got international players out who she's never played against before. I hope that she does get an opportunity to play again, that the bigger nations like England and Australia play the Associate countries, because it would do their cricket a world of good.

"Wini is a wee favorite of mine. I don't know if she'd be able to play in windy Wellington though. She would have to bowl into the wind and I'm not sure if she'd get through the crease. She's more than welcome to come to New Zealand at any point in time, but we'll just keep her away from windy Wellington."

Unfortunately, timings didn't allow for Martin to have a breast health assessment during the FairBreak tournament. But she has spoken to Suzie Bates (New Zealand's Captain and fellow White Fern) about her perspectives on the assessments conducted by Associate Professor Deirdre McGhee and Elyse Potter.

"It's such an important topic for a wicketkeeper. I've been hit so many times in the chest, where the ball has bobbled through, or a bad throw has snapped off the stumps. I did have a chat to them about breast protection and putting something in place, and I got some of the donated breast shields from them. I know there are a couple of girls in New Zealand who are going to reach out to Deirdre and Elyse.

"It's so important. Not just the breast support, but the actual protection aspect. In New Zealand there are a lot of conversations around periods and how the menstrual cycle impacts training, but no one ever talks about the breasts and how being hit in the chest is another injury. I've been playing games and felt sick and sore for a good hour after being hit. I just have to wait for the pain to go by.

"Something that normalises that an impact to the breast is an injury and is quite different to a pulled muscle. Marina Lamplough [a Hong Kong player] said she feels like she's far more supported when she plays now in terms of her chest area. It's an education piece that does need to go out wider. It's been good that players have been able to come back to their own countries and actually talk about it. Hopefully it will normalise those types of conversations in Asian countries. I'm sure it's a lot more challenging for them than it is for us."

Katey Martin is a Dunedin girl. Dunedin is a small city at the southern end of New Zealand's South Island and has a climate far removed from the intense heat of the United Arab Emirates. When I asked her how she coped with the heat she said, "You learn to sweat. It's intense when you have to wear black, like when we played in Dubai during the middle of the day on another tour a few years ago against Pakistan. It was just so hot. The sun shines on your back. At FairBreak, we played a lot of the 8pm games which was good. It was humid and still extremely hot, but you get used to it. We play all around the world. I would love a normal 20-degrees day. Now that's perfect cricket weather, with just a nice light breeze."

I asked Martin about her plans for life after cricket, and she told me, "I've had the benefit of playing during the amateur era before turning professional, so I have a consultancy career outside of cricket. I will step back into doing a bit of business consultancy as well as some commentary here in New Zealand and over in Australia. I will keep busy with that and doing some coaching of the young wicketkeepers here and doing some club coaching. There's plenty on. I'm working at a company doing a merger and acquisition with an insurance company. I do that full time and when it gets into summer, I'll manage my commentary with that.

"Having something outside of cricket, and keeping your brain occupied is important. Sometimes when you're so involved in the game and that's all you do, it can be a bit overwhelming at times. I found I managed better when I had a separation, something to focus on away from cricket.

"For some professional cricketers these days it's a bit of a challenge. If they haven't got the option of something outside of cricket when they finish up. It's crucial and an area I'd love to get a bit more involved with; to focus on the transition out of professional sport. Schedules these days make it really hectic. It's hard to get experience in business or whatever area players want to focus on outside of cricket when they have limited time for it. It's made my transition out of cricket a lot easier. Being able to commentate and do coaching, being involved in FairBreak. I'm still associated with cricket and I can give back to the game that has given me so much."

Writing player announcements in the lead up to the tournament, I was inspired by the diverse range of demanding careers that many of the women players who participated in FairBreak have outside of professional cricket. Lawyers, scientists, doctors, statisticians, and engineers, for example. Martin agreed about how multi-disciplined many of the female players are. She said, "The benefit of professional teams is that you get to spend more time playing cricket. But you can miss out on career opportunities outside cricket. Georgia Redmayne is a doctor and she worked in Queensland through COVID-19. It's wonderful that she has been able to represent Australia, to be able to manage that. It helps her within cricket too, if she can find that balance, and is able to spend time training, playing and being away.

"I'd love to see the Associate Nations have a bit more funding. FairBreak have given more opportunities to players from Associate countries. I'd love it if the ICC got on board with it and were able to help fund some of this. FairBreak are doing it pretty much off their own back. It's hard work to get sponsors, and the cost is quite extreme for a tournament like that. It just shows that you can get a number of people who have an absolute love of the women's game and see the importance of being able to provide opportunities to others who don't really get that in their own countries. This is so crucial to the development of the game.

"I've had heaps of conversations with players, like Tara Norris from the USA and Sita Rana Magar from Nepal, and told them if they want to come over and play in New Zealand, to just reach out. We would take anybody who wants to play over here or help them in Australia in the club competitions. Let's open up those channels."

Katey Martin looks forward to getting involved as an assistant coach for FairBreak at future tournaments and doing some commentary, she said, "For me it's finding whatever opportunities I can to give back. It was so important to finish my playing career at the FairBreak tournament. I knew the importance of the tournament for myself as a cricketer, and I felt fortunate to have the opportunity to be a part of it. If I can support the girls who were in Dubai in a coaching capacity or with mentoring in the future, I'd love to do that. Hopefully schedules will allow me to be a part of the next one, and to be part."

"I'm a #1 fairbreaker from the very beginning. FairBreak has had a massive positive impact on my career so far. Being part of such an amazing environment is crucial for Associate players like me. I will always represent FairBreak with pride!"

Sterre Kalis, Netherlands

Marketing and Social Media

Claudia Lamb and Kimberley Lee

Claudia Lamb has been working with the FairBreak team since 2020. She helps FairBreak share their equality and opportunity message and publishes illustrative player stories across all the social media platforms, Twitter, Instagram, Facebook and LinkedIn. She also collaborated on the establishment of FairBreakX. Through her business, Louder Now, Lamb helps businesses amplify their online presence. She manages FairBreak's requirements alongside those of other clients. She originally came onboard when Martyn reached out to her to assist with FairBreakX. She was already aware of the great work FairBreak was doing and jumped at the opportunity to get involved.

"I originally came onboard in 2020 to help with the launch of FairBreakX. In September 2021, I began managing the social media channels to share FairBreak's message. In May 2022, I was part of the on-ground team for the SDG FairBreak Invitational 2022 where I assisted with the stadium branding, social media, and communication as well as creating video content for the broadcasters, press, social media and FairBreakX. The SDG FairBreak Invitational in Dubai was the first of its kind. It was ambitious, and it worked. To see so many countries' flags displayed, and the diversity on and off the field, including the tournament's match officials and support staff, was phenomenal.

"I was also part of the FairBreak XI on Tour in the UK and Netherlands in August 2022 where I had the opportunity to capture footage of the matches, the players, management interviews and to manage the social media accounts."

Lamb says she is influenced and motivated by FairBreak's ethos, "A vision for creating a world with equal opportunities has always resonated with me. Growing up in England and Australia, I've been very fortunate to receive excellent education and work opportunities in the areas I'm passionate about. I believe everyone should have access to opportunity.

"The players are my motivation for being part of and staying with the FairBreak mission. It has been incredible to hear so many strong testimonies and see the impact the tournament and tours have had, not only on the women involved, but also the nations that have got behind them. Players from countries where people don't know cricket exists have been broadcast to the world, and their home nations have proudly watched and cheered.

"There have been many moments that have motivated and stayed with me. Conversations with the female players are defining moments for me. To hear how players never thought they'd be able to play with their cricket idols proudly showcase their country to the world or be given any opportunity as an Associate Nation player. Those stories have really resonated with me. It was also fantastic to hear how the Full Member Nation players learnt just as much as the Associates at the SDG FairBreak Invitational in 2022.

"I think if you're demanding change, there will always be people who fear it - especially anyone profiting from inequality. I think the biggest roadblock for FairBreak to date has come from individuals who are fearful of what change will mean to them and their organisations.

"The future of women's cricket is only upwards from here. It's only going to get bigger and better. In the years to come, I believe there will be additional opportunities and support available to female cricketers across the board. More opportunities, more funding, more support from friends, families and the broader sporting community. And to grow audiences, there needs to be greater understanding that women's cricket is not a cut down version of the men's game. Women's cricket is a stand-alone sport with a potentially huge global audience that needs to be engaged."

Kimberley Lee is a freelance communications consultant. Alongside that, she is also a private practitioner counsellor and therapist. She started working with FairBreak in 2016 on a pro bono basis until 2020 when she moved to a more formal, and paid, communications consultancy role. FairBreak is one of several clients she currently collaborates with in her capacity as a communications consultant. She recounted, "I originally took on the work pro-bono in 2016, lending my time and skills in communications to the early stages of establishing the organisation as FairBreak. In 2020, when we got closer to delivering the first global tournament, I shifted to a paid consultancy role so I could continue being involved with FairBreak.

"When I first met Shaun, he told me his vision and why it was so important for women, for cricket and for his mission to create opportunities in the sport. His passion and dedication to this vision was – and still is – inspiring and motivating. When we met, FairBreak as we know it today still didn't exist. I was part of the small team involved in the concept that was born out of Shaun and Lisa's original venture, Women's International Cricket League (WICL). I could sense the incredible potential for innovation, creativity, and real change, and it drew me in! Shaun has built a team of people from diverse backgrounds and experience who have spent many hours deliberating on decisions that stay true to FairBreak's values.

"My wish to see justice, fairness, equality, and equity comes from my upbringing in a family that teaches those values. It is also fueled by my experiences as an intercountry adoptee. Being involved with an organisation that creates new opportunities for people who may not otherwise have access to the resources needed to participate in their chosen profession resonated with my ethos.

"Seeing the impact FairBreak has had for female cricketers from less developed nations has been profound. Bearing witness to the change this organisation can bring about has been my motivation for remaining part of FairBreak's mission.

"Being part of bringing the first global tournament to fruition was a momentous time for me. It's what we've all been working towards for so long. It's been a wild ride of ups and downs with many challenges. Delivering a sensational event and experience has not happened without the hard slog of educating people, along the way, about the value of women's cricket. This has sociopolitical undertones about the importance of women. It's emotional on a deeper level."

Kimberley Lee believes that people paying lip service to the value of women and women's sport but not backing it with real and tangible support has been a roadblock. She said, "It's also been challenging finding people who genuinely believe in our ethos and are not trying to ride a wave of change and success for their own benefit in ways that don't align with or support FairBreak's mission and vision.

"It's taken a lot of time to assess, review and discuss how to best approach positioning and pitching this new product in sport. We've been met with loads of encouragement but we have also been let down by a lack of action. Finding people who genuinely believe in the bigger picture – one that goes beyond FairBreak – has been difficult.

"I'm probably the least cricket-minded of the team, but what I've learned along the way is the depth of story, character and meaning that exists around the incredible women playing cricket. These women are so passionate and dedicated to their sport. They can manage their cricket alongside full-time careers in other professions, and often motherhood.

"The FairBreak Invitational in Dubai is what we have spent the last 4 years working towards. It was a momentous time that has set the stage for things to come and is the beginning of an exciting journey ahead.

"In ten years, I hope to see women's cricket positioned as equal to or better than men's cricket and other sports. There are broader opportunities to take women's cricket into a space of its own beyond sport, into the world of business, education, and wellness. Here is a chance to scrap the rule book and the 'this is how it's always been done' mentality and get creative with how the sport is developed and delivered.

"For the sport to flourish, people who genuinely believe in the value of women's cricket, and the value of women in general, need to act and make change happen. To grow audiences, those who are marketing women's cricket need to position the sport as new and dynamic, and to tell the story of the women who play it in depth. Women's cricket is a human-interest piece."

"What, play cricket in England, Dubai, even Australia? That's impossible, stop dreaming young lady!!"

Those are the words I've heard from people over the years.

But hey, it did happen. It was possible. I was not dreaming.

If you have just one person who believes in you, even if you don't believe in yourself, that's all you need. Just one person.

I was so fortunate when I started playing cricket, I came across so many good people who encouraged me to always believe in myself. Even when I had nothing to play with. Not even a bat or a helmet. But I had patience, and I worked hard and that's what got me to play in England. I was so excited to play alongside Alex Blackwell, Charlotte Edwards and Suzie Bates back in 2018, because for a girl like me it was a dream come true. I am forever grateful for the opportunity.

This year (2022), I was fortunate to be able to play for FairBreak again and this time it was huge! I got to play with some of the best cricketers I've watched on TV and always wished I could watch them play live. To watch them live would have been enough. But there I was, playing in the same team and even against some of them! I was so full of emotion I couldn't believe it! I found myself holding back my tears when my coach told me that I was playing in the first game.

Now I can tell my teammates here in Vanuatu that it's possible. If you work hard and have patience. It happened to me. I believe it can also happen to them.

The Dubai experience has given me a lot of hope for women's cricket, especially Associate Nations like mine. One day if I stop playing cricket, I will look back and be happy that I played a part (even if small) to motivate at least one or two girls to play cricket.

If, one day, Vanuatu makes the World Cup, and I am no longer playing, I will not be sad because I will be happy that I experienced something like that in Dubai 2022.

FairBreak to me is hope. For many young ladies like me, FairBreak is hope, fairness and equality in everything. I really believe FairBreak is the future.

So, thank you FairBreak for giving hope, breaking barriers and changing the game for Associate Nation players. Even though some Associate Nations don't get to play in the World Cup, some players get to experience a World Cup equivalent through a FairBreak Tournament. FairBreak you really are a dream come true.

Much love from

Selina Iakia Kandy Solman

[Captain of Vanuatu's Women's Cricket Team]

PHOTOGRAPHS

Lisa Sthalekar and Shaun Martyn at Bradman Oval in Bowral in 2003

WIWCC Founders and Legends at Scotch College, Melbourne, 2004. L to R: Dean Jones, Geoff Lawson, Shaun Martyn, Merv Hughes, Paul Harvey, Bill Payne, Tim Caruthers, Colin 'Funky' Miller

Geoff Lawson sporting a WIWCC cap

Alex Blackwell and Paul Harvey in the early days

Alex Blackwell in the early days

Lisa Sthalekar in the early days

Paul Harvey, Shaun Martyn, Tony Wright. 14 Degrees Pty Ltd Tour of India in 2008

Geoff, Lisa and Shaun at Sydney Cricket Ground in WICL days

Shaun Martyn in a WICL shirt at home in Narooma, NSW

Vidya Rao and Shaun Martyn donate WICL cricket bats to Sri Ayyappan School in Bangalore

Divya GK, Lisa Sthalekar and Selina Solman at South Pacific Training Camp, Auckland, Oct 2015

Merryn Apma is an Australian Indigenous artist who used to live and exhibit her art in Central Tilba on Yuin country near Shaun Martyn's home in Narooma. In 2015, after following FairBreak's gender equality message, she offered to paint a signature piece of art to support the movement. This painting was purchased by Pymble Ladies College and hangs in the foyer of the school on Sydney's North Shore.

Merryn is one of Australia's Stolen Generation. Born in Murray Bridge, South Australia, she was adopted by a non-Indigenous family from Geelong, Victoria, where she grew up. She was 22 when she finally returned to her home, Arrernte country near Alice Springs (Mparntwe) and met her family.

The inner circle represents Australian Indigenous women joined by sport to all women in other parts of the world. Merryn paints the strong Aboriginal women of the desert. This painting has become the FairBreak lapel pin.

West Indies' Britney Cooper and Shamilia Connell with Shaun Martyn in Mumbai 2016

Isabelle Duncan. Cricket Historian, Player and Commentator

Shaun Martyn, govt lobbyist Greg Holland, Geoff Lawson in Parliament House, Canberra

Mignon du Preez (Minx), Shaun Martyn and Professor Shirley Randell attend a Women's Conference in Cape Town in 2017. Australian academic, Prof. Randell is a world authority on women's issues, gender and equality and has been a close advisor of Martyn and FairBreak for many years

FairBreak's Corporate Social Responsibility initiatives include distributing Solar Buddy lights to children living in energy poverty in India

FairBreak XI at Wormsley, May 2018

Shaun Martyn and FairBreak XI at Wormsley, May 2018

Akanksha to play exhibition match

TIMES NEWS NETWORK

Bengaluru: Karnataka cricketer Akanksha Kohli and Delhi wicketkeeper-batswoman Lakshmi Yadav are among 12 cricketers from 11 countries picked to play for FairBreak Global XI in an exhibition T20 match promoting gender equality on May 30 at the Wormsley Estate in London. The one-off twenty20 contest is a part of the annual day of gender equality promoted by FairBreak Glob-

GENDER EQUALITY

al and the Commonwealth business women's network in association with Sir Paul Getty XI, who are the home team and will field their first-ever women's squad.

The Fairbreak team will be led by former England skipper Charlotte Edwards and also comprises New Zealand ace Suzie Bates and Australian Alex Blackwell. It will be coached by Austra-

lian Saba Nasim and Khyati Gulani from New Delhi.

Former Australian cricketer Geoff Lawson, who is associated with the event said, "Hopefully this would be a bit of a revelation to what rest of the cricket playing world has seen from female players.

On the difference in men and women's cricket, the 60-year-old pointed out, "Lisa Sthalekar is one of our finest cricketers but in material terms, cricket treated her poorly. That was the genesis of my interest. In Australia we have the WBBL, just one small area where gender equality is recognized. The discipline, skills and commitment on show in the WBBL are fantastic. The WBBL is elite sport, the skills are terrific."

The FairBreak Global XI: Akanksha Kohli (Ind), Alex Blackwell (Aus), Diane Bimenyimana (Rwanda), Divya GK (S'pore), Divya Saxena (Can), Lakshmi Yadav (Ind), Mariko Hill (HK), Nadia Gruny (USA), Vaishali Jesrani (Oman), Selina Solman (Vanuatu), Shamilia Connell (WI) and Suzie Bates (NZ).

Times of India article – Akanksha Kohli and Lakshmi Yadav in FairBreak XI Tour, May 2018.

Alex Blackwell, Suzie Bates and Sana Mir reunite at Wormsley in 2019

Shaun Martyn and FairBreak XI before attending Garsington Opera, Wormsley in 2019

Shameelah Mosewu and Sterre Kalis open
the batting against an MCC side during
FairBreak XI Tour 2019

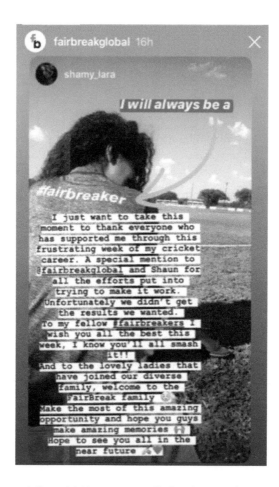

When Botswana's Shameelah Mosewu was initially denied an Australian visa in Feb 2020

FairBreak XI on Bradman Oval at Bowral in Feb 2020

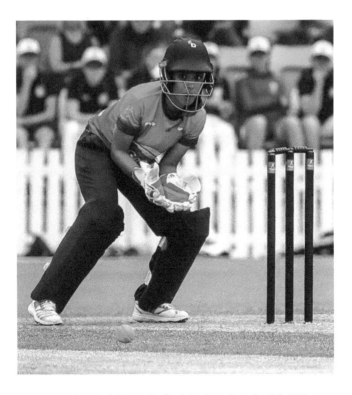

FairBreak XI Wicketkeeper Sindhu Sriharsha at Bowral in Feb 2020

Mariko Hill bowling for the FairBreak XI at Bowral in Feb 2020

Shameelah Mosweu and Sterre Kalis and Blackwell Mir Cup at Bradman Oval in Feb 2020

Sterre Kalis batting for FairBreak XI on Bradman Oval, Bowral in Feb 2020

FairBreak XI, Bradman XI, R. Venkatesh and Geoff Lawson outside the Bradman Oval Pavilion in Feb 2020

Sucheta Gorolay, Shaun Martyn, Kimberley Lee on Bradman Oval in Bowral, Feb 2020

Shaun Martyn and Vanuatu Captain Selina Solman

Welcome Drinks in Dubai – Diana Baig, Suzie Bates, Sophie Devine, Sune Luus, Laura Wolvaardtt

Anju Gurung of Bhutan bowling for Falcons at FBI22

Photographs

Assoc. Prof. Deirdre McGhee and Elyse Potter in Dubai Stadium

Bangladesh's Jahanara Alam demonstrates the Falcons' celebration

The Barmy Army Nails and Cap for Dubai worn by Vanusa Burnham @ladybarmy

West Indies' Deandra Dottin smiling in The Barmy Army shirt at FBI22

Pakistan's Diana Baig jumps for joy as a Tornadoes player at FBI22

Fatima Sana with The Barmy Army team

Rwanda's Henriette Ishimwe throwing for The Barmy Army

Henriette Ishimwe celebrating taking a wicket at FBI22

Jahanara Alam modelling facepaint and shades for Falcons at FBI22

Tornadoes' Katey Martin and The Barmy Army's Kavisha Kumari in action

The Barmy Army batter Kavisha Kumari

Falcons on safari in the UAE desert outside Dubai

Mignon du Preez and a falcon in the UAE desert outside Dubai

South Africa's Ayabonga Khaka bowling for Spirit

Lesego Pooe and Georgie Heath on the interview deck

South African girls unite! TV host Lesego Pooe and match official Shandre Fritz

Australian Umpire, Simon Taufel and Falcons' Britney Cooper

Jamaican Umpire Jacquline Williams and Spirit Bowler Nicola Carey

Mark Farmer, Shoaib Malik, Ramasamy Venkatesh and Ravi Nagdev in Dubai

The FBI22 7th Team: The Match Officials led by Simon Taufel

Falcons' Nannapat Koncharoenkai and Spirit's Nicola Carey

Shabnim Ismail, Gaby Lewis and Elyse Villani celebrate for Sapphires at FBI22

Sana Mir and Maryam Omar celebrate for Sapphires

Sapphires pose for a team photo

Nepal's Sita Rana Magar doing the Pushpa

Spirit Wicketkeeper Yasmin Daswani from Hong Kong

Spirit players Kaia Arua from PNG and Sophie Eccelstone from England

Tornadoes' Stafanie Taylor and The Barmy Army's Fatima Sana

Netherlands' Sterre Kalis batting for Tornadoes

Simon Taufel and Sapphires' Kary Chan

R. Venkatesh, Shaun Martyn, Roy Burton in Dubai Stadium

Vidya Rao presents Player of the Match prize to Nepal's Sita Rana Magar

Mignon du Preez and Warriors celebrate her catch

Friendship: Mignon du Preez, Hayley Matthews, Deandra Dottin

Esha's Bounce: Warriors' Sindhu Sriharsha, Esha Oza, Hayley Matthews, Mignon du Preez

The Commentating Desk – Adam Collins, Isa Guha, Isabelle Duncan

Winifred Duraisingam and Sita Rana Magar celebrate as Tornadoes

Photographs

Malaysia's Wini Duraisingam meets Adam Collins and Baby Wini

Suzie Bates bowling for Falcons in FBI22 Final

Katey Martin hugs Thailand's Chanida Sutthiruang after Tornadoes win FBI22 final

Tornadoes celebrate their win after the FBI22 Final

Jen Barden (Assistant Coach) and Sterre Kalis after Tornadoes win the FBI22 trophy

FairBreak XI Tour at Wormsley in August 2022

Isabelle Duncan signs a copy of her book *Skirting the Boundary* for Sonali Patel at Wormsley, August 2022

FairBreak XI Captain, Mariko Hill, shakes hands with Katie McGill after playing Scotland's national women's team at The Grange in Edinburgh. The first time a FairBreak team played a country

Essex XI v FairBreak XI at Billericay Cricket Club, Essex, August 2022

Claudia Lamb (FairBreak Videographer), Saba Nasim (Team Manager and Player)
and Elle Williams in Scotland, August 2022

Shaun Martyn and Karen Motyka edit the first draft of the FairBreak manuscript, September 2022

Elle Williams at Wormsley, August 2022

Burji Shroff, Chairman of Cricket Hong Kong, and Shaun Martyn, November 2022

Jahanara Alam and Suzie Bates reunite during Bangladesh tour of New Zealand, December 2022

FOLLOW-ON
REFLECTIONS
AND FUTURE

"Q&A with Geoff Lawson OAM
Former Australian Test Cricketer, Coach,
Commentator and Columnist"

You are just back from leading the 2022 FairBreak XI Tour of England, Scotland and the Netherlands. How was it?

"The progress of the girls during the FairBreak XI 2022 Tour and how their cricket improved was phenomenal. We finished with three games against the Netherlands' national team and we won all three of those games in different circumstances. The ability of the girls to learn quickly, to adapt and to understand what they need to do individually and as a team was fantastic.

"The tour was a series of highlights. The idea of the FairBreak XI Tour was to give the players opportunity and experience. We also had great weather, so the cricket conditions were good which really helps when you go to those parts of the world.

"The general improvement of individuals and the team and how strongly they played, even though we had a couple of injuries for the very last game of the tour was great. They played some good cricket and found a way to win. They were a good group and they enjoyed each other's company. We were forced into a few last-minute changes because of the visa situation where we couldn't get certain players into the Netherlands. It wasn't the team we originally selected, so we had to be flexible and adaptable. And that was our mantra for the tour: flexible and adaptable!

"We had players coming in and out and travelling in between, but they were terrific. They just love the chance to play the game. They don't complain about anything. Not a squeak of complaint about having to travel or play successive days. They don't complain about accommodation. They just get on with it and appreciate that they've been given the opportunities. The girls accept everything that's given to them. They feel like they're in a position of privilege. They don't take it for granted. They appreciate what they're getting.

"Male cricket tours have been going a lot longer so expectations are much higher. The quality of their accommodation and transport and all the other things that go with it. And that's understandable. But the girls, whatever you throw at them, "The bus is going to be late, you must wait around, we've got a long trip". It doesn't matter. They just embrace it all and move on, and that's a wonderful thing.

"For example, the first day in Amsterdam. They played cricket and it was a lovely day. But it was quite tricky for the bus to arrive in the right spot. It was a very difficult place to find. Finally, we finished the day and the game. They had a good win. The hosts put on a barbecue and drinks. It was lovely. We were expecting the bus to come, but it didn't arrive. The girls passed the time playing French cricket by the boundary with a tennis ball and kicking a soccer ball around. For an hour and a half! There were no demands to get back to the hotel. I was amazed by their energy. Even though they'd been playing competitive cricket most of the day, they were quite happy to enjoy the lovely Dutch evening and muck about with a soccer ball. I expected them to get sick of it at some stage, but they had fun. It was getting dark when the bus finally arrived and they hopped on. Not once did they say, "Where's the bus? Come on, we want to go". They were happy to keep enjoying each other's company and spending time with the opposition as well.

"Compared to the FairBreak XI Tours in 2018 and 2019, we played more cricket and had more travel, and there's always logistical issues with that. And the weather in the UK was terrific.

"We started at Arundel Castle. Played a couple of days there. We drove from Worthing to Arundel both days and then headed to Oxford after that. Then we drove down to Wormsley for a couple of days from Oxford. Then we went over to northeast London and played there. Then we had a nine-hour bus trip up to Edinburgh. It was about forty-five minutes into the ground every day to play at The Grange.

"Next was a flight to the Netherlands from Edinburgh. Turn up for the airport and go through immigration and security and fly to another country. Quite different to what we have been used to on earlier tours. The amount of travel and cricket compared to earlier tours was heavier. There were consecutive days of cricket, or sometimes we played doubleheaders. So, two 20-over games on one day. We played a mixture of 20-over and 40-over cricket.

"There was a lot more cricket and a lot less rest for the girls and sometimes that can be a challenge. Certainly, towards the end of the tour in Amsterdam they were starting to get a few injuries because they're just not used to playing five days a week and travelling on the other two days. That's unusual. But they didn't complain about it. They were just so happy to be playing every day and they were pleased with how much they learned. Coaching and talking about how to improve in certain areas, and then playing again the next day and getting a chance to put what everyone has learned into practice, is a very useful exercise. Playing consistently and constantly, they improved rapidly."

Some players are juggling demanding careers or study. How did you manage that on Tour?

"We had eighteen different players on the tour. So that was a challenge. Players coming in and out, some available, and at other times not available. Because they had to go off and do their real jobs, which is something that, once again, the men don't tend to have to do.

"Ruchi Venkatesh couldn't play the Dutch part of the Tour because she had to hand in her thesis for her Masters in Neuroscience. She finished playing with us on the Monday in Scotland, then on the Wednesday she had to hand in her thesis. That took precedence.

"While we were on the bus from Essex to Edinburgh, which took all day, some of the girls went to work in central London for the day. They worked all day in London and then caught the train up and met us.

"We had a couple of students. Ariana Dowse, who ended up getting Player of the Tour. She had just graduated in accountancy and finance from Solent University and hadn't got a job yet. Sonali Patel is a first-year computer science student. She was on holiday from University and missing the first week of term.

"We had a dental hygiene nurse who broke her thumb in Amsterdam in the second game but insisted on playing on and then got a couple of wickets. She was in trouble though. She was not going to be able to work for three weeks when she got back as she needs both hands to work. Zainab Khan, who is English, but she's from Pakistan and has captained the Pakistan side. She's a social worker in northeast London who deals with refugee issues and displaced people.

"These are the calibre of women we had in the team. They've got serious jobs and responsibilities in life, and they just love their cricket. In fact, they're passionate about their cricket. Passionate is a word that gets thrown around a bit too easily sometimes but these players display it. They want to play the best level they can. They're competitive. They're super competitive, and I love that. When I see them go about their jobs and go about their games. You've got those elements together.

"When we all meet as a team, there are many disparate personalities and people who haven't met each other before. But these girls, within about twenty minutes, are all best friends. It's incredible how they gel together. I had to pick up Poppy McGeown, who was flying over from France into Luton Airport. I had a car to go and pick her up at the airport. I didn't know her, but I had to find her at Luton Airport. She's an equine vet who has been all around the world and is currently working for a seriously important practice in the South of France. She has a Scottish father and French mother and was brought up in Belgium. She's worked in Australia and Hong Kong and is a seriously intelligent woman. Within about ninety seconds, we had cricket as our common denominator and we had things to talk about.

"We met the bus that was driving north to Scotland and Poppy got on and within a couple of minutes she was best friends with everybody on the bus. And that's how it works with all of the players. They just get on so well together and cricket's their common denominator. Next thing you know they're into TikTok songs and singalongs. It's a wonderful atmosphere that they create themselves. They create the environment.

"It's easy to coach them at cricket because they just want to learn everything. We could have done with three specialist coaches on that tour. I was doing fielding drills and running the nets. I was coaching all the time, giving hints about how to change their balance, their grip, all the little things they wanted to know about. Most of the grounds had practice nets, so they wanted to get to games early and do some work in the nets. They were quite demanding from that point of view because they wanted to learn all the time. I could have done with a couple more coaches to be honest. But it was just me. They made my life busy, which was good."

You have been a key member of the FairBreak management team since the early WICL days. How did that come about?

"Shaun was having his charity cricket matches and inviting male former Test players, and then inviting female international players like Lisa Sthalekar and Alex Blackwell. It fitted right in with what he was doing with his 14 Degrees Team and his mates from Chevalier College who just love cricket and were helping to raise a bit of money for local charities. I was invited to play in those games and it started from there. Shaun has always been keen to look after his equal opportunity piece and he was always talking in disgusted tones about how the best women players in the world we're being treated. He couldn't believe it. He was always aghast at the treatment they were receiving, and so those games were his way of helping the women make some extra income and making a contribution to helping the situation.

"We played these corporate charity style events, and they were always well organised. Shaun has an event management background. So that was the nub of the idea and it just grew from there."

The remuneration for female cricketers was such that they all had other jobs to pay their bills. As an elite player and coach were you aware of this?

"When I was coaching New South Wales in the mid-1990s, I was always aware of the female players, and thought they were treated reasonably well. They were given a good deal of recognition if not money. They were recognised as important players when I was playing, even in the late 1970s and certainly through the 1980s. But the fact that the women were paying their own way to play, even when they got to play for Australia was ridiculous. I don't know how that was allowed to flourish. Mind you, knowing some of the board members and their views, it was hard enough being a male player trying to get paid fairly.

"I remember a particular day, when I was coaching NSW, practicing at the Sydney Cricket Ground, after they built the indoor centre at the back of the nets. The women's team were practicing, and we were having an optional practice and there were about four nets available. We were only using two of them. A couple of the female players asked could they use the turf wickets, and I said, "Go for it. Absolutely".

"They were practicing next to my NSW men's state team, and we could see the intent and the seriousness of what they were doing and that they could seriously play. We could see their skills. They were very good cricketers. A couple of our state players bowled to them, and they were quite surprised about how fast they could bowl to them. The women could play the game at a really high level.

"Guys who used to dismiss women cricketers as not being particularly skillful were quite surprised that day. Lisa Sthalekar was there, and Alex Blackwell. Some of Australia's best female players were in that NSW Breakers team. One of the women said to me, "We don't often get to practice together. We all work and we have to try and get here from work".

"There's the difference. The men had gone fully professional, and the women were still amateur. Amateur with professional attitudes. That was the mid-1990s. They were seriously good cricketers still paying to play the game. Playing for NSW but paying for their own accommodation. I think some of their transport costs might have been paid for by NSW, but not very much.

"Bottom line, looking back, I still can't believe that the women were still having to pay to play cricket. They were being paid to play for the state but they still had to pay to play for Australia. They were forking out money and making sacrifices, while the Australian male players became full-time professionals and started getting paid serious money. The women cricketers were being treated incredibly poorly by the administrators who were, naturally, nearly all men.

"The administrators did not have the vision to see the value of women's cricket, whereas Shaun had a completely different vision, much broader, much deeper and a much better understanding of what contribution female cricket makes to the community. Maybe that comes from his school teaching background where he was dealing with males and females on an equal basis. He had a deeper and broader view than any cricket administrator at the time.

"WICL and then FairBreak have come a long way despite the barriers and the hurdles and the thumbtacks thrown onto the road in front of the organisation. It was a bit like *The Road Runner*, there was always someone trying to disrupt progress.

"Shaun sought to take FairBreak to a new level, and I was dragged along in the whirlwind he created, and I have always been very happy to be a part of it and to make some sort of contribution. I still have a WICL shirt in my cupboard. That will be a family heirloom in years to come.

"The big picture is Shaun's persistence and never taking no for an answer. His unlimited enthusiasm is extraordinary. After so many knock-backs from the ICC, Cricket Australia and the ECB, anybody else would have said, "You're making it too hard. You don't want women's cricket to flourish. I've got better things to do with my life". But not Shaun Martyn. He wouldn't take no for an answer.

"The WICL Auckland camp in 2015 was a nice start. Fortunately, some of those Kiwi players who were with us in Auckland are still big supporters of FairBreak. We had Kerry Tomlinson play in our games in the Netherlands during the FairBreak XI 2022 Tour. She played in that 2015 side in Auckland. She's a terrific player."

What's involved in unearthing all the hidden talent in the Associate Nations?

"For FairBreak, my part involves, and this takes years of experience, picking all the teams. Putting together six teams from Full Member and Associate countries. We have a committee to do this, Sana Mir, Alex Blackwell, Shaun, and myself. With some input from Julie Abbott in the United States and Mauhtisham Rasheed who was my assistant coach when I coached in Pakistan. He deals with Pakistan Women's Cricket. We also talk to Roberta [Moretti-Avery] in Brazil and Sian Kelly in Argentina.

"We talk to people about what's happening in Rwanda, Bhutan, Nepal, Brazil and Japan for example. There's a lot of networking. Take the players in Hong Kong. They will have played qualifiers against Thailand, Uganda and Japan, and they will have seen who the good players are. And because we are tied up with the Hong Kong players, like Mariko Hill, who is a very smart lady and the Global Innovation Manager at Gencor, she gives us names of potential players to have a look at.

We look up their *ESPNcricinfo* records and try to get some video. We'll send an e-mail to Japan Cricket asking to see some visuals or we look up the Bhutanese team. We ask, "Who are the best players? Who's got the most runs? Who's got the most wickets? Let's get hold of Bhutan Cricket. Have you got some footage of Anju Gurung?"

"We got astonishing stuff. Footage taken at cricket practice at the Bhutan Cricket camp. There were all these young women diving around on a black surface, I still don't know what it is, committing themselves to stopping a cricket ball or catching a cricket ball. The network gets wider and wider.

"We are lucky to have Roberta [Moretti-Avery] who works in that incredible environment of Brazilian Cricket. She knows some players. It just goes on and on. You can watch the Rwanda, Uganda, Tanzania, 3-way series being live streamed from Kigali. I've been to Rwanda to meet some of the players. I've been to the cricket ground. The fact that they livestream so much cricket these days is useful. It may only be one camera coverage, but we get to find out something about players and we can make some judgments.

"It takes a lot of time to find ninety players and put them into six teams and try to make those teams of equal ability. We were having a bit of a guess about what Gunjan Shukla from Sweden was like. Luckily, I have a contact in Sweden who is involved with cricket there, I asked him and Gunjan Shukla turned out to be terrific. She just played on our FairBreak XI Tour of the UK and Amsterdam.

"We do a lot of research. We ask for a lot of footage. Once we start asking questions, word spreads. People start contacting us. I just had an email from a guy in the United States asking me how his daughter gets to play in the FairBreak team.

"It's word of mouth, it's research, it's networking. It's people becoming enthused by the fact that players from their country, whether that's Uganda or Rwanda or wherever, will get a chance to play on the big stage and they'll get a chance to play with some of the best players in the world."

Dubai was a massive undertaking at short notice. Tell me your perspective.

"Dubai was one of those great labours of love and passion. Driven by Shaun to an enormous degree. The major motor mechanic of it all was Elle [Williams] who was tireless in terms of the issues she had to deal with. The relentless dramas! Just to get the players there was a bonus. There was still COVID-19 happening. There were visa issues. But we were there and we had an international stadium to play in. The original intention was to play in Hong Kong, but Dubai had a huge upside. It was a major stadium so we had all the issues to do with getting it ready to play on.

"My title is Director of Cricket, so I look after all the cricket issues, including the state of the stadium, what the pitches are going to play like, and working with the people who look after the ground. I organise all the practice schedules for all the teams and the venues. We change those multiple times. I get all those cricket issues sorted out so the teams and coaches can turn up and put their players through their paces and figure out who is going to be in their starting XIs and let them do their thing.

"I've got to provide the right environment to allow coaches, captains, and players to show us what they've got. That's basically my remit for the tournament. I also ended up doing commentary on every game, which wasn't originally planned. I've got a background in commentary for ABC Radio for over twenty years, lots of TV commentary around the world, and I write about cricket so that wasn't a problem for me. We wanted to have a lot of female voices, but Melinda Farrell got COVID-19 in the middle of the tournament, so I had to take over for her. She was doing the coin toss, some post-match interviews and conducting the pitch report. So that made my day busy.

"From time to time, I got a player from one of the teams to do a guest pitch report. It was a good way to give the girls some exposure and let them do a piece to camera. It worked well. They were all excellent at that.

"I commentated every day. We'd get to the ground about 1:30pm for a 4:00pm start. The first night, we all got back to the hotel at about 1:30am, completely exhausted. After that, it was between midnight and 12:30am, but we all got used to it. I remember after we bowled the very first ball, I made a point of grabbing Shaun by the shoulders and saying, "You've done it mate, you've got this thing underway".

"The cricket was absolutely outstanding. Whatever trepidations we might have had about the standard of the cricket and what was going to happen were forgotten. It was of the highest quality, and it produced everything you could possibly want it to produce from a cricket viewing standpoint. The daily traumas, the hurdles, the thumbtacks, the whatever, were justified by how the girls played the game and what they produced on the field.

"The pictures that went out were amazing. We had a great TV production company. We had a great mix of commentators, mostly female commentators who work in the women's cricket space. They gave different viewpoints from what we normally see in the commentary that's going around.

"We had Adam Collins there who does more research than NAASA does for a moon landing. He did massive amounts of research and he shared it with everybody. Whatever was going to make the coverage better for everyone. And he was happy to do it. He had his dossier updated every day and we could use it when we were doing commentary. I think that was incredibly valuable.

"I arrived in Dubai about two weeks before the tournament started. Originally, I thought I wouldn't need to be there that early but Shaun was adamant I had to get there to make sure things were all in place. And I'm glad I did because every day there were hurdles to jump over. The lead-up the tournament was frantic and hectic. Then it was a very tiring, consuming, intense couple of weeks when the tournament was on. But the result was absolutely outstanding.

"Hong Kong in 2023 will be a piece of cake compared to what we had to do in Dubai. Changing signage for example. One of the sponsors, a commercial group in India, pulled out a few days before the tournament started which was unbelievable. They'd agreed to sponsor a team and then said they'd only pay half of what they were supposed to. That was a major set-back a few days out from the tournament because we had to get rid of all their branding. It was on the clothing; it was on the grounds.

"Then BYD [Build Your Dreams] electric vehicles, their logo was on the boundary wedges and the team uniforms, their parent company decided they didn't want BYD on the signage, they wanted EVCrypto instead because that's their global brand. So, we had to change all of that, which was not easy. We didn't have the boundary wedges for the first two days of the tournament because the man who was in charge of changing the branding on them locked them up in his warehouse and went away on holidays for the weekend. Seriously, changing branding a few days out from the start of a tournament, in a foreign country, during Ramadan. It's not easy!

"Then the President of UAE died on the 13th of May. That nearly put an end to the tournament just before the semi-finals. We kept that information quiet because we didn't want to cause mayhem amongst the players and staff. The forty-day period of mourning started and we were waiting for an official to arrive at the stadium to tell us the tournament must end and everybody had to go home. But nobody came.

"Having the 2022 Invitational at the big stadium in Dubai was forced upon us. But everybody who was involved with the organisation made a success of it through their hard work. Hong Kong will be easier because the Kowloon Cricket Ground is smaller. It's the home country of Cricket Hong Kong who are the co-hosts and they know their home territory well. The commercial deals will be easier to do. Also, we will know how to improve practice schedules and how to get coaches and managers to better handle certain issues.

"And COVID-19 will not be hanging over us every day. There were very strict rules in Dubai around the reporting of COVID-19 and seven days of isolation in a hotel room. Four or five players had to isolate at the start of the tournament. They played at the end once their symptoms had gone. The

Dubai authorities came to the hotel rooms to check that anyone who had been reported to have COVID-19 was isolating in their room. We had to download Dubai's COVID-19 Awareness app. We were not allowed in the country unless we'd downloaded it. I still get updates on it now. I got an update today. They had four hundred cases in Dubai today. We all had to have a mask on anytime we were indoors in Dubai. So, if we were in the big shopping mall next door or in the hotel, theoretically we had to have our mask on and there were some serious fines if we did not.

"We were in two hotels, the Intercontinental and The Crowne Plaza. They're part of one complex about 30 minutes from the stadium. Fortunately, Dubai had a very cool May. The hottest it got was mid-30s. The matches were scheduled for 4pm and 8pm. So, we were playing late afternoon and evening. The heat in Dubai was flagged as a potential issue, but it ended up being quite bearable."

Explain pitch reports to me. Your guest pitch reports were a superb point of difference. How did they come about?

"In terms of the pitch, you don't want there to be too much difference. With 20-over cricket you don't want the pitch to change. But they did, and the curator at the ground had a great system. It was the end of his season, so the pitches had all been used a bit. He had a plan, he said, "We've got the first six games on this pitch, then we're going to move over onto this pitch, then we're going to move to another pitch for the final". He had it all mapped out.

"It doesn't matter about all the other work you do with things like marketing, team uniforms and sponsorship, if the cricket pitch is not good enough, you don't get a decent game. Fortunately, the guy at the stadium in Dubai produced some excellent pitches. So, for the second game, the pitch did change a bit, it got a bit slower. But it's not rocket science. And we were not doing a pitch report that is rocket science. It's not the CSIRO doing an agronomy report on the soil. It's what the players think. How is it going to play? How does it behave? The bounce has to be regular and high so the batters can play their shots. If it's low, you get very boring cricket. You need some good bounce. And you need it to stay the same the whole game, and you want it to be the same for both teams.

"Pitches can look very different in various parts of the world because of diversity in the soils. It's just how they behave and how they play. Bounce and pace are very important, particularly for women's cricket. The bowlers aren't as quick as the men, obviously, but you need pace for batters to play shots and to be able to hit the ball hard. You need the ball coming on to the bat. It can get a little bit complex.

"It was my idea to get the players to do the pitch reports because they were the ones who would have played on it the day before. Many times, the teams played consecutive days and the players could see what was happening to the pitch and how it was wearing under that heat. They could make their assessment and give their view rather than some other expert who wasn't playing on the surface. It also gave the girls a chance to be in front of a TV camera, to be seen around the world and to display their personality and knowledge.

"I took a punt and suggested the idea. On the second day, when we wondering who was going to do the pitch report, I asked Mariko Hill, one of the Hong Kong players, "Who have you got on your team who might be good at doing a pitch report?" And she replied, "Well we've got Yasmin Daswani. She loves talking".

"Yasmin Daswani plays for Hong Kong, she's a wicketkeeper batter and a litigation lawyer in London. She likes a good time and is a very interesting young lady. So, I said, "Yasmin, would you mind doing a pitch report?"

"And she was brilliant! A pitch report is only two minutes long. The person reports what they see. They get some guidance from the director who is down there on the pitch. The camera pans along it while they look at the pitch. They say what they see, look up to the camera and finish. It's not complicated. But if you're not used to having a camera pointed at you, it can get a little bit daunting.

"We got Yasmin on and she was outstanding. She injected a bit of humour into it. She wasn't taking it super seriously like some people can, and it made great TV. So, we decided that every day, we'd get a player to do this. And most of them were good. I'd love to string all the pitch reports together just to have a look at them. They were entertaining and informative. And not only did they get to showcase themselves, but they also got to showcase women's cricket and what it all means.

"Empowering those players to do the pitch reports was another example of how FairBreak gives opportunity and equality to people. Having the players do a pitch report worked well. It created a point of difference. And that is what the FairBreak Invitational was all about. Shaun didn't want it to look like every other tournament. There were points of difference all over the place, which everyone loved.

"There are so many tournaments around the world, and it is ordinary stuff. They start every game the same, there's no great innovation. It's the same people saying the same stuff. Our commentary team was a point of difference. The players' contributions to things like the pitch report were entertaining. We got lots of good feedback. People around the world really enjoyed it."

The Associates taking on the big guns made for great TV. As a commentator how did you feel watching the action?

"Sita Rana's Pushpa and some of the other reactions and celebrations the girls displayed during the tournament made for great insight into their cultures. You never know what you're going to get. You've done all this homework on players and you think they can play, but you're not sure how they're going to go against the big-name players, so you've got your fingers crossed a little bit. Take Henriette Ishimwe, I'm pretty sure she got a wicket in her first or second over of the tournament. Which was great. If you get a wicket, you're in the game! All the people who are in your team relax about what you can do. The scrutiny of the superstars diminishes just a little bit.

"A lot of the Associate players got wickets very early on. Sita Magar, Henriette Ishimwe, and Winifred Duraisingam were in fine form. Henriette's most memorable moment occurred when she rattled Nicola Carey with an exquisite in-swinging yorker. That was one of the highlights of the tournament, and Nicola's incredulous look at this brilliant delivery! An unknown Rwandan player bowling the Australian superstar. And then the celebrations! It was priceless television. The girls' celebrations became trademarks. I think they started those spontaneously. But they were all a part of the FairBreak point of difference."

What are your hopes for FairBreak and women's cricket in the immediate future?

"In the coming years, I would like to see two or three FairBreak tournaments happening each year. And one or more FairBreak XI Touring teams in Asia, the United States or South America. Roberta [Moretti-Avery] is keen to get South America involved, especially Brazil, Argentina, and Chile. There are all these exciting prospects of taking cricket to locations that are not mainstream. Imagine if we had a tournament in Brazil! In Roberta's hometown, which is a big cricket town. I think it would be incredible if we had a FairBreak Americas tournament in the middle of Brazil. It would be unique!

"Cricket is a fast-growing sport in Brazil. They have full-time, contracted, Brazilian women players. They send the players and coaches to university to get sports science degrees. If they want to be full-time coaches, they do a full-time coaching degree within sports science, so that they can become the future coaching staff of Brazilian Cricket. Being on a contract enables them to study. That's the way Brazil is propagating the game of cricket, particularly through the women, more so than the men. There's a coherent program in Brazil to widen regional cricket. Obviously, soccer is the major sport in Brazil and goodness knows how much money is poured into that. But cricket is getting some traction.

"We are one tournament in. And we've had a couple of tours and games. But FairBreak's reputation is already spreading widely. We get mentioned in mainstream cricket broadcasts now. We were mentioned during the England v South Africa Men's Test series recently. We get mentioned in all the female cricket broadcasts regularly. FairBreak is virtually considered a major component of women's cricket worldwide now.

"We still need to keep working at it. We now need big institutions to put their hands in their pockets and support it fiscally, not just verbally. There's a lot of talk about corporate responsibility and equal opportunity. FairBreak is walking that walk and it needs support from enlightened organisations.

The wheels are turning, slowly but inexorably towards greater opportunity for women. Not just in cricket.

"Cricket Australia is doing a good job with the WBBL [Women's Big Bash League] to a degree. There's still some limited thinking, and they certainly lack creativity with what they do, but at least they've funded the WBBL and it's been very successful. Let's see how India go with their women's version of the IPL [India Premier League]. They've certainly got the money to do it. But do they have the will to do it properly? The BCCI have not shown a great deal of support for their women players up until now. However, they do seem to be getting dragged, kicking and screaming, towards equality in cricket in India. Not allowing the Indian players to come to FairBreak in Dubai was disappointing but not completely surprising. That's why we had a backup plan."

"I feel so privileged to be guided by the likes of Geoff Lawson who gave us valuable insights into every game. A highlight...was the memories and friendships made with the wonderful women on tour. These off-field moments are as important as what's gained on the field, and [they] will always be treasured. These friendships around the world are a big part of what makes FairBreak special."

Ruchitha Venkatesh, Hong Kong

" Alex Blackwell
Former Australian Women's Cricket Captain "

Alex Blackwell is a former Australian cricket captain who has "lived and breathed" the sport for thirty years. She represented Australia 251 times across Tests, One Day Internationals and T20 Internationals. Since retiring in 2019, she has remained involved in the sport as a board member, commentator and spokesperson. She is also establishing a post-retirement career in genetic counselling and has started a family with her wife, Lynsey.

Considered a treasured and highly regarded member of the FairBreak management team, I asked Blackwell to tell me about what she brings to the table. She said, "Starting from the beginning, I was invited to be on the touring party for the FairBreak Global XI in 2018. I was a senior player, a mentor. I was there to guide, encourage and inspire other players who were in that same team. Interestingly, I received some of that back. For example, I was inspired by Selina Solman who was courageous enough to open the bowling and she did a fantastic job. This was a young woman who had travelled all the way from Vanuatu, a tiny island in the Pacific Ocean, and had never caught a taxi before in her life. She had to take herself from Heathrow Airport, by black cab, to Wormsley Park in Buckinghamshire, which is a significant journey. And when she arrived, we ended up opening the bowling with her against some of England's most established players in the opposition. Players like Charlotte Edwards, who is a legend of the game.

"My initial role was to be side by side with cricketers from all around the globe and to help them feel like they could do it. Because they can. It's just that they haven't been exposed to these experiences before. And once Selina bowled that first over at Wormsley, I think she understood and thought, "Yeah, I can do this". It's just overcoming that fear factor at the beginning.

"Ongoing, what I bring to the table for FairBreak is my strong reputation in the game which I have established over decades. That takes a long time to build. I bring my reputation to the organisation to endorse it, to say this is a really worthwhile project, and that I really believe in what FairBreak is trying to achieve. Me being alongside what FairBreak is doing brings a level of kudos to everything. I've been that well-respected person across many different cricketing nations. I've done development work in cricket as well. I'm known for trying to level the playing field, to create opportunities and encourage cricketers from emerging nations like Mongolia and Japan. Who would have thought that cricket could take me to those places? I've been to both those Associate Nations as an ambassador in a development role to encourage and lift up players.

"I've been to Japan twice for cricket. Firstly, to work directly with the Japanese team and the second trip, in 2014, involved being an ICC ambassador across the East Asia Pacific Tournament. The ICC East Asia Pacific Women's Trophy was the first stage of the qualification process for the 2016 World T20 in India. The Cook Islands, Vanuatu, Samoa, Papua New Guinea and defending champions, Japan, were the participating nations.

"I absolutely loved it. I got to sit in each of their tents on the sideline and talk tactics and help players debrief after their performance on the field. I helped lift them up. Each team brought their culture to our global game. It's a standardised game across the whole world, but each team plays it slightly differently and has a unique perspective on it.

"The Cook Islands have never won a game. Ever. And they would sing before the game. A beautiful song that I don't know the words to. I did not know what they were singing but I could feel what they were singing. There was such joy in what they were doing. They were coming together for a common purpose. There was a respect for what they were accomplishing and for their opposition. And then they would go out and, typically, lose their game. And then after the match, they would sing again. I got a very different perspective on cricket and how valuable it is to bring all sorts of people together, and that while winning is important, what is more significant is the social impact of it all. I was really inspired by that tournament and all the women who took part.

"After I retired from the Australian team, there was an opportunity for Cricket Australia to send someone to Mongolia. Our wonderful first Australian ambassador to Mongolia, John Langtry, wanted to help promote cricket in Mongolia, and especially within schools, to help create a sense of teamwork.

Because Mongolian people are nomadic and individual, there is not a lot of team sport that goes on in Mongolia. Cricket is emerging as a really great tool to help create those valuable life skills in the young people. So it was a sports diplomacy program through the Australian government that helped get me over there for about six days and I absolutely loved it.

"I went to schools and ran cricket clinics. I met with the Education Minister to talk about cricket going into the curriculum. I went on live news. I played a game of cricket at the only cricket ground in Mongolia. They have a special pavilion called a "ger-vilion". A ger is the animal skin tent they use as housing in Mongolia, and because of their nomadic culture, they can pack it up and move it. So there was a ger as the pavilion and it was the most picturesque cricket ground I've played on. Unfortunately, the cricket field is built on a riverbed so there were plenty of rocks out there.

"I learned that cricket is played all year round in Mongolia. It's generally played in the indoor halls of the schools rather than on this outdoor cricket pitch, the only one in the country. Their equipment is second hand and is sent over from Australia and elsewhere because you can't buy cricket bats in Mongolia. Anyway, these bats are stored in a shipping container. During the winter when the temperatures can fall to minus thirty degrees, the bats stored inside the container dry out. So I was using this terrible bat. It was probably the best bat they had, but I couldn't hit it off the square. I was trying to hit boundaries to show off a little bit and inspire the kids, but I couldn't hit any boundaries because the bat was no good.

"This made me fully comprehend how important the quality of equipment is to play properly. That's another way FairBreak is helping out. By providing equipment to women from Associate Nations which helps them train and perform when they get their playing opportunities. Whether that's at an Invitational or representing their own countries.

"FairBreak is a natural fit for someone like me because I've already really enjoyed working with Associate Nation cricketers. And I've got a pretty good eye across the whole cricket ecosystem from being a player and an ambassador in development roles through to sitting on the boards. I was a board member for Cricket NSW for three years. So I have a good sense of the whole of cricket all round the world.

"I watched, with great interest, the FairBreak Invitational in Dubai on the television from my couch. I would have loved to have been there, but I had a brand new baby and my wife had had a serious medical event. She's fine now, but there was just no way I could be there. And COVID-19 as well. Travelling during that time wasn't something I wanted to do. But I sat back and watched the product as a spectator and as a fan and I thought it came across beautifully. It demonstrated that if you invest in the production side of things any cricket really can be entertaining.

"The production needs to adequately display the skills of these cricketers. If you have terrible camera angles and awful production, anyone, even the Australian men's team is going to look bad. I thought FairBreak got the production side of things just right, and it was really entertaining to watch. It was quite emotional to see some of the players whose names I had put forward to be considered for an invitation, to see them out there taking their opportunity. And some of them getting Player of the Match awards. It was awesome. I loved it".

I shared with Alex Blackwell how emotional I can get just writing about the tournament and listening to the perspectives of the diverse cast of characters who were there and who helped make it happen. For example, Deirdre McGhee, the Associate Professor from the University of Wollongong who ran the breast health research trial during the tournament. I recounted that McGhee spoke to me about how she welled up with tears watching the final when all the teams came running on to the field and everyone was singing, laughing and crying. She was deeply moved by it all. She felt this extraordinary camaraderie which completely aligned with her ethos around working in breast health.

Blackwell concurred. She said, "There is definitely a deep feeling of camaraderie. I guess it goes back to why I was so hooked on FairBreak from the first moment I was involved on that Global XI tour. Playing a few matches alongside some very established cricketers, like Sana Mir, who was normally my opposition. I have the utmost respect for her. It has been an honour to be a teammate of hers in FairBreak, and to learn so much from her, and to understand the unique challenges as well as the joyful things that come from being a female cricketer in Pakistan.

"I was invited to be that star player. To usher along the emerging players. When you are side by side in a team you are an equal to everybody. I loved being teammates with people from all around the world. Some of whom do not share the same language necessarily. But we do share the language of sport, and the language of humour, and the language of determination and effort. Those things are all the same. There is something quite special about FairBreak in that it is truly global. And it gives people like me and Heather Knight and Sophie Devine new experiences and new ways to love our game. Because it is a wonderful game, and it's so nice to be an established player and still be able to find new ways to get joy from it".

Over the years, Blackwell has suggested the FairBreak management team extend invitations to play to a number of Associate Nation players. I was keen to hear how she had unearthed these promising female cricketers. She revealed, "Some of them I've seen directly. For example when I was in Japan and Mongolia. Also I did a coaching session in Canada just recently. I am always out and about looking around. Also being able to watch women's cricket. It's fantastic that there is now more opportunity to watch, say, the World Cup qualifiers. So I am looking at Associate Nations competing. I am analysing stats and score cards that come through, especially *ESPNCricinfo*. I am keeping an eye on players who really stand out.

"Take Mary-Anne Musonda…she scored a hundred for Zimbabwe in her first or second ODI. Once her team had achieved some international status and could play in a One Day game, she scored a hundred in one of her first matches. So that's an example of the sorts of stories that sing out and get someone like me to pay attention. Social media is a big part of it as well. Female sport uses social media quite well because we know that the mainstream media doesn't cover women's sport as well as they could. Through social media you can hear what is going on, even in some of the most remote places. An example of that is our lovely left arm bowler from Bhutan, Anju Gurung.

"She was training in the lead up to the FairBreak tournament and was out there on her own bowling in the street. It's just so cool to see that no matter how remote a player is, it is possible to play on the biggest stage. I think that's what is most exciting about FairBreak. We are making a conscious decision to go to the most remote corners of the globe to try and find talented cricketers who deserve an opportunity to test their skills.

"There are a number of ways I contribute on the management team. Shaun and I are in constant discussion, bouncing ideas. And occasionally I challenge Shaun on some of his thinking. He's someone who thinks big and sees all the things that are possible. I have to remind him that sometimes our players aren't quite ready. He sees the skills in them. And he sees that they would dominate in other competitions. Sometimes I need to remind him that it does take a long time to be a toughened cricketer, to become match-hardened and to be able to perform under pressure, and not to devalue the competitions that are already in existence.

"I get that he is frustrated by the way women's cricket has been delivered over many, many years. And that is admirable. That's why he has created the amazing innovation that is FairBreak. His frustration is a good thing. But at the same time, some of what has already happened in women's cricket is also fantastic, and we need to continue to remember that. It is important how we communicate with the CEO of Cricket Australia for example, and the WBBL. The way we talk about that is vital. It's not necessarily that we know how to do it better. We've got great ideas on how to do things better, but it's crucial not to get them off-side. I think I've helped bring some balance to that. But without Shaun stretching us all to think bigger this innovation would not happen. Maybe I'm a little bit of the handbrake.

"What I continue to encourage us all to talk about is the fact that women's cricket is fantastic as it is. Yes, it can certainly get better. But men's cricket is not, necessarily, the gold standard that we should aspire to. And I know that Shaun and Geoff understand that. I believe it is important that women mentor women, and that we create more ways to mentor women within the sport.

"For example, our coaching mentors. There are fantastic male coaches in the world, but there are also fantastic female coaches. Unfortunately at this point in time, there are fewer female coaches available to be mentors. So what I want to ensure is that we are not mentoring our coaches and our players through a male lens. While skilled coaches from the men's game are valuable, if they don't have a women's cricket perspective and experience, it's maybe not the right recipe to have them mentoring and advising coaches who will be coaching women.

"Coaching men compared to coaching women....there are a lot of similarities, but there are some differences too. We shouldn't just assume that if you've coached men's cricket, that you'll be the answer for the women. I advocate for gender diversity across our coaching and leadership teams at FairBreak. Which is, of course, embraced as a concept by Shaun and Geoff.

"Shaun very much understands that. He wants more women running the ship, which is great. I'm excited about being involved and it aligns with my values. I have no hesitation about being a part of this. I bring a different perspective and that's what we need to continue doing. Our management team is diverse, and that's excellent because decision making is always better when there are different perspectives.

"I don't want it to sound critical, the coaching through a male lens. I'm happy to work with FairBreak to create opportunities for female coaches. Then there will be more female coaches to coach future coaches. At the moment we don't have all that many experienced female cricket coaches, because of historical disadvantages for women in the game. It's understandable why we have more male coaches, and it's awesome to see male coaches want to be involved in the women's game, because they see it as cricket. And they're passionate about cricket. They don't discriminate between working in the men's game or the women's game. They're just passionate about improving cricketers and helping people get better. It's understandable that there are more male experts available to the FairBreak movement at the moment. But we will soon change that through the work that we're doing by creating opportunities for women.

"It will take time for there to be more women to choose from for coaching roles. In the meantime we need to ensure that we are not just picking people… when we select candidates, our biases are interesting to examine…we tend to see a man and he looks like what a cricket coach looks like. We've been used to that for so long…and then to potentially have a woman interview for the job… the people selecting for that job may have unconscious bias towards picking people that they've seen do the job before. They have confidence in that person because they've seen people who look like that do the job.

"We just need to be mindful of not seeing men's cricket as the gold standard that women have to measure up to. They are two different products. They're quite different and each have their own charm, history and appeal to different people. We shouldn't necessarily try and force one to be the other, or vice versa. They can learn from each other. I get irritated that the cricket world doesn't seem to look at the women's game as something to learn from in terms of the men's game. We always look up to the men's game as a place from which to draw learnings to help the women. But what about the reverse? There could be amazing lessons in the reverse.

"In terms of what the men could learn from the women, a great example is how female bowlers are potentially more skillful than the men because they have to defend the cricket field with fewer fielders out on the boundary. The women are only allowed to have four out on the boundary, whereas men can have five. The men have more fielders to be able to defend the field with.

"Additionally, women do not have as much pace at their disposal to be able to defend or to be able to attack and get wickets. So you could argue that female bowlers and captains of women's cricket have to be more skilled in certain ways to be able to combat that. So it is a very different game, it has different rules. It's got different attributes like pace, boundary size, the size of the ball, and playing conditions such as fielding restrictions. Women play the game in a different way. That's my whole point around why the experience of having played women's cricket is of value and having coached women's cricket is of value to guide the sport. Outside views are really important of course. But I question whether we have that one traffic direction view that men guiding the women is valuable, but it's not necessary in the reverse.

"All people are different and within a team it's difficult to cater for everybody. I worked with a fantastic coach called Richard McGinnis. He and I were successful as an Australian coach and captain combination for a period. I was captain for about eighteen months and, together, we won a T20 World Cup. Our very first one. We won an Ashes Test match, and we won multiple Rose Bowl series against New Zealand.

"He has experience across both men's and women's Australian cricket at the highest level. He used to say that his observations are that women win when they are happy. And men are happy when they win. So maybe there's a different focus.

"It is important to ensure that women feel a sense of connection and feel really valued and supported. Potentially there's an extra element of nurturing them just as people which helps them with their performance. And that may not get the same focus in men's cricket. Potentially, the men are just happy when the performances are good and it doesn't really matter what else is going on within the team.

"To answer your question regarding what the men's game can learn from the women's game…I think that our young men coming through are showing that emotions and mental health are important, and that they are willing to be vulnerable. Historically, women, as a whole, have had practice in dealing with that and have embraced that side of working with people within teams.

"Male coaches may gain great benefit from working in the women's game and observing how there's more sensitivity required in the way that women are coached effectively. Our young men may, as time goes on, be more sensitive, and that's great. They will reveal themselves as more vulnerable and willing to talk about their struggles. There could be some learnings there around compassion and nurturing. Maybe it's more person-first coaching, rather than cricketer-first coaching".

Earlier in this book, I interviewed Rina Hore from the Bradman Foundation, and she observed that there can be some intense hustle amongst young male players coming through, whereas the girls work more collaboratively as young players. Hore also spoke about the inaugural U/19 Women's World Cup in early 2023 and how the boys have had this competition in place for thirty years. When I shared these observations with Blackwell, she commented, "The U/19 Men's World Cup has been around for a long time and has helped produce players like Virat Kohli and Steve Smith. It's fantastic that this new tournament is coming for the girls.

"I think girls get into the game to play with their friends and they're not that competitive. I know that sounds like a generalisation. There's going to be some girls who just want to win, and just want to score fifties and hundreds or take fifers. Girls and women who play cricket generally like club cricket. For them, it's about that social connection. Doing something together and having that common goal of trying to win together, trying to perform together. That's what the FairBreak Invitational highlighted. How much joy these women got from playing alongside each other. It was more than just winning. There was much more to it. It was about creating opportunities that should be there for these talented women from wherever they come from all around the world. Our very best players in the world really resonated with that.

"It's quite unique. I think the FairBreak Invitational is really well suited to the women's game. I'm not sure that it's something we even need to think about for the men. They have more opportunities. Certainly, there's discrepancy and equality of opportunity, but generally speaking, female cricketers, even in the best, most developed cricket countries still experience inequality.

"There was some fierce cricket played at the Invitational in Dubai, but when you hear the players talk about that tournament, it's about the connections they made with women from all over the world, and what they learned from each other".

I asked Blackwell whether she will be attending the FairBreak Invitational in Hong Kong in April 2023 and she said, "I am hoping I will be going to the Invitational in Hong Kong as an advisor and a spokesperson and a mentor. It's not settled yet. My role is not defined as a coach nor as a selector. I'm across it more broadly. At the moment, I'm involved in helping to create really great squads that are going to achieve a nice element of competition. In its second iteration, we need to keep the core of the teams together and to maintain the team cultures we see developing.

"We are only one tournament in, but each one of the teams is starting to build their own unique identity. That's something we are very conscious of. We have a group who are putting the names together, and right now, we are thinking about other women we would love to give opportunity to. It's an Invitational, so we can invite whoever we want really.

"I have articulated on paper what our coaching and selection philosophy is so that the four of us who are picking the teams and players have a reference point. We know what we're all about. We just need to make sure that we are consistent with that. I thought that was really important. Because outsiders might think, "Well, how are they picking the players? What are they basing all this on?"

"It's a privilege to be invited to FairBreak, and we are not going to be able to provide opportunities for everyone in each tournament. Obviously, there's a limit, but we are trying to provide opportunity for as many people as possible from all around the world. And we are unearthing some incredibly vibrant cricketers who are very entertaining. And it's their endeavour that is entertaining to watch. Their back stories are also compelling, understanding their journey. Maybe that they didn't have anyone to train with, that they do all their training on their own.

"For example, we followed up on Anju Gurung from Bhutan. We followed her development and her training program through social media. We could watch what she was doing and this got a lot of engagement and built up our excitement around watching her in the tournament. Then we saw her opening the bowling for the Falcons, doing a great job against some of the best in the world, and she held her own".

Blackwell and I discussed the forthcoming launch of this book and Martyn having suggested to me that I interview all the players for their back-stories for a follow-up FairBreak "coffee table" book. She smiled with me and said, "Shaun continues to think big. I've witnessed people like that in the game. I see the way Christina Matthews has thought big around inclusion in Western Australia and the way that she has stood firmly for representing cricket for everybody with the statues that are being put up around the new development at the WACA. She is someone who sees that there is work to be done to make the game appealing and to be fair to everybody. Every person should see that there is a place for them in the game. And Christina does that work against the tide, and without the support of some of the board.

"I love seeing that. I loved that many years before the 2020 T20 Women's World Cup was due to be hosted in Australia, Nick Hockley and Belinda Clark approached the Australian Women's team. They asked us where we thought the final of the T20 should be played in Australia. I was the vice-captain at the time. We were saying to them, "North Sydney Oval is pretty good, or Hurstville, or the Junction Oval in Melbourne". They replied, "What about the MCG?" And we all just thought, "There's not going to be anyone there. It's going to feel terrible". And look how that turned out! The #FilltheG campaign resulted in the biggest audience for a women's cricket match ever. Just under 87,000 people in the Melbourne Cricket Ground watching the final of a T20 Women's World Cup!

"Sometimes you need people like Nick and Belinda, like Christina Matthews and like Shaun Martyn. People who stretch our thinking about what is possible. I think Shaun has done an amazing job to bring so many people along. Potentially it's not that hard because FairBreak has a great philosophy and vision around creating opportunities for women and especially in sport. Who knows where it might go.

"Cricket is one of Shaun's great passions. It's a great sport for women because of the social connection. In cricket, you spend so much time together and you go through extreme highs and lows. You can be out there on your own sometimes and you have to bear the brunt, good or bad, of individual performances. It's about celebrating or commiserating as a team. It's a great social game. Those interpersonal connections are probably the highlight of it. It's a very skillful game where you can find your little niche. No particular body type is required. It's quite an intellectual game and it requires lots of different tactics. For those reasons, it's fantastic for so many people, but particularly for women and girls.

"Shaun thinks ahead a lot and we are lucky as female cricketers that he has taken charge of this and been an innovator and a mover and a shaker. Going back to what I was talking about earlier regarding communication, what I have learned is that when you are an innovator, or you challenge the status quo, it's easy to put people offside. I have had that experience. As someone who has challenged the status quo around the treatment of gay cricketers, it isn't easy. So perhaps my experience in doing that can assist in FairBreak's mission to challenge the status quo, to create new opportunities and to do things differently. By doing that we can highlight the inadequacies or the gaps where others have not provided opportunities or have not thought creatively enough or have not taken risks to get things done.

"Shaun is an innovator. And by being an innovator, he can quite easily put people off because he has shone a light on what they haven't done. And the proof is in the pudding. He has done a marvellous job of bringing people together and communicating the vision. If he wasn't good at doing that, we wouldn't be at this point. We wouldn't be looking forward to our second tournament.

"Shaun looks at cricketers as more than just cricketers. Especially our #fairbreakers. Not only has he presented them with cricket opportunities, but he has provided other types of opportunities for them to learn from each other and to experience new things that may not have been possible back in their home country. I mentioned the story about Selina Solman catching a taxi for the first time. There was also the Wormsley trip where we all went and watched the opera after the cricket match.

"The point being that he provided the opportunity for us to have a wonderful time and to experience a different culture. He left space in the schedule to allow adult women to go and spend time together. To take a trip into London and explore the city on their own. It was not about him dictating how we spent our time because we had been brought over for this amazing tour.

"I've experienced the amateur to professional era in women's cricket and I really don't want us to lose some of the charm of amateur cricket. The excitement of being picked for an Australian tour and travelling to a new country and having the time to go and see the sights and try the local food. FairBreak advocates for that. What are the memories we take away from playing sport? It's not really the runs and the wickets so much as the time we spend together as a team. And we are very lucky to have cricket as a vehicle to provide this opportunity to travel and meet so many different people. It's also about making good memories and building sports diplomacy with other parts of the world".

Concluding our conversation, I asked Blackwell if she was happy for us to publish some photographs of her from the early days when she participated in some of Shaun Martyn and Paul Harvey's corporate and charity cricket matches. She happily agreed and said, "While I don't remember that time very clearly, it was an absolute shock to get an invitation to come and play a charity or corporate game and get paid. I was like, "What are you serious?" Because we would always be asked to play those types of things and to promote the game and we never really got paid for our time. So when Shaun invited us to play in his corporate cricket matches, while it wasn't a whole lot of money in the scheme of things, it was a respectful demonstration that our time was valuable".

"Q&A with Sana Mir
Commentator and Former Captain of
Pakistan's Women's Cricket Team"

Sana Mir is a highly respected Pakistani cricket commentator and former trailblazer cricketer who captained Pakistan's national women's cricket team in One Day Internationals and T20 Internationals. She played in 226 international matches including 137 as captain of the squad.

At a glittering ceremony in New York in 2019, Mir was awarded the Asia Society Game Changers award in recognition of her impact on cricket in Asia and worldwide. While growing up in Pakistan, Mir saw few girls or women playing Pakistan's national sport. Refusing to let this hold her back, she joined the country's newly formed women's cricket team, went on to become the captain and was regarded as one of the world's top female cricketers. Universally admired for her stance on discrimination and the protection of human rights, Mir dedicated her award to those fighting for climate change, children from war-torn nations and women helping each other.

Sana Mir retired from international cricket in 2020 but came out of retirement in May 2022 to captain the Sapphires at the FairBreak Invitational in Dubai. I spoke to Mir in her home in Pakistan over Zoom and WhatsApp. A poor internet connection conspired to interrupt our conversation a number of times.

Shaun consults closely with you because it is vital that what FairBreak does is well received in Pakistan and the wider region. Why is seeking your counsel so important?

"In my working relationship with Shaun, and most of my professional relationships, it is extremely important for me to remain authentic and to say what the right thing is. We come from different backgrounds…there are a lot of cultural differences…along with many similarities. It's really good that we have a relationship where we can discuss things very openly…where I can be honest about whether something will sit well with our people here or not. We have that level of trust with each other…we are only going to suggest whatever is best for the bigger cause. I think this is an underlying trust which myself and Shaun share.

"When we met the first time, I was really blown away by what he was doing and how he was doing it. I saw a lot of honesty in his whole idea of making a difference for Associate Nation players, and players who do not get…the kind of opportunities that he was giving. Myself…coming from a country where we really struggled hard to be where women's cricket is right now…I understood the struggles of those players, and I realised how important and how significant it is to have someone looking after you at that time of your career…when you are not in the top eight teams or not in the top six teams… but someone is still supporting you…so we connected through that.

"With my whole experience of leading my country at an international level…you have to be culturally sensitive…travelling to different countries, interacting with different people along the way and then checking with my own roots in Pakistan about what people thought about those things and how we can collaborate and find a way where we can all get along together…Shaun really respects that. He sees that in me and he respects that. That's why I'm able to contribute in whatever way I can…because he acknowledges that. I think that because we acknowledge each other…whatever we are doing…that makes it a very healthy relationship professionally."

You are an esteemed member of the FairBreak team. How did you and Shaun first meet?

"Shaun did call me for the first time when he was trying to set up a tournament for women. I think it was back ten years ago. I don't remember exactly the time. I thought it was just a random phone call. Someone was offering big amounts of money to play in a league, and there was no league in women's cricket. I didn't know whether to trust or not, so I just didn't take it very seriously. And then five or six years down the line I saw Charlotte Edwards and Suzie Bates post on social media their videos and pictures of being involved in FairBreak at Wormsley in 2018.

"That's when I first knew that there was something happening under FairBreak. I started researching it a little bit, and in 2019 Shaun contacted me and asked if I would like to be a part of the FairBreak XI Tour. I was travelling to the Men's World Cup. I was on the ICC Women's Cricket Committee, so I was already travelling to the UK to watch the final and be part of the ICC Committee. Shaun said the FairBreak XI Tour was right after the World Cup and asked would I like to join them. I thought, "It's a good opportunity. I'll go and see what they do and how things work for them.""

"Once I went there, I really enjoyed everything that was happening. I got involved with the players. I got involved with the whole campaign. I saw that this is something where we can really make a difference. That one week of work with the Associate Players, we saw their rapid improvement. Initially they lacked confidence, they didn't feel like they belonged there. Within a week they started expressing themselves on the field way better than they would have ever…because they had mentors around them. People who believed in them. So that made a huge difference. That's when I felt that this is something I want to stay connected with."

Do you get involved in player selection? Do you suggest emerging players for invitation?

"Myself, Alex Blackwell, Shaun and Geoff interact with each other, sometimes on a monthly basis. We suggest players…and discuss how players got along in the previous season. So there is a nice discussion about that. It's only with the pool of players, generally, that we talk. With the setting of the teams…because I'm still playing in the tournament…I generally do not take part in that too much. It's only about the balance of the teams and the overall pool of players… who we are inviting. I basically suggest players from Pakistan or Bangladesh or Sri Lanka where I've really played a lot with them…I know which players are coming up…what contributions they've had throughout their career…it's easier for me to suggest those from here."

The FairBreak Invitational in Dubai was watched by millions in Pakistan. What was the reaction from the viewers when you and the other players came home?

"I think it was shown on the national television station, Pakistan Television, PTV. And because of that, a lot of people watched it, and at that point, not a lot of other cricket was going on. And because the timing was good…we were in the same time zone…Dubai and Pakistan…people were watching it in prime time. There was a lot of people following it because of the time zone and it being on national television…and then there were five Pakistani players. Nearly every FairBreak team…had one Pakistani player in it. So that generated the interest also…people watched it pretty keenly.

"The show that I do on PTV [Sports 360]…they covered it throughout the FairBreak tournament…it's on Monday to Thursday…we have a one hour show every week…so viewers were keenly following it because I was part of it… some people were following because of me…or because of Bismah [Maroof] or Aliya [Riaz] or Diana [Baig] or Fatima [Sana]. Because they are top players from Pakistan. Pakistani players do not get a lot of opportunity to play in cricket leagues abroad. FairBreak was one of the very first…and they all did pretty well in their teams…so it was pretty good for the Pakistani people… and also the players…and other players still keep asking me how they can be a part of FairBreak. So there's a lot of interest, not only from players, but physiotherapists, managers, coaches. Everyone keeps asking me how they can be a part of FairBreak because they know that I work with the management. I just direct them to Shaun or Geoff or the website…yes, it generated a lot of interest."

How did the players feel on returning to Pakistan after Dubai? Were you all on a high? What was the general vibe amongst you?

"I think mostly the players were really, really touched by the overall spirit of FairBreak because it brings together players from the top four nations with the top ten nations and then down to the Associate Nations. And then on the cricket field we are all equal. And that's exactly what sports should be all about. When we are competing as nations, because of different resources, different infrastructures, we do feel that big gap between nations. But when we are playing within a team then we feel on par with each other and then we get to experience the dressing room environment with people from different cultures, different faiths, different backgrounds…and at the end of the day we realise we are all human beings and pretty similar. We have the same fears. We have the same dreams…there's so much similarity. I think that was the biggest take away for everyone.

"From the cricketing point of view, they were tested in different conditions. They played under different captains. They interacted with different coaches. They played under different circumstances…like their batting order would change. Their bowling positions would change compared to what they were doing in the Pakistan team…so, I think, this all was a big learning for them… how to handle that and how to be on their own…because generally they travel as a team, so they don't get a lot of exposure in the leagues…so it was a great exposure for all these players."

And they all got to do press conferences and pitch reports?

"I'm not sure about the pitch reports from the Pakistan players. I did a bit of commentary. I was in the box. I got to do my first stint with Isa Guha [English cricket commentator and former England cricketer] which was pretty memorable because I really look up to her as far as commentary is concerned. She has made a huge name for herself, so it was really nice sharing the box with her. I think the Pakistani girls did a lot of press conferences, so handling media…just adds to their growth as players."

The opening ceremony featured Zeb Bangash. Was it your idea to have a Pakistani singer perform?

"Yes, I did suggest Zeb because Shaun was thinking about having an opening ceremony. I first met Zeb in 2011 after hearing one of her songs. In 2008, she had a huge hit in Coke Studio so she was the brand name at that point. And then after a couple of years, I met her at an airport and that's how we became friends. What I really liked about her is, of course, her voice and her ability to sing in different languages. She can sing in seven or eight different languages. Shaun was trying to have an opening ceremony catering to all different nationalities…I thought having a female singer who can sing in seven or eight different languages would be good…the other thing was she has been a big supporter for women's cricket in Pakistan when we were in a struggling time….she was a celebrity in her own right…she put a lot of weight behind us at that time and connected us with corporate sponsorships…we didn't have a background or knowledge of things like that….we just wanted to play cricket. So Zeb connected us with a lot of her contacts".

At the FairBreak Invitational in Dubai, despite not playing for a couple of years, Mir enjoyed being back in the middle. She admitted she felt "nervous" at first but once those feelings had settled down, she took some wickets and got right back into it. Mir skippered the Sapphires, a team that included Australia's Elyse Villani, Jade Allen and Grace Harris, South Africa's Shabnim Ismail, England's Natasha Farrant, and Ireland's Gaby Lewis and Kim Garth. There were also seven Associate players in her squad.

Mir wants to see, through FairBreak, many female Associate Nation players becoming leaders in their own right. She believes that FairBreak is acting as the catalyst for making cricket truly global because sport transcends boundaries and nationalities. Looking to the future, she sees women's cricket not being dependent on the men's structure. She would like to see further tournaments for women and the building of fifty strong cricket nations. With the ICC broadening their horizons, she knows that consolidating those cricketing nations needs to be done collectively.

Mir draws immense satisfaction from helping emerging players grow and acting as a role model for those who do not have senior players around them. At times in her early career she experienced "a feeling of being lost". Fortunately, Mir benefited from mentors towards the end of her career and considers herself blessed to have had them around her. She loves FairBreak because the concept allows her to give back by mentoring young women not only from Pakistan but from all around the world.

"

Lisa Sthalekar
Former Australian Cricketer,
Commentator and President of FICA

Lisa Sthalekar spoke to me from Dehradun in the far north of India, near the Himalayas. Today, she is a cricket commentator, pundit and host at cricket matches around the world, and sits on a number of boards and advisory councils, including the Federation of International Cricket Associations (FICA) where she is the recently appointed President.

I asked for her perspectives around where FairBreak fits into women's cricket now that they've delivered their first tournament. She said, "What's evident is that things have dramatically changed from when the idea first popped up between me and Shaun. There wasn't a lot of cricket taking place, and players weren't getting paid. That has drastically changed. There are a lot of professional female players now around the world. It's a great concept to allow Associate players to be able to rub shoulders with some of the best players in the world.

"Where it fits in the calendar is the question. It's going to be a tight one as the years progress, simply because the Women's IPL might come in, plus we've got the WBBL and The Hundred. The CPL have their own women's domestic competition. Then you've got South Africa looking to do similar in a couple of years. Then you've got your bilateral cricket, and then you've got an ICC event every year, so we're starting to find that there's not a lot of time within the calendar.

"If we look at the men's game, it's a bit of a mess. The calendar is full. We are seeing a lot of players retire from international cricket, or a certain format of cricket, because they can't fit everything in. Where it [FairBreak] fits...it still has a place for Associate Nations and Associate players, but how often they are going to be able to access the best players, only time will tell.

"On the future of women's cricket in general, compared to when I retired in 2013, and on the day [8th March 2020] when I was at the MCG for the final of the Women's World Cup 2020 and there were 86,000 people in the stadium, I didn't think that there would be that many people there just to watch a women's game. So, it has certainly accelerated at a great speed.

"COVID-19 has probably played a role in slowing that progress, but you get a sense that things are starting to get back to normal now, and I'd like to think that in the next couple of years we will see more acceleration in the women's game. The Commonwealth Games were amazing for the women to be involved in. There are some real high points still to come within the women's game. It's still got a long way to go. But it's in a very good place at the moment.

"In terms of Associate Nations like Thailand, they showed us in 2020 how good a team they can be. Unfortunately, their game against Pakistan, where they scored 150, got rained out so we didn't get to see, potentially, their first victory in an ICC event. They play with real passion. They play because they enjoy the game. The game has gone from an amateur sport where you play it because you love it, and now it's become an income for some players in certain countries. So, there's extra pressure. We're seeing a lot of players take breaks from the game because they're mentally burnt out, whereas Thailand comes in with this fresh approach. And it's lovely to see.

"They're playing just for fun. They're playing for love. They're not professional, as in they're not earning big money like other countries. It's not their full-time job. I don't know their structure, but they keep pinching themselves every time they get to play against an England or an Australia. They can say, "I have just watched this cricketer play and now I'm playing against them on the same field". Whereas players for England, Australia, New Zealand, India, think, "I'm playing for my country, I'm playing for my spot."

In terms of what FICA does for players, she explained, "Every country, apart from the Asian countries, has a player association whose job it is to be the voice of the players, and to work with the national boards on remuneration and commercial rights. Alot of them house the IP [Intellectual Property] of the players and they do a lot of work with welfare, they do work with underage players, current players and, obviously, past players. We have the Australian Cricketers' Association and FICA is the international body of all those player associations coming together.

"Each country is slightly different in terms of where they are in women's cricket and how they see their female players. I guess the main thing is about equality and what that looks like in each country. New Zealand recently announced a new agreement where all international players, male and female, will get paid the same match fee.

"They won't be paid the same contract because the men play more than the women, but if they play a one day international, then Kane Williamson will get the same as Sophie Devine. Each country is doing things slightly differently around the word equality. And then also learning and sharing from each other about what's working and what's not working across different countries. It takes money, it takes people, it takes investment. It takes looking for commercial dollars. It's about getting the structure right in domestic cricket so that you're not just putting all your money into the top group. That you're filtering it down to ensure that you're producing the next generation, so when cricketers retire, a country is left with nothing.

"Perspectives on what needs to change or adapt in women's cricket over the next few years? It's going along well. The Future Tour Program is the first time that's been put in place for women's cricket. We're going to see at the next few ICC events, an increase in teams participating, so that will be good. Women's cricket is going in the right direction. Historically it's taken a good 150 years for us to get to where we are now, so we're going at a good pace now. There are more pressing issues in the men's game now. That's probably taking up more time for a lot of people involved in cricket.

"The growth of audiences watching female sport and women's cricket has been fantastic. The viewing numbers for the Commonwealth Games were huge, and it was cricket, most of all, that embodied the strength of women's sport at the Games. Some of the hottest tickets in town in Birmingham, were for the Women's T20 games.

Asked for comment on the success of the FairBreak Invitational and its future, Sthalekar said, "I haven't really been involved with the organisation [FairBreak] for a while. For a very long time, so I don't know what their strategic plan is. I don't know what the future looks like for the competition, how their funding models work. The talk was that the players enjoyed themselves, a chance for Associate players to play with some of the best players in the world. That's a good thing."

Thank You Letter from a young French Cricketer Poppy McGeown

Dear Shaun,

I am Poppy McGeown from France (and yes, a bit of Scotland...my surname is a bit of a giveaway) on the FairBreak XI 2022 Tour this summer.

Firstly, I would like to apologise. I meant to email you before to thank you, but life (work really) got in the way a bit. But here I am now. Spoiler alert, it is a long email. I am more of a letter writer myself, but I know from experience having written to my Australian friends in the past, that a letter can take a long time to reach "Straya" and I would hate it to get lost.

I have followed FairBreak, I admit only recently, with the tournament in Dubai this year. I few of my German friends were playing and it was an absolutely amazing set up. Without being dramatic, I thought, at the time, if one day during my life I am ever invited to FairBreak it really would be a dream come true and something to work towards and motivate more training and more cricket. But it was a possible-but-may-not-happen type dream, and if it were ever to happen, I was expecting it to be after a few more years of training and hopefully performing in the French national team.

I certainly was not expecting a phone call mid-August asking me if I was available to come on tour only a few weeks later. It was surreal, and the best thing was that in my current job I could get sufficient annual leave at short notice to come on tour. The stars aligned and I was absolutely in awe at the opportunity. When the news came out, I received a lot of messages (more than anticipated) from fellow players in France. All of them were, firstly, genuinely happy and excited for me to go. But it very quickly became clear by their comments that the fact that a player from France was going was truly horizon-opening for them.

This meant that we, like many other Associate Nations, feel there is something more we can dream and hope for. Playing for our countries gives us immense purpose, pride, and joy but it is sometimes difficult to get the support, the opportunity, the infrastructure to grow and progress. We don't have many players, but when we look back and see what we can achieve with the training we have access to, it really is something I think we can be proud of despite it not always being easy. Do not get me wrong, we don't complain, we love cricket so much we are happy to give it time. We buy our kit and finance most of our transportation to the few club games we get a year. It is just to illustrate what a huge deal it is for one of us to be invited to FairBreak, and what it means to us as a community, not just the person who is invited.

I joined the FairBreak XI 2022 Tour in Essex. I had followed the previous games and was looking forward to meeting everybody and get stuck in. Of course, at first there are always the questions going through your mind, "Will I fit in? Will the team be nice? Will I be good enough to find my place in the team?"

All of these were immediately relieved on the first day. It was clear, very quickly, that what FairBreak claims to represent is a reality. The players and the staff where immediately inclusive, kind, fun and all very devoted to representing FairBreak to the best of their ability. I could see that most of the girls on the team were at a slightly higher level than me but that did not seem to matter. I got support and advice at training, kind words, and really felt included like a full member of the team every single second. I room shared with Roberta [Moretti-Avery, Captain of Brazil] and being able to discuss our cricket stories, and our challenges and triumphs in our home countries was again, horizon-opening. I really felt like we came from similar backgrounds and settings, and to hear how in Brazil they have addressed these challenges and solved them, filled me with ideas and hope to try and contribute to cricket in France.

Training with Geoff [Lawson] was amazing. He always gave me time and consideration and I received advice that will truly stay with me for the long term.

The thing I benefited most from during the Tour was being around the other girls, hearing how they approached each game, how they went about their business, how the skipper spoke to the team, and how they were constantly seeking to play their best cricket as a team. Even when a game was won, they were always thinking, together, "How can we get this batter out? How can we make her play a shot she doesn't want to play?" And any player could pitch in. There were never any issues or debates about who batted at what number, who bowled how many overs, who did this or that. Every run, wicket and good play was celebrated together, for the team. I have heard coaches try to explain this countless times, but you cannot really get it until you see it and are part of it, and this really has impacted how I approach each game and my own cricket.

In France, getting decent amounts of good quality cricket can be a struggle and I was happy to go on Tour and be 12th woman if I wasn't up to scratch to play to the team's standards. But again, I quickly realised the team's standard was playing their best cricket whilst giving players opportunity. We all felt fully included and part of the team and so proud to represent FairBreak.

And did I mention the time off the pitch? Dinners together, cinema, days off spent exploring. In Edinburgh, especially, I had a wonderful time. We mixed and met in different places, planned things together (we did a Harry Potter Escape Room which was fun). Simple things like travelling together from England to Scotland, getting to the pitch on the bus in the morning with the music on, sharing the hotel rooms and gathering in the evenings for relaxation inside or outside the hotel.

It really was an all-inclusive experience. As I said, I learned a huge amount with regards to cricket but also genuinely felt like I was on a holiday with a bunch of friends I have known for a long time. Being valued regardless of where you come from or your background or your skill as long as you are passionate and embody the values of the team, is something that you cannot teach or impress upon a group if it isn't happening. To stand alongside all these amazing players and people, in the ranks, with the flag of my country on my back ... there are no words for that.

So, thank you, it was important for me to tell you directly but also hopefully, to give you a little bit of insight as to how I experienced the Tour.

It gave me so much inspiration, motivation, and ideas about how to get better myself, train harder but also bring more cricket or different cricket back to France. I do not want this Tour to be just about me having a good time. I want to bring the benefits back to France. I hope that this has opened a door for good things to happen and I am intent on doing my bit as much as I can. I am planning more coaching sessions (going to the UK and getting coaches to come to us for weekends), buying a bowling machine for us to be able to use, trying to get a team together to go to La Manga for a seven-aside tournament, maybe even joining a club in the Netherlands and travelling up [from southern France] once a month during the season to get more games. Maybe one day I will take a year off and travel the world to play cricket. I thought you had to be a top-level player to do that, but now I know if I am brave enough and willing to do it, I can definitely do it.

This may all sound very obvious to people from big cricket countries. I could see that most of the players on Tour had sponsors for gear, a number of different coaches for different skills, training camps (in the UK or abroad) etc... this is not the case in France. Every game, coaching event, little tournament or tour, new piece of training kit etc. is invaluable to increase access and improve our players' skills set.

On that note, the kit was a great surprise, the pads and thigh guards are wonderful and the bat I was given at the end of the tour meant so much (in 12 years of playing cricket it's only my 4th bat - I still have and use all the old ones). I will use it well!

Receiving the invitation for FairBreak 2023 was both unexpected and extraordinary. I describe it as the cricket equivalent of receiving a letter to go to Hogwarts! You probably know from Elle [Williams] that my current job may mean that I cannot make it. Of course, this is something that I worry about, but speaking to Elle on the phone she reminded me to give myself some time just to fully enjoy the pleasure of being invited regardless of whether I can come or not. Best advice I could have ever received! I feel very honoured, privileged, and proud to have received an invitation and I really do hope I can come. I remind myself that although this time around my job may prevent me from going, this same job allowed me to go on the FairBreak XI 2022 Tour in the first place.

The FairBreak website says that every player should get their fair break. Well, I got mine this year and I could not have hoped or dreamed for better, and I only feel grateful. I would love more, but if that is to be my fair break, I would not swap it for anything else. Being the bearer of the French flag into the FairBreak family is something I will always be proud of, and I really hope the door has been opened for me. I wish every player, regardless of their country, their experience, or their skill to be given an opportunity like I have been given.

All I can say is thank you for creating FairBreak, I hope that I get to meet you in the flesh and give you a heartfelt hug someday. I mean every single word of what I have written above. And thanks for having me in the FairBreak family.

Take care,

Poppy McGeown

Letter from America
Julie Abbott, USA Cricket Coach

Julie Abbott, originally from England, is an avid cricketer. She manages and coaches CanAm United Women's Cricket Association which is helping to promote first-class women's cricket throughout the Americas. Abbott has also managed Team USA and is currently one of three selectors for the USA national women's team.

Members of CanAm get lots of match experience while promoting the spirit of cricket in a variety of settings and cricketing conditions. Players sign up with CanAm for different reasons; some wish to simply enjoy the camaraderie of cricket, while others are aspiring to play at the highest level, because CanAm is a development platform helping players gain more exposure to benefit their cricketing careers.

As a Master Educator for the ICC, Abbott also works closely with Fara Gorsi the ICC's Regional Manager for the Americas. She said, *"The Americas Region is home to many passionate female cricketers who constantly yearn for competition and the opportunities to Play More! The West Indies aside, this geographically vast continent is home to several ICC Associate Nations, and their representative female players are vehemently living for that next opportunity to train and play.*

"In the North, Canada and the USA are fierce competitors, as are Brazil and Argentina in the South. Collectively, the players have a deep, common bond and an understanding of the importance of advancing the women's and girl's game within the region. They know that the stronger they become, the stronger their neighbours will become. And they want that. They are thirsty for growth!"

"FairBreak has made this region feel significant because players from the USA, Canada, Argentina and Brazil were invited to play in Dubai in May 2022. They now feel engaged and included. Fast forward to October 2022, and the chatter about this "wonderful movement" has expanded to other areas within the region such as Peru, Chile and Mexico. The all-important conversations about how to prepare for next year's South American Championships, or the ICC Regional

Qualifiers, now also include players chattering about how they too can get involved with FairBreak."

The USA had four players participating in the SDG FairBreak Invitational 2022 in Dubai. The USA Women's Captain, Sindhu Sriharsha, skippered The Warriors. Sriharsha was the only captain who represented an Associate Nation. The other USA players were Tara Norris, Shebani Bhaskar and Geetika Kodali.

As USA Women's Cricket Coordinator, Julie was invited to the FairBreak Invitational in Dubai to be Team Manager for the Warriors. When asked to reflect on the Dubai Tournament she enthusiastically remarked that the event offered players from the USA the opportunity to be exposed to "first-class everything".

She added, *"The opportunities in the USA for our female players to play regularly, let alone on noteworthy grounds, are rare and challenging. Our country is vast, and we currently have only a handful of good facilities like Moosa Cricket Stadium in Pearland, Texas, Broward County Stadium in Florida, Woodley Park Cricket Complex in California and Church Street Park in Morrisville, North Carolina.*

"While we have made significant strides to establish a solid women's domestic pathway and our future looks bright, there are still numerous challenges for our growing pool of young talent. In the USA, the girls rarely get to play on turf, and they often have to board an airplane, at their own expense, to take a four-hour flight to play at a competitive level. This will change once we begin to see more players competing locally and coming up through our development pathway, but for now it remains difficult and costly.

"FairBreak offers our more talented players the opportunity to play at a higher level, and truly experience what that next professional step-up looks and feels like. What better way to bridge the glaring gap between Associate Nations and Full Members by inspiring Associate players, coaches, umpires and managers to learn and grow by participating alongside some of the most widely known names in the sport?

"The Warriors Team had players of thirteen different nationalities participating. This immediately created an air of fun and challenge for the players, captain

and Head Coach, Julia Price. While there was a varying degree of talent and experience on the team, everyone benefited. The girls learned about breast injury and the impact it has on player well-being and performance from Australian breast health expert, Associate Professor Deirdre McGhee. The less experienced players acquired more game awareness and absorbed knowledge from the best coaching staff and players in the world of women's cricket. Plus, they simply shared stories and experiences with their teammates and built enduring bonds. For the USA players, the FairBreak experience in Dubai was life changing."

Letter from Georgie Heath
Sports Journalist, Commentator and Podcaster

It's hard to find the right words for something as unique as FairBreak, and what it means to be part of it. It's like nothing else I've ever seen in sport, and to even play a small part in a cog that is whirring at a faster rate day by day is unbelievably special.

From the moment I got to Heathrow and caught up with Adam Collins and his family, I was fully engrossed in the movement, what it could be and the display we were about to put on at #FBI22. Despite not being seated together, Adam and I chatted about all things FairBreak, cricket, commentary, women's cricket and more, most of the way to Dubai. So, when we landed, I was even more certain we were in for an incredible couple of weeks at the inaugural FairBreak Invitational.

For me, it was my first proper foray into a truly global competition – and what is more global than having over 35 countries represented?! And that, too, is part of the beauty of the FairBreak movement, it celebrates players, coaches, support staff, media, and everyone in between and provides opportunities to showcase the reach of the game.

What it did for my own growth is incomparable to anything else I have experienced, and I'm sure I speak for others in all areas of the FairBreak family. That's the beauty of FairBreak.

I won't ever forget that first stint on commentary alongside Collo. Everything was new to everyone. What was coming? Would it be the success we knew it could be? Well, when I had the chance to call the first FairBreak Invitational six as it was launched off Sri Lanka's Chamari Athapaththu's bat, I knew we were in for an incredible ride.

There was an energy around the hotel, the cricket ground and on social media sparked by what FairBreak is and what it means. We were all fully aware of this, but to see the response around the world, and the reach the game could have, it still gives me goosebumps.

Never did I think I would witness a Rwandan teenager claiming the scalp of an Australian International plus two run outs in the same innings. But when Henriette Ishimwe launched herself on the scene in Barmy Army's game against Spirit, that's exactly what I did see. There were far too many moments like that to pick them out.

On a personal note, the individual growth my involvement allowed me was indescribable. I have drawn on much of the learnings from FairBreak regularly, in my work, since and have also made some friends for life, both on the pitch and off it. Being part of the FairBreak family is beyond what I could ever have imagined, and I cannot wait to continue this ride behind the mic and on the camera alongside some of the best people I've ever met.

You never know, maybe next year I'll brush the dust off my pads, and we can have a media match too. Although I might need some winter nets sessions first!

Georgie Heath

@GeorgieHeath27
listen to Women's Cricket Chat on Spotify

Coffee at the MCG with BBL Coach Greg Shipperd

In early September 2022, during the writing of this book, Shaun Martyn and I met for coffee with Greg Shipperd at the Melbourne Cricket Ground's café. Shipperd coaches the Sydney Sixers in Australia's Big Bash League (BBL). He has also coached the India Premier League's Delhi Daredevils, plus he has coached Tasmanian and Victorian squads. He and Martyn first met back in the 1990s when Martyn was working as a player manager, and they "tussled" over player contracts. Shipperd and Geoff Lawson were cricket opponents in the 1980s when the former played for West Australia and the latter for New South Wales. Lawson was Shipperd's assistant coach for a while and they have gone from being on-field opponents to friends.

Over coffee, Shipperd told me that he has been "listening in the shadows" to Martyn and Lawson "plotting and planning this FairBreak notion". He has provided them with many ideas over the years. He told me he has a "fertile mind" when it comes to marketing, and he has his finger on the pulse of all things cricket. For example, he recently recommended Martyn purchase FairBreak's next line of sustainably produced cricket uniforms from Tsunami Sport whose teamwear eco apparel is made from recycled plastics. He is also able to give direction when it comes to TV deals, coaching, and those important relationships that need nurturing when an innovative women's cricket tournament needs to be organised. "Having Greg Shipperd's imprimatur gives us serious credibility", Martyn informed me.

Solar Buddy is a charity helping children living in energy poverty by providing them with solar lights and is FairBreak's Corporate Social Responsibility (CSR) partner. Solar Buddy lights are small renewable-energy powered units invented by Brisbane man, Simon Doble.

With the generous assistance of corporate funding (they cost approx. 1500rupees/AU$28 to make), FairBreak distributes Solar Buddy lights in India where millions of homes are plunged into darkness every night. Energy poverty on the sub-continent is permanent. Through Martyn, Greg Shipperd learnt of the millions of Indians who die each year from breathing in the fumes from kerosene or paraffin used for cooking and lighting. Women and children under fourteen are most affected and they end up with the lungs and health conditions of heavy smokers. Four to five million die every year.

Before the pandemic hit, Shipperd spear headed the Captain's Cause initiative by getting Australia's cricket captains to unite to end energy poverty. Today, he would like to see the Captain's Cause extended to the coaching space to engage cricket coaches in Australia and around the world to raise the profile further. Shipperd told me he wants to get Virat Kohli and Rohit Sharma, the former and current Indian national captains, photographed in a Solar Buddy Captain's Cause shirt. He is hoping to enlist the help of current Australian Men's Captain Pat Cummins for this.

"A Solar Buddy light is as precious to an Indian child as a cricket ball", Shipperd said. "The Solar Buddy lights are also important to women in India who use them for security when they leave their homes at night to use the toilet."

Martyn added, "Naresh Patel, of ANP Solar is another collaborator of ours in India. Patel studied for an engineering degree in India and came to Australia to do his Masters. He lived and worked in Australia for fifteen years where we got to know each other through cricket. When Patel moved back to Ahmedabad to set up his successful solar business, he brought Australian installation standards and expertise home to the Indian market. Patel grew up in a little house in India with no light. As a child and teenager, he used to go and stay at a friend's home during the school year because there was a light at their house, and he could study there. Patel understands the lived experience of energy poverty."

Shipperd is looking forward to mentoring and providing cricket intellect to FairBreak's coaches, assistant coaches and managers. It was hoped that he would act as a coaching mentor in Dubai, but other obligations meant he could not go to the United Arab Emirates with the FairBreak management team.

During our meeting, Martyn, Shipperd and I discussed the FairBreak Invitational in Dubai. Martyn told us, "The two teams that made the FairBreak Invitational final may not have been the strongest on paper, but they successfully used the experience and skills of every player in their squads to best advantage. The captains, coaches and managers need inclusive personalities and the ability to adapt to having thirteen different nationalities in their team and to approach the play with an open mind. This is not a place for thinking about the result MORE than the players. We want our captains and coaches to think about the players AND the result.

"The Associate Nation players lifted quickly. Within seventy-two hours of arriving, they were different players. And the established players got performance anxiety. Because all these Associate Nation players were looking at them and thinking, "Well you're supposed to be pretty special, when are you going to do something special". Players from the Tier 1 countries talk about this. Sophie Devine, for example, was nervous. She told me that.

"There is expectation from all the other players. And this is healthy. It's a learning experience for them having to overcome that performance anxiety. When you are the No.1 player in a team there is innate pressure on you to perform. So, the whole standard lifts. And that's what happened for the two teams in the final. They had included everyone. Nobody felt that they were not an equal.

"At one point in a Barmy Army game, Kavisha Kumari was massively outscoring Deandra Dottin at the other end, and it was hard to pick who was the global superstar. The Associates are not intimidated once they get out there. Sterre Kalis is now a world class player, she was outscoring Sophie Devine.

"FairBreak will retain a large cohort of the players who were in Dubai and keep the core teams. It's important to create and maintain team identity. Hayley Matthews has said to me, "Don't put me in any other team Shaun, I'm a Warrior. Don't put me anywhere else". They've already identified with their teams. In the Asian qualifiers recently, there were groups of FairBreak players from different countries, who had all played in Dubai, being photographed together in their national uniforms posting on social media things like, "Falcons Together Again". They are now identifying as much with their team brand after two and a half weeks in Dubai as they are with their own countries! We will keep that strong cohort and change out a couple of the coaches. Charlette Edwards is now available. She wanted to coach in Dubai but couldn't get a release from other duties."

As an individual with little knowledge of cricket, I asked Shipperd to explain what managers and coaches do. He informed me, "The manager's role involves a bit of everything. Transport, accommodation, uniforms, wellbeing. Ensuring players are where they are supposed to be at the correct time with the right kit. In terms of injuries, they liaise with the physio. The team manager is the all-encompassing problem solver. Not just the principal of the school, they are the teacher as well. They are the fixer.

"If players are not on a down day, the coach will be doing match reviews and match previews. They run the meetings leading into games. After a game they will review what has occurred. They run the trainings. They deal with every player's emotional and physical wellbeing. They must be a soft landing for players. The coach picks them up and gets them ready mentally, emotionally and strategically. The coach will have a planning strategy with the captain around team leadership. The coach will be problem solving issues with the manager. The coach plots the course. The manager comes into support that, along with the assistant coach who might have a particular skill set. They might be a specialist bowling or batting coach."

Martyn told us that he had a specific request of his coaches and assistant coaches in Dubai. He did not want players selected or non-selected by text. He wanted players spoken to by their coach and the reasons explained, in person, why they were or were not playing. He believes that is a respectful thing to do. With fifteen in a squad. Only eleven go onto the field. The other four are expected to be at the ground watching, doing warmups, learning, participating, observing, running stuff out and supporting their teammates. The coach picks a squad of players with a variety of skill sets to win the game.

Another rule Martyn introduced in Dubai, which will be repeated in Hong Kong, was that every participant had to play a minimum of two games. He expanded, "Although this creates a strategic issue for the coaches, I wanted to ensure that in a tournament like FairBreak's, we were not flying a player from somewhere like Vanuatu or Bhutan to have them sitting on the sidelines for two and a half weeks, and then going away feeling deflated because they never got on the field or put under the microscope."

On player performance, Martyn also said, "Players get bowling maps and batting charts and watch a massive amount of footage on other players. They get exposed to large amounts of intelligence about their opposition. Then they get to a tournament like FairBreak's, and there are no bowling charts on Anju Gurung from Bhutan or Henriette Ishimwe from Rwanda. So elite players are facing bowlers they have absolutely no knowledge about. They don't know what's going to happen. It's like Day One all over again for them. It's a challenge for the experienced cricketers because they are being faced with players they've never seen or heard of before. They must think on their feet and respond quickly to the unknowns.

"Suzie Bates is an experienced player and has been part of FairBreak from the start. She opened the bowling in every Falcons game with Anju Gurung from Bhutan. The first ball of the whole tournament was bowled by an Associate player from Bhutan. As soon as Suzie saw Gurung in the nets, she knew she was too good not to use. She immediately forgot about where the player was from. That had no relevance to Suzie. She only saw what Gurung could do. And that is exactly the attitude we want. Gurung bowls amazing left arm in-swingers. Medium pace. In Bhutan she plays men's cricket. She isn't intimidated by anyone. I have footage of her bowling to the men, and they can't hit it.

"She'll be in the FairBreak WBBL team if we can get that happening. The WBBL need to use FairBreak as a resource. We've got all this knowledge about all these players around the world.

"The beauty of the FairBreak Invitational was that the players loved that they were in the same hotel for the whole tournament. They could play, have a break, then play again. Four days in a row was too much for everyone. Not just the players but the broadcasting team, umpires, commentators, everyone. Three days consecutive play is best.

"In the lead up to Dubai, we had a Zoom call with all the managers to introduce them to each other. We did the same with the coaches. Then we released the teams to the managers and the coaches so that they could have communications with all their players. Two weeks out from the tournament, the coaches and managers were in touch with all their players.

"In Dubai, we brought everyone together and handed the teams over to the managers. We didn't want to be overly influential in what was happening.

I had a private meeting with the captains and Mignon du Preez [who will be FairBreak's Head of Marketing from January 2023] and I spoke to them about our expectations and what we stand for. Suzie Bates and Sana Mir were there, and they are steeped in what we do. But the others were not. It was a fantastic meeting. We also had a welcome function, and players were asked to come in cocktail attire not team uniform. Again, I spoke about what it all meant, and our expectations."

Shipperd told Martyn he considered the media interaction after the games outstanding. He said, "The storytelling was fantastic. It exposed the girls to the experience of being put in front of a camera and asked questions. That's a learning experience right there."

Martyn shared with us that another requirement they introduced for the after-match media involved the team captain bringing along the Player of the Match. And if the Player of the Match was not from an Associate Nation, then another Associate Nation player had to attend the press conference so they could be asked questions and get media experience. In that way, there was an Associate Nation player in every press conference.

We also spoke about the commentating team, and Martyn told us, "Annesha Ghosh has been writing for *ESPN* for the last six years. She got her job at *ESPN* through winning a commentary competition, yet they have never let her commentate. She did a lot of the media for FairBreak, and we put her in the commentary box. We also gave Georgie Heath a stint at commentating. Georgie was brilliant. She applied online and directed me to her podcasts. She was a sensation as an interviewer, running the press conferences and her knowledge of the game.

"Isabelle Duncan has always commentated for BBC Radio, but she had never done television commentary. We tried to give opportunity right across every aspect of the tournament. And we unearthed all this talent. Lesego Pooe applied through the website. Henry [Geoff Lawson] and I had a Zoom call with her. We initially thought we'd give her sideline interviews, but once we had interviewed her on Zoom we wanted her as the host. Now she is the face of FairBreak.

"For Hong Kong 2023, most of the teams will remain the same or similar. If the coach isn't retained, the manager will be, so there will be some continuity. There will be three days of training and net sessions. The women engage as a team much faster than the men. Within thirty minutes of meeting, they've got a WhatsApp group sorted and have their whole social agenda organised. Men tend to break off into smaller groups. Every time we bring the women together, they bond in a different way."

I asked Shipperd how he sees FairBreak fitting into the landscape of world cricket. He said, "It's a great steppingstone. It's the flower blossoming. FairBreak are spreading awareness of the awesome talent in the Associate Nations."

We discussed FairBreak's next move and Martyn shared with us, "The next step is to get a FairBreak team into next year's WBBL. A squad of fifteen from between ten and twelve Associate Nations. The number of eyeballs that we can bring to that tournament from a broadcasting perspective is huge. If Cricket Australia want to continue to grow their support base and their broadcasting revenue, then they must look outside of Australia. We only have twenty-five million people here.

"They need to look at players like Sita Rana Magar from Nepal. When she did the Pushpa in Dubai, we got 100,000 views in twenty four hours. We are taking the game further. We can base the FairBreak team in Canberra where they have access to all the consulates. Manuka Oval is virtually unused. It's a white elephant. We can engage with all those consulates and the business community of Canberra.

"There are no teams in the WBBL with that kind of reach. Here's an opportunity to grow the WBBL's broadcast base and revenue. Today, I posted off Tornadoes uniforms to a guy and his two daughters in South Australia. They are massive Tornadoes fans. They've already got Tornadoes backpacks and now they will be wearing Tornadoes shirts. Imagine what we could do from a merchandising perspective if we have players from ten different countries playing under a FairBreak banner? Cricket Australia would be sending gear all around the world.

"The WBBL team can be an aspirational goal for the Associate Nation players taking part in the FairBreak tournaments. We keep building their profile and skill set for a WBBL spot. And then I want to win the WBBL with a FairBreak team! How amazing would it be for global women's cricket if a FairBreak team won the WBBL? If Cricket Australia take a big picture view, just imagine how competitive the next season could be? That's the goal. It's achievable and within our capabilities."

AFTERWORD

What's Next for FairBreak?

It's late October 2022 and I have just returned from a meeting with Board members of USA Cricket, and representatives of the ICC. It is particularly pleasing that we now have such a supportive relationship with the ICC. As I have said, right from the start, our intention was always to work closely with cricket's governing bodies. I am looking forward to a very strong and collaborative partnership with the ICC. We have all come to understand our roles and the part we play in the development and advancement of cricket and specifically, in our space, women's cricket.

While I was on the US West Coast, I also spent time at the U/19 National Women's Championships in Los Angeles. FairBreak has contracted two players from those championships, and they will appear in Hong Kong in April 2023. We also hope to have a second FairBreak Invitational each year in the USA.

The United States is an incredible market and has enormous cricket potential. Men's cricket in the USA will always struggle to get a foothold because baseball plays too big a role in the fabric of American life. The women's game, on the other hand, is a sleeping giant. Women's soccer is huge in America, and I believe that women's cricket will follow a similar trajectory. There is no competition.

FairBreak has also had very productive meetings with Cricket Australia with reference to having a FairBreak XI in the 2023 Women's Big Bash League (WBBL).

Olivia Thornton, the CEO of ACT Cricket, has been an enormous help with this, as has Greg Shipperd, the coach of the Big Bash League's Sydney Sixers. If successful, the FairBreak team will play out of Canberra. A squad of fifteen female players will be invited from Associate Nations. It seems appropriate that a FairBreak WWBL squad should be based in the national capital. A FairBreak team will bring a large global audience to the WBBL, and Cricket Australia can lead the development of inclusion and diversity though the women's game.

If FairBreak can host two fortnightly tournaments each year and field a team in the WBBL we can create enormous opportunity. Emerging female cricketers can showcase their skills in a tournament setting and then move into a WBBL squad. When they return to their national teams they go back as fully formed players with a wealth of experience to impart. Having this system in place would accelerate the development of many Associate Nation teams and create a stronger and more diverse global program. FairBreak sees this as being a complementary program in concert with the programs now being run by the ICC.

It is a testament to the magnificent work that everyone has done that we are now being spoken about as a significant feature in the landscape of world cricket.

FairBreak will continue to innovate, and we look to lead the discussion around creating opportunity, diversity and inclusion. We will continue to work to reduce our environmental impact at tournaments and to support sustainability in sport.

There is a bright future ahead.

Shaun Martyn

'We haven't come this far, just to come this far'

Shaun Martyn

FURTHER READING

10 May 2013

Clare Connor
Head of England Women's Cricket England and Wales Cricket Board
Lord's Cricket Ground
London, NW8 8QZ, England.

BY: Email

Dear Clare

I refer to our recent discussions regarding the possible inception of a women's twenty20 international cricket league, proposed to be conducted over a 10 day to two week period in early 2014 (the **T20 Tournament**) by Women's ICL Pty Ltd (**WICL**).

Just to recap on what we have discussed, at this stage, WICL can confirm that the T20 Tournament is likely to involve the following key components:

(a)   Six competing teams, comprised of international and domestic players from the ICC's member countries (subject to their board approval to participate). The teams will be sponsored by six corporate partners, and the names of such teams (eg Olay 'Whites'). By doing this, it will provide us with flexibility as to where we schedule the T20 Tournament.

(b)   The T20 Tournament will be conducted over a 10-day to two week period in one location.

(c)   WICL will work with the ICC and each of the players' home boards to schedule the Tournament at a time that does not conflict with each player's international commitments.

(d)   Players who express an interest in participating in the T20 Tournament will be allocated to the competing teams based on an auction process.

(e)   Players who are ranked in the top 50 Twenty20 players in the world (based on ICC statistics) will be invited to participate. The remaining 28 places will be available to all female players who advise WICL of their interest in being a part of the auction selection process.

(f)   Players will be ranked as either a 1st, 2nd or 3rd tier player and will be paid a participation fee based on this ranking. ICC and home board statistics will be used to determine the rankings of the players.

Prize money will be awarded to the team which wins the T20 Tournament. We are proposing to conduct the tournament on an annual basis.

We are confident that we have a commercial model that will sustain the event, whilst have the benefit of providing an additional event on the women's international calendar. It will assist the players financially, as well as providing a unique learning environment at international players get to play alongside each other in the teams. However, running a financially viable cricket competition is not WICL's sole or only focus.

Importantly, we are seeking to work in tandem with the ICC and all cricket boards so that we can support each of their endeavors in growing the women's game. We certainly do not wish to conflict with any aspect of the current calendar and will work with all key stakeholders to ensure this continues.

A major tenant of our business plan is to, through the ICC, direct a percentage of our profits back into women's cricket development programs. Our view is that the ICC is the right body to do this through because:

(a)   by directing such funds through the ICC, we will be able to ensure that the fund reach the appropriate programs for women and girls wherever the need is greatest; and

Women's ICL Pty Ltd (ABN 74 162 744 989) – PO Box 426 Coogee, NSW, 2034 Australia

(b)   the ICC has the greatest insight into where investment is required to develop the women's game, whether that be through more players or more fans.

Further, in addition to having 78 contracted players to six teams, we are also looking to allocate one additional player to each team for the purposes of player development. We would ask the ICC and the ICC member boards to advise us of any emerging player under the age of 25, to which they would like us to consider to allocating such an opportunity. We are going to brand this as our "Pathways Initiative". The Pathways Initiative would be comprised of the following basic components:

(a)   allocation to a competing team;

(b)   paid a scholarship fee (such fee not yet determined;

(c)   opportunity to participate in all briefings, meetings, trainings, preparation and match day activities.

Further, by having been a Pathway Initiative recipient, such players may impress themselves to make their way onto the team list of 13 in future years.

We have also identified 12 marquee players who we want to be the face of the T20 Tournament. We have had initial discussions with such players and to-date, all are very enthusiastic and excited by the prospect. Our sense is that a T20 Tournament of this kind will provide the players with valuable financial support, important media and public exposure, as well as a unique learning environment. We are looking to present a tournament that gives fans a unique insight into the talents of international and domestic women's cricketers, including interactive ways to broadcast the T20 Tournament and the innovative positioning of camera placement.

Of course, it goes without saying that in conducting in such event, player welfare issues will be given the highest of priorities and we will be committed to working with both ICC member boards and relevant player associations to ensure everyone is comfortable that the players are in strong, supportive high performance teams for the period of the T20 Tournament. WICL has a well-balanced management team in terms of commercial and high performance sport experience and this blend ensures the players interest are at the forefront of any decisions made in relation to the T20 Tournament.

In summary, what WICL is seeking from the ICC is support, not in terms of funding, but rather in terms of consultation and dialogue.

As I have stated earlier, and I am firmly on record as stating, WICL wishes only to work in conjunction with the ICC and in support and growth of women's cricket.

WICL looks forward to a long and constructive relationship with the ICC and I look forward to further opportunities to discuss this with you over the coming months as we further progress our planning and preparation.

Best Regards

(not signed as sent electronically)

Shaun Martyn

CEO

Women's ICL Pty Ltd

18 October 2013

Mr Shaun Martyn
CEO
Women's ICL Pty Ltd
PO Box 426
COOGEE NSW 2034

Dear Shaun

Women's ICL

I write to confirm the support of the Federation of International Cricketers' Associations (FICA) for the proposed Women's ICL.

FICA, and our individual member associations, are strong supporters of women's cricket and we think the Women's ICL concept is a brilliant one for the women's game and all female cricketers, now and in the future.

Women's cricket is undoubtedly on the rise and the skill level of the players nowadays is exceptional. Bringing all of the best players in world cricket together for a tournament will showcase just how good our female players are and we believe the flow on effect will be substantial for the women's game moving forward.

We are also thrilled at the level of priority being given to the welfare of the players and the commitment you are giving to working with the ICC, its member boards and the player associations in putting this event together. This commitment will ensure the players will be well looked after and the tournament will run smoothly.

We look forward to working closely with you on this initiative as you progress towards your launch date.

Please call me at any time if we can assist.

Kind regards

PAUL MARSH
Executive Chairman

cc   Lisa Sthalekar, WICL

FAIRBREAK

David Collier
Chief Executive

DGC/kjh/01-14

20 January 2014

Mr Shaun Martyn
Womens ICL Pty Ltd
PO Box 426
Coogee
NSW 2034
Australia

Dear Mr Martyn,

Thank you for your letter of 19 January concerning the women's cricket concept.

As Ms Connor explained in her email of 27 May 2013, the priority for the ICC Women's Cricket Committee is to firm up on bi-lateral cricket for the next few years and those proposals are now with ICC and its Members. As Ms Connor commented 'We have a significant amount of work to do to scope our potential structure/costs to then progress within ICC and our own home Boards. This is a priority as it will address one of our strategic aims of closing the gap amongst the top eight teams and will provide us with a clear World Cup qualification pathway. The view was that if this process is to be successful over the next 12 months, the introduction of a privately run T20 league at the same time would not be helpful.'

We share your desire to support the growth of women's cricket but under the ownership of ICC and its members and in line with the priorities the ICC Women's Cricket Committee has determined for the best way to grow women's cricket. I am afraid your proposal does not appear to reflect those priorities and hence I am afraid at this time we cannot support the proposal.

Yours sincerely,

David G Collier
Chief Executive

CC: C Connor, C G Clarke

England and Wales Cricket Board

* * *

From Playground to Test Arena

Lord's Cricket Ground, London NW8 8QZ, England. Tel:+44(0)20 7432 1211 Fax: +44(0)20 7289 5619 www.ecb.co.uk

 England and Wales Cricket Board Limited Registered Office: Lord's Cricket Ground, London NW8 8QZ, England. Registered in England No.3251364

https://www.theguardian.com/sport/2014/jun/04/england-womens-international-cricket-league-ecb

THE GUARDIAN

ENGLAND WILL NOT RELEASE PLAYERS FOR WOMEN'S INTERNATIONAL CRICKET LEAGUE

By Andy Wilson 4 June 2014

England have increased the rhetoric against plans for a privately run women's cricket tournament and stressed that they will not be releasing their centrally contracted players to play in it.

Sketchy details of the Women's International Cricket League, a Twenty20 competition which would theoretically be staged in Singapore, have emerged from Australia over the last couple of months, with the former Southern Stars all-rounder Lisa Sthalekar named as the driving force behind the plans alongside her business partner Shaun Martyn, and a variety of cricket names claimed to be in support including Clive Lloyd, Geoff Lawson and Paul Marsh, who is the head of the Australian Cricketers' Association.

The England and Wales Cricket Board has dismissed claims that the competition has endorsement from Cricket Australia and the International Cricket Council, stressing instead that the development of the women's game should be left to the ICC and national governing bodies.

Clare Connor, the ECB's head of women's cricket and chair of the ICC women's committee, said: "There has been a lot of misleading and as yet unsubstantiated information around how far advanced the proposed WICL is. I stress that from an ECB perspective this competition is not on our agenda.

"The immediate focus for international women's cricket is the ICC International Women's Championship, which the ICC board approved in January. For the first time ever, the top eight ranked women's teams in the world will play each other in a bilateral competition, with results determining qualification for the 2017 ICC Women's World Cup. This is a real game-changer for the women's game."

She added: "The ICC and its members do not recognise privately owned tournaments or leagues in the men's or women's game. The ICC and the members have made significant investment into women's cricket over the ten years to create a commercially viable product. In particular there is recognition that a Women's World Twenty20 every two years will be the vehicle through which to build commercial investment in the women's game, and it is for the ICC and the members to capitalise on this and take it forward.

"Any Twenty20 tournament that features the best players in the world outside ICC competitions would need to be run and controlled by one of the full members, as opposed to by a private operator."

Giles Clarke, the ECB's chairman who has been a leading advocate of the women's game, said: "Put simply there is no support or interest for this proposed event. Women's cricket has made enormous strides in recent years with great investment in the game from the grassroots to the international level. At the same time, thanks to the ICC global events and member investment, we have seen new and exciting players emerge on the world stage. This has to be the continued route for the women's game, not a privately run competition."

https://www.cricket.com.au/news/southern-stars-cricket-australia-ecb-have-not-endorsed-female-ipl-wicl/2014-06-05

AAP AND CRICKET.COM.AU

WOMEN'S ICL NOT ENDORSED

5 June 2014

The two biggest governing bodies in women's cricket, Cricket Australia and the England and Wales Cricket Board, have both insisted they have not endorsed a female cricket equivalent of the IPL run by an Australian businessman.

Shaun Martyn is proposing to launch a Women's International Cricket League (WICL), with the aim of attracting the world's best players just as the lucrative Twenty20 Indian Premier League does for leading cricketers in the men's game.

The proposed tournament, which sees Martyn in partnership with former Australia World Cup-winner Lisa Sthalekar, could see players earn AUD$42,800 in 12 days - small change by IPL standards but a huge amount of money in terms of women's cricket.

But England, who this year put their women's team on a full-time professional footing, remain wary of Martyn's plan which has yet to be endorsed by a major national governing body or the International Cricket Council.

Instead, the ECB has put is faith in the new ICC International Women's Championship, a one-day tournament which will lead to qualification for the 2017 World Cup.

"There has been a lot of misleading and as yet unsubstantiated information around how far advanced the proposed WICL is," said Clare Connor, the ECB's head of women's cricket, in a board statement issued on Wednesday.

Connor, a former England captain who is also chair of the ICC women's committee, added: "I stress that from an ECB perspective this competition is not on our agenda."

The ECB comments are in line with Cricket Australia's position on the proposed tournament.

"We are working hard to professionalise the women's game," said Cricket Australia's Executive General Manager of Team Performance Pat Howard.

"Last year's restructuring of the contracting system for female international and state cricketers has seen our elite players become some of the best paid female athletes in the country.

"We are continuing to provide our elite players with further opportunities. This includes developing a model for a women's T20 Big Bash League, which is seen as an important step in further professionalising women's cricket.

"As a result of these efforts, female cricket participation at the grassroots level is at an all-time high, with a 18% increase from 2012-13 taking us to 180,000 female participants.

"In relation to comments by the Women's ICL, CA has not endorsed the competition in any way.

"The proposed Women's International Cricket League has also recently been discussed by the International Cricket Council and its Members and was not supported.

"However, we are highly committed to developing female cricket at all levels of the game as we work to make it Australia's favourite sport for women and girls."

SINGAPORE CRICKET ASSOCIATION
The governing body of cricket in Singapore

4th June 2014

TO WHOM IT MAY CONCERN

This is to confirm that Singapore Cricket Association has been in discussion with Mr Shaun Martin and Ms Lisa Sthalekar from Women's International Cricket League (WICL) for the last 12 months in regards to hosting the inaugural Women's International Cricket League event in Singapore.

Should WICL, get necessary approvals from the International Cricket Council, Singapore Cricket Association would be happy to have the tournament staged in Singapore through the Singapore Cricket Association.

Should you have any queries on the above, please feel free to contact the undersigned.

Prakash Vijaykumar
Chief Executive
Singapore Cricket Association

SINGAPORE CRICKET ASSOCIATION, 31 Stadium Crescent, Singapore 397639
Tel: (65) 6348 6566, Fax: (65) 6348 6506, E-mail: cricket@singnet.com.sg
Website: www.singaporecricket.org

FAIRBREAK

15th August 2014

Dear Lisa

Re Womens ICL

Many thanks for your recent correspondence on the proposed new T20 Women's ICL and the information provided as well as the associated press coverage that has been evident.

When we first saw this announcement like many we were overjoyed at the possibility of some of our best female players being given the opportunity of playing with and against the top players in the game at super venues with quality opportunities for support staff and coaches.

We were also delighted to see the initial support from some leading players in the game who thought likewise about the future of Women's T20 Cricket. Despite the set-backs that have occurred in getting approvals for the event we urge you to push on with your Cricket and Commercial plans to create something truly special for the Women's game of which we hope to be a part of when it is all finalised.

Although these are testing times for you and the organising team we hope that you can finalise a proposal that is ICC-compliant with all of the FM countries in agreement that this is the next bold step for women's cricket across the world.

We wish you the best of luck and look forward to further information on the event in due course where we hope that the Netherlands will have a presence in and around the teams.

With best wishes

Richard Cox

CEO
KNCB (Cricket Netherlands)
31-48 Wattbaan
Nieuwegein
Nr Utrecht
The Netherlands.

Koninklijke Nederlandse Cricket Bond
Wattbaan 31-49 · NL-3439 ML Nieuwegein · P.O. Box 2653 · NL-3430 GB Nieuwegein · The Netherlands
[T] +31 (0)30 7513780 · [F] +31 (0)30 7513781 · [W] www.kncb.nl · [E] cricket@kncb.nl
Bank 47 36 10 598 · BIC ABNANL2A · IBAN NL62ABNA0473610598

http://womens-cricket.blogspot.com/

EXTRACTS FROM WOMEN'S CRICKET BLOG

By Martin Davies

Sunday, 19 January 2014: Breakaway Women's T20 Tournament

Saturday saw the official announcement of the creation of the Women's International Cricket League and the launch of the www.wicl.org website. To many who follow the women's game it was no great surprise. There had been rumours that something was afoot for a few months. The WICL's stated aims are to create sporting opportunities for females - not only in cricket but starting with that. The main opportunity it seems is to play sport professionally and to make a living from it.

The faces behind the WICL are former Aussie all-rounder Lisa Sthalekar, and sports and events management specialist Shaun Martyn. Their plan is to host a T20 tournament, probably initially in Singapore, as they have been working with the Singapore Cricket Association, made up of six "franchise" teams, consisting of a mix of players from around the world. In addition to the teams who will be competing in the T20 World Cup in March - Australia, England, New Zealand, West Indies, India, Sri Lanka, South Africa, Pakistan, Bangladesh and Ireland - players would be drawn from all the cricket playing nations in the world, which might include players from Papua New Guinea, UAE, Holland and Japan for example. They might not be that strong as a team, but they may have individuals who could hold their own against the best in the world. With six teams you would expect the player pool to need to be in the region of 75/85 players.

The website suggests that WICL are still looking for partners - people to sponsor the teams, broadcast partners and the like. They are also presumably looking for players. It is obviously still very early days. Lisa Sthalekar says they are "working with the ICC on a number of matters", and that they "still have some work to do". No dates are yet being publicly banded about for when the tournament might be or how long it might go on for, but one would guess that it would be a three/four-week tournament on a league basis, culminating in semi-finals and a final perhaps all played on the same "finals' day". If it is to succeed than you would guess that it will need to be sanctioned by both the ICC and the various boards of the countries involved. That could take some doing. Clare Connor, in reply to a question asking what she thought of the WICL announcement, tweeted that "IF it gets off the ground and stacks up commercially, it could be an exciting addition to the international women's calendar."

It is a big "IF". Some analogies can be drawn to the emergence of Kerry Packer's World Series Cricket, back in late 1970s, when Packer took on the "establishment" ostensibly to improve the lot of players, but in reality, to obtain the exclusive television rights to Australian cricket for his company. The opportunity to make substantial amounts of money led many leading players to sign up, despite that meaning that they would be banned from playing for their countries. Here too money would be the over-riding factor for the players. Currently very few players in the world actually earn their living from playing cricket, although one or two of the Aussies who are now centrally contracted have the potential to earn $70,000 to $80,000pa. Some are also suggesting that England may also announce some improved central contracts for their players later this year.

It may be quite attractive to some boards to allow their players to play in the WICL, thereby supplementing their Board incomes. It means the risk of the competition flopping falls squarely on WICL, but the best players in the world get paid some decent money, and the profile of women's cricket and women cricketers is enhanced. On the back of that, boards may be able to get more people to watch their own international matches, both at the ground and on television. It would be a win, win situation.

As Clare Connor says it is a question of whether it stacks up commercially, which means that a broadcast company has to be involved and has to be willing to pay out some pretty big bucks to get the rights to the tournament. It is a nice idea, but it may just be a little early in the commercial-viability graph of women's cricket. The fact that anyone is even talking about it is testament itself to how far women's cricket has come in the last five years, and it may inspire boards to have the confidence to invest even more in the women's game for the benefit of all players.   MD 19/I/14

Tuesday, 3 June 2014: Can the WICL Succeed?

UPDATED 4th June 2014 - ECB issued a statement today which said that it does not have any support for WICL - Clare Connor "Any Twenty20 tournament that features the best players in the world outside ICC competitions would need to be run and controlled by one of the full members".

So where does that leave WICL now? ECB contracted players will presumably not be able to play, depending on the wording in their contracts. Will Cricket Australia and others follow suit? Will ECB or CA organise their own Women's T20 event? Will WICL try and go ahead without English and Australian contracted players? I'd expect an announcement from CA in the near future....

Trying to build a sustainable business based around women's cricket is a bit like trying to build a house without foundations. There is simply no money in women's cricket. The only reason players are currently being paid anything (and there are only a handful who are genuinely full-time professional players) is as a result of money from the men's game or generous sponsors (take a bow Momentum in South Africa).

So, you have to applaud 14 Degrees, the company behind the proposed Women's International Cricket League, who are trying to stage a Women's T20 tournament for six global teams, playing 17 matches over 12 days in one location, with all the players being paid between $5,000 - $40,000 for their efforts. They obviously believe that they can do it. As Shaun Martyn, Director of WICL says "It's a big project, but we are a long way down the track".

Each of the six teams will be owned by a separate business and Martyn assures us that they are well-advanced in signing up two companies to this role, with a third not far behind. Discussions have already been had with some of the star players in the world and they are naturally excited about the prospect of earning $40,000 and perhaps becoming a global star in the process. This is hardly surprising considering most of them have earned next to nothing from the game they have played almost full-time for several years, let alone $3,333 a day.

So how will WICL achieve what others have so far failed to achieve – i.e., revenue? The answer seems to be the reach of the internet and the huge possibilities of new cricket markets - China, the USA and South America for example. WICL are committed to including a "pathway player" in each of the six teams. These will be players from emerging nations - they will also probably be players from emerging markets for women's cricket. "I'm looking for the 6-foot 4-inch Papua New Guinea fast bowler that no-one has ever seen, who's been spearing fish in some remote river somewhere", says Martyn, tongue firmly in cheek. You can see the appeal to the competition and potentially to all the people with internet access in Papua New Guinea. They would have their own star on a world stage.

Martyn is keen to emphasise the importance of developing the image of the individuals involved. He is right. Women's cricket needs heroes. People seem to need to have the back story to buy into the product as a whole. He rightly says that beyond the four of us in the room - him and the Three Bloggers - very few people would be able to name the top 20 women cricket players in the world. That is something he would like to change. And that is something which he thinks WICL 1 and beyond can change.

He is naturally tight-lipped about the current negotiations with the major cricket boards. There have been meetings and there have been negotiations. He first spoke to Clare Connor in her role as Chairman of the ICC's Women's Committee 18 months ago. He is keen to point out that all the WICL is doing is creating an opportunity for 78 women cricket players to earn some cash, something that all the international male cricketers can do in abundance. He does not see WICL as a threat to women's cricket and the various cricket boards, but an opportunity for women cricketers to make realistic money from the game they play. He is hopeful that a suitable window can be found for the tournament and that the boards will all buy into the project. He says the tournament will go ahead in the next 9-12 months.

The tournament will have its own range of sportswear, created by Masaba Gupta, the daughter of the great Vivian Richards. We are promised some "funky designs", perhaps even personalised lids (as F1 drivers have perhaps). Martyn says the girls want this. They are fed-up of wearing cut-down men's gear and rolling up trousers that are far too long. Apparently some of the girls have already had some input on designs. This won't make the cricket any better of course, but it is a realisation that women's cricket has to appeal to a broad market. If you take a look at women's tennis and how far that has come in the last 40 years and the importance of fashion and design in the current game, then you can see where WICL is coming from.

Cricket aficionados may be horrified by what they see if they tune in in a year's time. But then people were horrified by Kerry Packer and his World Series Pajama Cricket back in 1977. The game has had to progress. Coloured outfits, white balls, spider cam, numbered shirts, switch hits, scoop shots, the IPL. We may not like them all, but it has made the men's game a viable product. WICL 1 hopes to do the same for the women's game.

Ultimately though the tournament will come down to the quality of the players and the quality of the cricket played, but don't expect to see all the players in the ICC rankings invited to the WICL. Emerging talent is an important part of the WICL brief. The question might be whether the emerging talent can hack it with the best in the world? There are in fact only 77 slots for players. We know one player and the captain of the 14 Degrees team already (the company are keeping one of the teams back for themselves) - none other than Lisa Sthalekar herself.

The next few months are going to be very interesting.   MD 03/VI/14

Sunday, 17 August 2014: A Chat with Clare Connor on The Future of Women's Cricket

No-one can deny that women's cricket has come a long way in the last few years, and by "a long way" I mean from a true minority sport for women to a sport that now attracts 60,000 women to play it every week and where those at the top can genuinely call themselves "professionals". A great deal of that development in the game can be put down to the work of Clare Connor, the Head of Women's Cricket at the ECB for the last seven years, and the huge injection of cash that has come from the ECB themselves. She is a massive supporter of England Women's cricket and works tirelessly for the sport she so clearly loves.

But there is always more to do, and the growing number of women's cricket fans always want more, so I took the opportunity at the Test Match at Wormsley to have a chat with Clare about what the future may hold and how the women's game can develop further. We covered a range of topics and here is what she had to say.

WICL

Earlier in the year a company called 14 Degrees announced that they were trying to put together a two-week T20 tournament featuring all the top women players in the world, akin to a cut-down version of the IPL. The players, who had been promised sums of up to £20,000 for their efforts, were naturally excited at the prospect. However, the ECB and Cricket Australia seem to have kiboshed the whole idea when they stated that they would not support the competition. So where are we now?

CC: "I think we have shut the door on it if it is only going to be a privately run tournament, because the powers that be at Cricket Australia and ECB jointly won't condone privately run cricket. Some of the privately run stuff in the past has set some rather strong alarm bells (ringing) for certain people.

I think there is a strong feeling from Australia and England that such a tournament is worth considering, once we have really established the ICC Women's Championship, which has been the priority for the last 12 to 24 months, but only if it was run by probably England or Australia. We want everything to be for the good of the game. We want the money to go where the money is most needed.

There are concerns around corruption approaches now; other regulatory stuff; medical support; players actually being paid. A huge amount of effort has gone into integrating women's cricket into the ICC, which I would argue has been a huge benefit to the top eight and the developing nations in terms of how women's cricket is run and developed and in terms of what the future looks like for women's cricket. And the joint World Twenty20 has been a big part of that in terms of profile and opportunity, and it is felt that, at the moment, we are not quite ready for another Twenty20 operation or competition. That is not to say that we would feel the same in 12 or 24 months." MD 17/VIII/14

Thursday, 13 November 2014 (extract)

While England were winning the Ashes (that always sounds so good) a breakaway T20 tournament called the WICL was proposed, akin to the

IPL but for the top women, where they would earn a decent wedge for two week's work. Much excitement ensued until the ECB and Cricket Australia effectively kiboshed the idea when they said that they would not sanction such a competition run by an outside agency. Plans are apparently still afoot for a women's T20 Bash in Australia next season, but the WICL lies dormant for the time-being.

Towards the end of May, the MCC Women played a Rest of the World team at Lords to help celebrate Lords' bicentenary. It was a splendid event, but, played on a working Monday, attracted almost no crowd. Great for those that played, but a huge waste of money that could have been better spent on grassroots cricket. It also gave me a chance to rant about radio commentators that are unable to identify women players and fail to pronounce their names correctly. The commentator concerned shall remain nameless in this blog entry as he got a bit miffed about the last one!   MD 13/XI/14

Hangin' With ... Women's Int'l Cricket League Co-Founder, CEO Shaun Martyn

BY ANNA HRUSHKA, STAFF WRITER

8.21.2015

SHAUN MARTYN

SHAUN MARTYN is the co-founder and CEO of the Women's Int'l Cricket League. Martyn, along with his business partner, former Australian cricketer **LISA STHALEKAR**, was inspired to create an elite women's league after noticing the lack of opportunity and financial reward for women on the int'l cricket stage. The proposed two-week long Twenty20 championship is partnering with Edinburgh Business School, Hindustan University and the University of Western Australia to create scholarship opportunities for top players and Martyn is currently seeking investment in a documentary series around the WICL's global search for talent. Martyn spoke with SBD Global about the WICL's goals, creating opportunity and the viability of women's cricket.

On the WICL's goals ...

Shaun Martyn: What we're about is creating opportunity, education and performance for women. We've used cricket as a catalyst because it's the sport that we as a group understand the best. And also because of my business partner, Lisa Sthalekar, who is arguably the best female cricket player of all time. She was an Indian orphan by birth who went on to captain Australia. This whole beat that we've created, the WICL, is about just that -- creating greater opportunity for women in professional sport and opportunity in general. This for us now has become a much bigger issue than just a cricket issue. It's now become an issue around those things for women.

On women's cricket opportunities ...

Martyn: If you think of men's cricket, they have multiple opportunities around the world to ply their trade and play. Women don't. We're trying to create that opportunity for them so that they can gain greater financial independence but also to set an example around what can be done in women's sport and to also prove the point that there is a large audience there that's very interested in women's sport. A lot of the things that you'll see me write and tweet about is that sport tends to be seen and driven by the media as stronger and faster as opposed to being about the contest. We've seem to have lost that notion in the sport -- that sport's about the contest, not everything being bigger, stronger or faster. If you think about what's happened with tennis over the years and golf, we're looking to do the same thing with women's cricket -- make it a proper product. We've got fashion designers working on what the women will play in and we've got some new technology that we'll introduce into the game that the men's game doesn't have. We'll create a proper product which is what we believe it should be. And then of course, running off the back of all of this, is the fact that we're creating opportunity for women.

2 All Access articles remaining | **SUBSCRIBE TODAY** ▶

On partnering with Sthalekar ...

Further Reading

Martyn: About 10 years ago, I was looking for a female guest speaker for a function and I got introduced by my great friend [former Australian cricketer] **GEOFF LAWSON** to Lisa Sthalekar. She spoke and I got more interested in what she was doing and who she was. I became the first manager of a female cricketer, which was Lisa. But, it wasn't a financial decision because she was hardly getting paid. So you can't take a fee as a manager from someone who is virtually not getting paid. It just got more interesting in terms of finding out more and more about cricket. ... The interesting thing then was to see how much she was expected to train and perform like a professional athlete but was not remunerated anything like the men were. It was just ridiculous, in terms of the difference in financial reward and opportunity in comparison to the men. That sort of progressed and progressed. Then I wrote her book with her in 2012. I helped her write her biography. Then she retired from international cricket after the Women's World Cup in 2013. While this was all going on, we were looking at the quality of women's play and how much it had improved, and also what we saw was the size of the audience around the world that was interested in watching women's cricket. That's how we decided that we would create the WICL with a view to creating those three things, opportunity, education and performance for women. It wasn't just about creating a tournament, it was about the bigger picture of how to make it sustainable over a long period of time.

On finding a place for the WICL ...
Martyn: We've been working very hard to work with the boards of all the countries around the world and the ICCs so that we're working with them, not trying to do something in opposition to them. It's not about that. It's about finding the appropriate window in the calendar that allows something like this to go ahead where we can support the work of the boards and the ICC. That's been our intention from day one. It's never been to set up something in opposition to someone. It's about, "How can we help develop women's cricket globally?"

On the viability of women's cricket ...
Martyn: We've built a really strong business case around the viability of what we're doing. There's always doubt about whether women's sport is monetary so to speak from a business perspective. And it is. It absolutely is. But you have to create a real product around it. The product has to be one that encompasses a lot of different dimensions, not just bigger, stronger, faster. I think that's a very outdated notion in sport. I also think that women and men view sport differently. Lots of women see sport as participation where men, obviously, a lot of the time see it purely as competition. And I think that's a significant difference.

Hangin' With runs each Friday in SBD Global.

;

FAIRBREAK

27 October 2015

Mr Mark Stafford
President
Vanuatu Cricket Association
PO Box 240
Independence Park, Port Vila, Vanuatu

Dear Mark,

I wanted to take this opportunity to firstly thank you for allowing your players to be part of the WICL's 'Fair Break' program and to give you a brief report on how the camp went.

Overall we feel it was a great success with the 12 players attending from Fiji, New Caledonia, PNG, Vanuatu and Singapore (**Regional Players**). Throughout the 2-day camp, the Regional Players were exposed to coaching from Geoff Lawson and I, comprising of skills sessions, theoretical instruction, as well having the chance to participate in game scenarios during two T/20 matches organised through the assistance of Ingrid Cronin-Knight. The most interesting observation for me was that the tactical and skills execution improvement between the 2 different game scenarios was significant and impressive.

For the Regional Players to be able to play against a stronger opposition was extremely useful for them. The fact that the team they competed against was comprised of two players that have represented New Zealand, two Samoan internationals and a number of Auckland Heart players, gave the Regional Players a real insight into where their standard of cricket needs to improve to. Whilst the Regional Players were able to compete in the bowling and fielding department, it was in their batting that they struggled to score runs against better deliveries.

As you will see in the attached documents, we have complied a report on each of your players. The report is an assessment of their skills and physical status, plus video footage of what they did during the game scenario matches.

Thanks to our sponsors, all of the Regional Players received a Fitbit Surge watch and some received a pair of skins. We are hoping this will be a small but meaningful way of inspiring them to get fitter in order to compete consistently at the next level

Related to this, the Pymble Ladies College students and teachers who attended the camp as part of a co-curricular initiative between WICL and the Pymble Ladies College were thrilled with the opportunity to start their project of filming and producing a short documentary as part of their work experience requirements.

I have also attached a document that indicates the general observations that WICL Staff made of the Regional Players. Please feel free to share it with your High Performance staff and we are more than happy to discuss with them any observations/recommendations that were made in the documents.

From WICL point of view, we certainly don't want this to be the end of our relationship between us, so if there is anything else that we can do to assist you or your players please do not hesitate in contacting us.

Thanks again for your assistance.

Regards

Kind Regards

(not signed as sent electronically)

Lisa Sthalekar
Director
Women's ICL Pty Ltd

Women's ICL Pty Ltd (ABN 74 162 744 989) – PO Box 426 Coogee, NSW, 2034 Australia

https://www.theguardian.com/sport/2016/feb/29/ecb-chief-giles-clarke-icc-takeover-commons-select-committee

THE GUARDIAN

ECB CHIEF GILES CLARKE TO EXPLAIN ROLE IN ICC TAKEOVER TO MPS

By Ali Martin 1st March 2016

Giles Clarke, the England and Wales Cricket Board president, will be summoned to answer questions by the Commons culture, media and sport select committee over his role in the controversial "Big Three" takeover of the International Cricket Council.

Clarke, the former ECB chairman, was central to the reforms in early 2014 that led to India, England and Australia taking greater control of cricket's governing body and allocating themselves 52% of revenues generated by international events.

With the select committee having spoken to Greg Dyke, the FA chairman, over Fifa corruption, the athletics chief Sebastian Coe regarding doping and Chris Kermode of the ATP on the subject of match-fixing in tennis, it will now turn its attention to cricket's governance.

"The committee has decided to look into the conduct of the ECB in relation to the governance of international cricket, in the context of the other investigations it is undertaking," a spokesperson said. "The committee has already looked at football, athletics and tennis, as part of a wider group of investigations into sports governance and, in relation to cricket, the ECB is an obvious choice to call in."

Damian Collins, the Conservative MP for Folkestone and Hythe who sits on the select committee, has also emailed the ECB chairman, Colin Graves, about the ICC issue, having been part of a protest outside The Oval by the Change Cricket campaign last summer.

Shashank Manohar, the new ICC chairman, has already vowed to review the 2014 restructure before the annual conference in June, with Collins now asking Graves how he and the ECB envisage change.

"This is a crucial moment for cricket," Collins said. "We have put six key questions to the ECB, because the cricketing public deserve to know how their game is being run.

"England, along with India and Australia, are the most influential boards at the ICC. In August I accused them of orchestrating a back-room power grab that saw these three countries taking over the game at the expense of the other 102.

"We welcome the news from the recent ICC board meeting that the ICC is considering governance reform but we want to know what the ECB thinks that reform should look like.

"It is hugely important that cricket does not miss this opportunity to embrace meaningful reform, and that the ECB are at the forefront of ensuring that the international game gets the independent, transparent and accountable governance it deserves. And if the ECB disagrees, we need to know why."

Collins' email to Graves was sent last week before a special screening of Death of a Gentleman at the House of Commons on Monday night, the award-winning documentary by filmmakers Sam Collins and Jarrod Kimber that charts the so-called "Big Three" takeover of the ICC.

"The England & Wales Cricket Board is aware of interest from the Select Committee for Culture, Media & Sport to look into the governance of international cricket," an ECB spokesman said.

"The Committee has already spoken to a number of sports bodies in their on-going enquiries into the governance of international sport and we would welcome the opportunity to talk with them in the coming weeks."

https://www.dailytelegraph.com.au/sport/swoop/australias-mens-team-can-learn-from-our-women-cricket-heroes/news-story/529d961e092f9fb937e3990fa559aece

THE DAILY TELEGRAPH

AUSTRALIA'S MEN'S TEAM CAN LEARN FROM OUR WOMEN CRICKET HEROES

By Fiona Bollen 30 October 2018

THROUGH all the assessments of the shambles that cricket finds itself in, it probably should be acknowledged that there is area that is clearly working well – women's cricket.

AS everyone began sifting through the cultural review into Australian cricket, perhaps there should have been further clarification to it all. The Australian cricket culture review: men's.

Because through all the assessments of the shambles that cricket finds itself in, it probably should be acknowledged that there is area that is clearly working well – women's cricket.

Cricket Australia could do worse than to rebuild around that pillar but given the press conference to announce the findings was scheduled for the EXACT time the women's third T20 against Pakistan began, it might be wishful thinking.

What they have in the Australian Women's team and the women's competitions, though, are successful, driven and honourable athletes working hard to produce entertaining and quality cricket.

They are players who win matches with their skill, not mind games and belittling.

They are humbled when they lose and take the time to analyse, find improvement and then go out and do it.

This is a team that has just swept New Zealand in a T20 series at home and added whitewashes of Pakistan in one-day and T20 formats as they prepare for the World T20 in the West Indies next week.

They're a good chance to bring that trophy home. Why? They're one of the best teams, firstly, but it's also likely because of their recent failings in the past two world tournaments.

They exited last year's World Cup in the semi-final after India exposed their bowlers. The Windies outplayed them in the World T20 the year before that when they cruised to victory going just one wicket down.

The Australian women's cricket team is historically extremely successful, but they have learnt they need to earn their wins.

They have worked through that the past two years and are ready to stamp their authority again.

Boasting some of the most talented players in the world and this team and the WBBL are helping to keep Cricket Australia's participation figures looking healthy. Girls are picking up bats and want to play. They want to be Meg Lanning, Ellyse Perry, Ashleigh Gardner.

The external review no doubt has some valuable take aways for Cricket Australia, but many are common sense.

On top of all that, they had an example of how players should handle themselves sitting within their organisation all along.

But maybe they missed it because they were at a press conference, rather than watching the stream of the women's team's third T20 win.

https://www.smh.com.au/sport/cricket/how-women-are-helping-cricket-become-the-new-world-game-20200118-p53sk9.html

SYDNEY MORNING HERALD

HOW WOMEN ARE HELPING CRICKET BECOME THE NEW WORLD GAME

By Geoff Lawson 18 January 2020

It's a confusing time in the cricket world – in a good way. Confusion caused by so much activity from the flannelled fools; a plethora of fixtures and formats that would make Roy and HG shudder. Just when is too much cricket not enough?

We have already had two Test series, completed a domestic 50-over competition, the Sheffield Shield is three-quarters done, half of the WNCL has been played, the WBBL is done and dusted, we're just past the halfway point in the BBL, the Australian men's team is on a trip (couldn't really call it a tour) to India – and that's all before Australia Day.

Reverse sweeping towards us is the women's T20 tri-series against India and England, followed by the Women's T20 World Cup – which will be opened, slogged, swatted and closed between February 15 and March 8. For the aficionados, you can even follow Australia A versus the English Lions men's series.

Plenty to pontificate about or just sit back and watch as the various spectacles unfold on our screens or up close and personal in the stands. And that's just the home fixtures. Australia are also contesting the Under-19 World Cup now in South Africa against the likes of Nigeria and Japan.

Hosted this year by Australia, Thailand managed to claim one of just two spots up for grabs through a qualifying tournament.

The absence of the men's national team on home soil at this time of year is partly a quirk of India's need to rule the cricket empire, but karma has suggested (on the Mumbai result at least) that India's playing dominance on their own patch is waning.

No matter what the disruption to the "normal" Australian summer, the financial gains for CA will be substantive and that should help the bottom line and support the sport at the foundation level. After all, it is the middle of the subcontinent cricket season as well, a time when those fans expect to see their own stars in action.

The global village of cricket has no summer or winter these days, nor does it have the geographical boundaries within which the British empire spread the seed. The crammed international summer will come to a climax at the MCG on March 8 with the final of the Women's T20 World Cup.

Australia, as titleholders and a team very much in form and full of outstanding players, will be expecting to be there. England want to copy their famous Lord's victory of 2017 (albeit in 50-over style) when the stands were packed to capacity, but their ageing stars have been waning in recent times. Perhaps Thailand will rejoice in their finest moment by coming from the qualifiers at a cold and windy Scottish club ground in front of a hundred or so to the final at the east Melbourne coliseum in front of 90,000. Now that would be a story!

Thailand beat Papua New Guinea in the final play-off match to get into the World Cup. Two teams from south Asia battling each other and frostbite in Forfarshire for a shot at immortality. I can see a screenplay forming ...

A World Cup in any sport shapes its relevance around the concept of inclusivity: the smallest country gets a crack at the Leviathans. There is always hope of an upset and courageous losses can be magnificent.

The main issue with Thailand reaching the World Cup is that only 10 countries are competing at a time when women's cricket is blossoming. The ICC has seriously missed a trick with this one. The shortest format is easiest to organise, and the expenses are relatively light, yet the upside in exposure and development in the associate countries is enormous.

Even Ireland and Scotland don't get a gig, when the inclusion of Vanuatu and PNG would be a terrific fillip for the Pacific game.

Fortunately, the FairBreak organisation (an international advocate for gender equality) has taken up the cudgel to promote opportunity through the sport in a number of the forgotten cricket-playing countries.

As an adjunct to the World Cup, a FairBreak team will play the first match against a Bradman Foundation team at Bradman Oval on February 22. The FairBreak team will be comprised of players from 10 different countries and include arguably Australia's finest player Alex Blackwell, and representatives from Vanuatu, the Netherlands, Botswana, Singapore, the US, England, Hong Kong and Ireland. The match will be live-streamed (http://fairbreak.ion-sport.com) and there will be an early match against a first SCG XI women's team. The main game starts at 2.30pm and the pipe opener is at 10.30am.

Middle-order batter and German gynaecologist Stephanie Frohnmeyer played in a recent FairBreak match in Britain before jumping on a flight back to Munich to deliver four babies. Having made those deliveries, she returned two days later to face some more deliveries on the field. The dedication and love of the game is unparalleled from these women.

The WBBL is really a domestic competition but would be well served by including players from associate or affiliate countries on their rosters. The result is a win-win for the franchises, giving women who otherwise don't get an opportunity the chance and spreading the game globally without leaving home shores.

Cricket is growing through central Africa, especially in Rwanda, Botswana, Uganda and Tanzania, countries that border the Great Rift Valley and Lake Victoria. The teams travel on rough roads for many hours to play fiercely contested tournaments. The MCC charity program has helped fund the building of a beautiful ground in the Rwandan capital, Gahanga Stadium, the "Lords of East Africa", with turf practice pitches on the outskirts of Kigali looking over to the emerald Murinja Hills.

Following the genocide of the mid-1990s, the country is peaceful and ordered and majority-run by women who see cricket as a powerful community sport. Imagine if Rwanda played a match at the WACA (just as the unlikely contest of Thailand versus the West Indies will make history at that ground on February 22).

Nigeria and Kenya have had longer cricket traditions (Nigeria have qualified for the current men's Under-19 World Cup and Kenya were famously the first non-Test playing nation to make the World Cup semi-finals in 2003).

Hong Kong have produced some excellent players, such a Mariko Hill, who will be in the FairBreak team at Bradman Oval, but perhaps the most exciting development in Asian cricket is the rise of China. That country will host the 2022 Asian games, of which cricket is a participant and the Chinese are keen for a medal.

It's drawing a long bow to suggest that China will become a force in world cricket, but with the right incentives and help to develop they could easily be central to the progression of the game through northern Asia and who knows what the diplomatic consequences of leather and willow might bring? Remember the effectiveness of "ping-pong diplomacy" in the Nixon era when a table tennis tour became integral to breaking down Cold War tensions? I can just see ScoMo and Xi Jinping doing a trade deal over a party pie during the tea break at a one-dayer in Hangzhou.

While Australian women's cricket has a historical base from which to emerge, the countries well off the beaten track need playing and coaching support, and the ICC to show they are fair dinkum about women playing their sport all over the globe – not just in the established countries or in elite tournaments.

Young players in Australia have certified heroes to look up to, whether it was Mollie Dive in the 1940s and '50s or Belinda Clark, Blackwell, Lisa Sthalekar, or current superstars, such as Ellyse Perry, Meg Lanning or Alyssa Healy. The game is healthy and professional in Australia, but battling and amateur almost everywhere else. Giving third world and associate countries a goal of World Cup qualification would have been rational and forward-thinking.

This Women's T20 World Cup should produce some memorable cricket, and much of it is likely to come from the home team. The title is theirs to lose. The rest of the world needs to get bigger and better.

https://www.cricket.com.au/news/choose-to-challenge-womens-cricket-contracts-pay-conditions-professionalism-iwd-part-1/2021-03-01

CRICKET.COM.AU

CHOOSE TO CHALLENGE: THE LONG PATH TO PROFESSIONALISM

By Laura Jolly 1 March 2021

None of the 86,174 people who were at the Melbourne Cricket Ground on March 8 last year will forget watching Australia's triumph over India in the T20 World Cup final.

The record turnout on International Women's Day was the result of years of investment in the women's game, and the dedication of those who believed Australia's women deserved to stand on the biggest stage.

Drawing on the theme of this year's International Women's Day – Choose to Challenge – cricket.com.au is exploring the strides made in the women's game, and by women working in cricket, while also shining a light on the areas where work remains to be done.

We will cast an eye on the elite game, coaching, media and broadcast, administration, participation and pathways, as well as looking at the broader picture internationally.

First up, part one of an examination into the game at the elite level.

The path to professionalism. What's the current situation?

CONTRACTS AND PAY

From players having to pay their own way to go on tours to the nationally contracted group that is now the highest paid women's team in Australia, the professionalisation of the elite game has undergone a transformation across the past two decades.

Prior to the summer of 1998-99, players were forced to pay their own way to represent Australia; fast-bowling legend Cathryn Fitzpatrick famously worked as a garbage collector and a postie during her career.

The arrival of a ground-breaking partnership between the Australian team and the Commonwealth Bank in 1998-99 proved a gamechanger, with tours, uniforms and time off other work all subsidised.

"I thought I was one of the lucky ones," former Australia captain and CA executive Belinda Clark told The Scoop podcast earlier this year.

"I had to pay to play for Australia, but only for half of my career.

"We'd get a dreaded invoice at the end of a tour, anywhere (up to) a couple of thousand dollars.

"Then in 1997-98, Commonwealth Bank came on board so from there I no longer had to pay to play so I thought I was in the lucky bucket."

It would take another decade for contracts above and beyond basic expenses to be introduced, with retainers of $5000-$15,000 introduced, while female players became full members of the Australian Cricketers' Association from 2011.

"All of us still had to take annual leave (to play cricket)," Lisa Sthalekar explained last month.

"I never got a holiday; I never got a chance to chill out by the beach because all my annual leave was taken.

"I had to take annual leave to represent my state, even though it was the state association I was working for. It was difficult and challenging times."

In 2013, CA announced a major pay rise for the national team, with contracts ranging from $25,000- $52,000, plus tour payments and marketing bonuses.

But the greatest step to date came in 2017, when the latest memorandum of understanding was agreed, and female players were included alongside the men in the revenue-sharing model for the first time.

Female player payments surged from $7.5 million to $55.2 million, and men and women share the same base-contract remuneration.

It took the minimum retainer for a CA-contracted woman from $40,000 to $72,076, while the average player was earning $180,000 – making them the best-paid Australian national women's team.

Domestic players also achieved semi-professionalism, as the minimum retainer leapt from $18,000 to $35,951 for someone holding both a state and WBBL deal.

CONDITIONS

As far as conditions are concerned, Australia's female players now rightfully enjoy a standard of travel and accommodation consistent with their male counterparts.

Australia led the way in that regard – at the 2016 World T20, when the ICC housed female players in twin-share rooms and flew them in economy, male players competing in the same tournament had single rooms and arrived in India on business class flights. Cricket Australia paid the difference to ensure their players, at least, shared the same conditions as the Australian men.

Since 2017, Australia's national sides have been referred to as the Australian Men's Cricket Team and Australian Women's Cricket Team, to ensure consistency, with the former 'Southern Stars' moniker shifting to a more colloquial nickname. For both teams, the series they are playing carries commercial partnership naming rights.

The women's development team, the Shooting Stars, is now referred to as Australia A, in line with the men.

PARENTAL LEAVE

A new parental policy introduced in 2019 saw maternity leave introduced in Australian cricket for the first time, supporting professional cricketers through pregnancy, adoption, their return to play and parental responsibilities.

It allows players who give birth or adopt to take up to 12 months of paid parental leave, while it also supports players who are primary carers after they return to the field, covering the costs associated with caring for their child and a carer – including accommodation and flights – until the child is four years old.

Parental policy a 'game changer': Healy

Players who take maternity leave will be guaranteed a contract extension the following year, while they will be able to transition into non-playing roles while pregnant until they give birth. They can then return to the field any time after giving birth, subject to medical clearance.

It also entitles players whose partner is pregnant or adopting, and who are not the primary carer, to three weeks of paid leave, taken anytime within 12 months of either the birth or adoption of their child.

PRIZEMONEY

Cricket Australia topped up the prizemoney won by Australia's women's at last year's T20 World Cup to ensure parity with the men's equivalent winnings.

The ICC increased the prizemoney pool for the 2020 event by 320 per cent on the 2018 tournament, with Australia as winners receiving US$1 million (A$1.278m) – a figure still well short of the US$1.6m men received at their last event in 2016.

As a result, CA made up the shortfall, tipping in a further A$767,000 to ensure parity.

The prizemoney on offer for the KFC BBL and the Rebel WBBL is equal.

WHERE DO THE GAPS REMAIN?

A disparity remains between the minimum retainers for men and women, both internationally and domestically.

For male internationals, the minimum retainer in the final year of the current MOU in 2021-22 will be $313,004, where the women's will be $87,609.

Domestically, the men's minimum state retainer will be $74,557 (the women's will be $27,287), and in the Big Bash, the men's minimum BBL retainer will be $40,064, and $11,584 in the WBBL for 2022.

This difference is due to the 'Base Rate of Pay' model used by CA and the ACA in the MOU to achieve gender equity. The model considers hours worked and then applies premiums for Australian players and commerciality of each competition.

Put simply, men play more cricket both internationally and domestically, therefore work more hours, while other factors including higher ground attendances and TV audiences also impact the pay model.

Even during the Australian women's team's busiest year yet, from June 2019 to the start of the pandemic in March 2020, they played a total of 33 matches, including one Test, nine ODIs and 20 T20Is – 33 days of cricket in total.

The Australian men played 10 Tests, 17 ODIs and nine T20Is across the same period. Taking into account Tests that finished early, there was a total of 69 days of cricket played (of 76 scheduled).

Where male state cricketers play in the Marsh Sheffield Shield and Marsh One-Day Cup, females only play in the 50-over Women's National Cricket League.

If a male cricketer played every possible day of cricket for his state in a normal non-COVID impacted season (including the final), he would play 44 days of Shield plus eight Marsh One-Day Cup matches: a total of 52 days of cricket.

Each WNCL side plays eight games per season, with the top two sides contesting the final, providing a maximum of just nine days of state cricket per summer.

As such, Australia's female domestic players are still classed as semi-professional, with many holding down jobs alongside their cricket.

In a column for Nine newspapers in mid-2020, Alyssa Healy expressed concern over the juggling act performed by her domestic counterparts, saying she believed players felt pressured to train above and beyond the hours they were paid for, and the number of matches played.

"Domestic female players are experiencing increased pressure to train 'over and above' their contractual obligations; many training for nine months of the year for a handful of WNCL and WBBL games," Healy wrote.

"With such expectation and increased demands from state associations and WBBL clubs, there is limited opportunity for many of our female domestic cricketers to build a second career outside of cricket.

"An increase in demand has not been matched with appropriate remuneration.

"As a result, many players are finding it very difficult to have a balanced life, which is resulting in an increased level of wellbeing concerns with the stress of finding a second income to cover daily living expenses."

The fact female players do not play multi-day cricket, with the exception of one Ashes Test every two years, also means fewer women are offered contracts by Cricket Australia (15 in 2020-21 compared to 20 men), or by the states (14 in 2020-21 compared to 19 men).

BBL teams can hand out contracts to 18 players, compared to 15 in the WBBL.

Increasing sponsorship, attendances and viewership of the women's game – not to mention an increasingly busy international calendar – could influence the next MOU, set to be negotiated ahead of the 2022-23 season.

https://www.cricket.com.au/news/feature/jess-jonassen-international-womens-day-break-the-bias-australia-cricket-world-cup/2022-03-08

CRICKET.COM.AU

LITTLE THINGS MATTER: CRICKET'S ROLE IN BREAKING THE BIAS

By Jess Jonassen 8 March 2022

I was the first girl to play cricket for my primary school.

But for me to do so, we had to get permission from Catholic Education Queensland – just to let me play school cricket.

At that time, it wasn't even called schoolboys' cricket – it was just the school's cricket team – and there was nothing stipulating what gender I had to be, yet I still had to get permission purely because I wasn't the "normal" gender that participated in that sport.

It was just one of many hurdles, but early on all I cared was that I could play.

As I got older, there were different times I was exposed to sexual harassment from the boys we played against. As an example, I even got asked, 'How are they hanging? Have they dropped yet?' It was almost like they were threatened.

Sure, they were immature teenagers, but they had to learn those attitudes from someone.

There were underage boys' teams that I wasn't selected in, even though there were no rules against it, purely because the male players' parents complained that they didn't want a girl to be picked – because it meant their son might miss out. Even though I was better than them.

These stereotypes about women being inferior to men are still entrenched in society: it's what's portrayed out there in media platforms, in day-to-day conversations, and how people have been brought up. And we're lucky; even though we face a lot of bias, we are in a decent situation where we live, compared to some other countries.

Genetically and biologically, women are different to men, you can't escape that. You can't hide it and you can't sugar coat it, we're different. But being different doesn't mean being less skillful, or less athletic. It's just different.

Female athletes can still work just as hard as male athletes and get the most out of their bodies.

I've always been a big one that if you're good enough to perform a certain skill or job, then your gender should be irrelevant, and I think these constant comparisons between men and women do more harm than good, particularly in traditionally male-dominated areas or sports.

You are constantly compared to a different gender, rather than where the women's game was 10 or 20 years ago. People say, 'this guy can bowl way quicker than this woman', and it's probably always going to be the case. Genetics and biology suggest that, and just because it's different, doesn't mean it's worse.

I see comments online saying, 'I'd love to see them try and face 150km/h'. Well, I'd love to see the person typing it try and face 120km/h, let alone 150km/h. I've done bowling machine sessions where it's got up to 140km/h and I've played it fine. But I don't face that, and you need to be just as skilful at playing the speed you typically face.

Then there's all the online comments about how female athletes look, or their sexual orientation. If we can get to the point where we're no longer talking about how somebody looks out on the field, and it's all about how they actually performed, then we'll know that we're heading in the right direction.

Some male athletes potentially feel like they're put into that same category, but I'd say it's only the minority. The positive thing is that over the last few years, there has been an increase in commentary around how the team's performing and how individuals are performing, and people saying they're watching because they play an exciting brand.

Society and the world is changing, and it's time that we all catch up. Simple shifts actually matter massively, more than the people who are making those decisions actually think.

Language is so powerful and there are really simple changes that don't require much effort but have such a powerful message – something as easy as using 'chairperson' instead of 'chairman'.

When you hear people say 'the international summer of cricket is starting' ahead of the first men's Test in November, when we've already played a series, it makes you as a female athlete feel like what you do doesn't matter.

Things are improving – when we started playing state T20 double-headers with the men, our matches weren't even listed on the tickets. Now the WBBL is a standalone competition.

When I think back to my experiences growing up, the best thing was that as soon as I told our coaches and a few of the boys on my team about the harassment, they were quick to jump in my corner and dish it back to those boys twice as hard. I knew those guys were on my team and they didn't care about my gender.

And those other boys, they've since had daughters of their own and I think they've now realised that how they behaved or how they acted wasn't a positive thing.

They realise they would never want their child to be subjected to those things, or have opportunities taken away or not even given just based on their gender alone.

If we want to break the bias, that is the sort of support we need. Strong, positive male allies.

A lot of the time, it is women standing up for other women – and we do need people in positions of power that have experienced bias, females on boards within organisations to be an advocate for other females.

But sometimes that's not enough to change things – especially when we're talking about attitudes entrenched so deeply in society.

I know that there's some really strong allies in our men's team – Mitch Starc has been a really good ally for us, and it helps that his wife is in our team.

Men with daughters is really powerful thing as well: you can teach them they have a genuine pathway; they will have people in their corner, and they will have people that will support them irrespective of them being a female.

Hopefully the more we speak up, the more people will be aware of the impacts of bias and how some simple changes or subtle shifts in perception can make an enormous difference.

https://www.smh.com.au/sport/cricket/india-what-are-you-waiting-for-why-cricket-needs-a-women-s-ipl-20220506-p5aj2t.html

SYDNEY MORNING HERALD

INDIA, WHAT ARE YOU WAITING FOR? WHY CRICKET NEEDS A WOMEN'S IPL

By Daniel Brettig 6 May 2022

This week, a privately funded women's Twenty20 tournament kicked off in the UAE.

The players are being well paid (about $20,000 for two weeks each), the prize money on offer is rich, and the playing stocks are drawn from an impressively wide selection of the world.

But with due respect to the FairBreak Invitational 2022, in which Australians such as Nicola Carey, Grace Harris, Georgia Redmayne and Elyse Villani are taking part (and available to watch on beIN Sports in Australia), this is not quite the women's T20 event the world is waiting for.

Instead, the game's richest board, India, continues to hang back on launching a full women's IPL of its own. Since 2018, the BCCI has elected only to play a "women's T20 Challenge" comprising three teams and four matches.

Earlier this year, as FairBreak's organisational efforts were ramping up for the tournament, the BCCI did discuss the possibility of "making an effort" to play a larger scale women's event from 2023 onwards. Around the same time, numerous Indian cricketers dropped out of FairBreak, including the national T20 captain Harmanpreet Kaur.

But any such plans were balanced against questions about how difficult it might be to "find a window" to hold the tournament, and that it may not be possible to do so at the same time as the men's IPL. It still sounds a bit too hard.

These sentiments were consistent with the views of a board that has shown scant interest in genuinely investing in the women's game, despite a surfeit of cash with which to do so. And after all, the president Sourav Ganguly had previously stated that the expansion of the T20 Challenge should take place in 2022. The outcome? No change to the tiny exhibition format this year.

Some of the opinions expressed in opposition to a full WIPL revolve around old and hugely outdated attitudes, about the women's game not being a financial draw, or that the Indian national team should have to win a World Cup before the BCCI "rewards" its players with an IPL.

These views stand in sharp contrast to some pioneering work done in Australia and England in particular, where the WBBL and the women's edition of The Hundred are now fixtures on the domestic scene. The collective view of players and administrators alike was summed up by Ellyse Perry.

"I actually think it is even more so an encouragement for other boards to seriously look at introducing professional women's T20 competitions, particularly the BCCI and a full IPL for women," Perry told The Age and The Sydney Morning Herald last year. "Because there is a wonderful opportunity there and it's increasingly becoming a great commercial opportunity for cricket boards to bring in a women's side of the competition.

"Not just from a spectacle or entertainment point of view, but also because growing the game in their country and getting more young girls playing cricket and being involved is so important to the viability of the sport in the future."

For now, numerous key figures in the women's game - such as Alex Blackwell, Lisa Sthalekar and FairBreak's founder Shaun Martyn - have lost patience in waiting for India to do something meaningful. The outcome has been the FairBreak Invitational, a tournament whose organisers fully acknowledge it may have a limited life if its major effect is to spur the BCCI into action.

Certainly, this time next year, India's administrators will have even more cash than usual to redistribute. The IPL broadcast rights are expected to fetch somewhere in the region of US$1 billion per season when they go to market in June.

TORNADOES

W (Saph 17r) W (Warr 13r) L (BA 8w) L (Spirit 75r) W (Falcons 7w) W (BA 4w)
Captain: Stafanie Taylor. Coach: Anju Jain (India). Assistant: Jennifer Barden (Eng)

STAFANIE TAYLOR (WI) ©: vSaph: 19 (23) & 0/12 (2). vWar: 31* (21) & 1/18 (3). v Barmy: 78* (54) & 0/9 (1). vFalc 1/26 (4). vBarmy 12 (12) & 0/6 (2)

30 / Current WI captain / Over 200 WI caps / Over 8000 international runs and 200 wickets / Jamaican / RHB/RAoffbreak Allrounder. Teams: WI debut 2008, Southern Brave, Sydney Thunder, Adelaide Strikers, Western Storm, Southern Vipers / Talented footballer / In 2013 only player ever to achieve no.1 ODI ranking in both batting and bowling / Opener – determined accumulator of runs / At 19, youngest woman to reach 1000 runs and later 2nd cricketer to 3000 runs in T20I / 145ODI 44av 7x100 37x50 HS171, 152w@21; 111T20I 35av 21x50, 98w@16 / Captain of World T20 winning team in 2016 - player of the tourney, too.

SOPHIE DEVINE (NZ): vSaph: 10. vWar: 48 (35). vBarmy 4 (5) & 0/8 (2). vSpirit 11 (9). vFalc 52 (29) & 0/5 (2). vBarmy 37 (26) & 0/11 (1).

32, RHB/RAm Batting Allrounder / NZ White Ferns debut 2006 / Teams: Adelaide Strikers, Perth Scorchers, Wellington / Leading allrounder & destructive batter / In 2020, 1st player to score 5 consecutive T20I 50+ scores – now 6 / Made NZ Cpt 2020 / Rep. NZ at hockey / Type 1 diabetic / Play golf in downtime / 128ODI 31av 6X100 14x50 HS145, 87w@37; 102T2OI 29av 1x100 15x50 HS105, 98w@17 / Mental health missed Aus series in 2021 / Third NZ to play 100 T20s (Satterthwaite/Bates the others) / WC: 309 @ 44 w/ 108 in losing effort v WI in WC opener; just 1wkt only bowling 11 overs in the comp

STERRE KALIS (NED): vSaph: 32 (29). vWar: 58 (57). vBarmy 0 (3). vSpirit 7 (13). vFalc 50 (47). vBarmy 34 (41)

22, RHB (RAm) Top Order Bat, NL debut 2018 / Teams: Northern Superchargers / Played in 100 and RHFT / Played for Fairbreak XI in Eng & Aus / Dutch cricket sensation / 17T20I 37av 1x100 2x50 HS 126*, 4w@13 / Bowls RAMF / RHFT ave 41 for Northern Diamonds playing all 9 games; lost final / Started WT20 qualifier well in Harare with 68 v SL and 47 v Ireland before the whole thing got called off

ANDREA-MAE ZEPEDA (AUT): vFalc 1/22 (2).

26, RHB/RAm / Int debut 2019 / Team: Austria CC of Vienna / Recently named the ICC Women's Associate Cricketer of the Year / Zepeda has led the development of women's cricket in Austria and captained their first ever side in the #WT20I in 2019 / 19T20I 37av 1x100 2x50 HS101, 10w@33 / Is a doctor by training having practiced for the last year / Found cricket because her father lived around the corner from a club in Vienna / Has taken annual leave to be involved in FairBreak / Half Philipino

KATEY MARTIN (NZ): vSaph: 22 (22). vSpirit 2 (5). vFalc TFC/WK. vBarmy 2 (2).

37, RHB/WK WK Batter / Int debut 2003 / Team: Otago / Confesses to loving a bit of banter on the field / Fun fact: has a cat with no tail / 1Test 49runs; 103ODI 22av 7x50 HS81; 95 T20I 18av 4x50 HS65 / 199 matches for NZ - will decide if she's going to keep going after FairBreak / Only NZ player to have Test Match experience; drives Bates to distraction that she's never been able to play one herself / Also works in NZ with Spark Sport doing TV comms / 149 runs in WC @ 30 HS 44

CHANIDA SUTTHIRUANG (THAI): vSaph: 0* (1) & 1/17 (2). vWar: 0/22 (3). vSpirit 0 (1) & 1/21 (2). vBarmy 1/22 (4)

28, RHB/RAm Allrounder / Int debut 2018 /42 T20I 13av HS46*, 43w@10 (!) / BB 5/4 v Indonesia in 2019 / Nickname: Ked / 1st cricketer in Thailand to take a hat-trick in a WT20I / In 2019 named ICC Women's Emerging Player of the Year / Member of Thailand squad at the T20 WC in 2020 / Lethal inswing per Schutt or Schubsobe and gives it a whack down the order - aggressive cricketer

MARY-ANNE MUSONDA (ZIM): vWar: 7* (5). vSpirit 12 (19).

30 / RHB(RAoffbreak) Zim debut 2019 / First Zimbabwean woman to score a ton v Ireland in 2021 / Team: KwaZulu-Natal Inland Women (South Africa) / Hundred on ODI debut - 103* v Ireland in Harare / Nickname: Mumu / Middle order bat & Cpt of Zim / Ex-basketball player / Master of Commerce degree in Development Finance / 8ODI 26av 1x100 HS 103*; 27T20I 24av 2x50 HS60

SUNÉ LUUS (SAf): vSaph: 5 (8) & 0/15 (4). vWar: 1 (2) & 1/22 (4). vBarmy 66* (58) & 0/25 (3). vSpirit 34 (33) & 0/23 (3). vFalc 13* (9) & 0/14 (2). vBarmy 26 (19) & 1/24 (3).

26 / RHB/Legbreak Allrounder / Int debut 2012 / Teams: Northerns, Velocity, Brisbane Heat (WBBL04), Lancs Thunder & Yorks Diamonds in the KSL days / Talented tennis player but chose cricket as a career / Jacques Rudolph told her to take up legspin at 16yrs old / In 2017, named Women's Cricketer of the year at Cricket SA annual awards / In 2020, 1st bowler to take 2x 6w hauls in WODIs / In 2022 named SA Cpt for the WC in NZ in DVN's absence / Scored 1686runs and taken 109 wickets in 100 ODIs / 100ODI 24av 12x50 HS83, 109w@21 5x5w; 83T20I 4X50 HS71, 47W@21 2X5w / South Africa made semi-finals under Luus losing just one group game but smashed by Eng in semi / Made 270 runs at 34 in the WC w/ 3x50s - 13th most

SITA RANA MAGAR (NEPAL): vSaph: 1/19 (4). vWar: 0/23 (2). vBarmy 1/24 (2). vSpirit 4 (4) & 1/26 (4). vFalc 18* (25) & 0/19 (3). vBarmy 1/18 (3).

30 / LHB/LA spin / Allrounder / Int debut 2019 / VC Nepal team / 21T20I 27av 1x50 HS82*, 21w@10 / Second highest run scorer in WC qualifier in Dubai last year / Opening batter in that comp

ALIYA RIAZ (PAK): vSaph: 20* (25). vBarmy 0/28 (2.5). vSpirit 1 (2) & 1/25 (3). vBarmy 15 (13).

29 / RHB/RAoffbreak Allrounder from Rawalpindi / Int debut 2014 / Teams: Rawalpindi, Federal Capital, Lahore / Leading wkt taker for Pak in 2018 Women's World T20 / In 2020, shortlisted for Women's Cricketer of the Year PCB Award / 45ODI 23av 5x50 HS81, 7w@95; 48T20I 18av HS41 17w@34 / WC22: Just 74 runs but included 53 v Australia v Shutt/Perry/King/JJ/Wellington/Carey / ODI HS 81 v SAf in 2021

DIVYA SAXENA (CANADA): TFC early in comp. vFalc 3 (7) & 0/5 (1).

28 / RHB/RAmf / Int debut 2021 / Calgary & District Cricket League Women's Alpha and allrounder on the Canadian Cricket women's team / A right-hand batter and right arm medium pace bowler, Saxena was named MVP during the ICC 2021 T20 World Cup Americas qualifiers in Mexico last year / Major foodie / 6T20I 60av 1x50, 2w@27 / HS of 70* on international debut v Argentina last October

WINIFRED DURASINGAM (MALAYSIA): vSaph: 2/20 (4). vWar: 3/24 (4). vBarmy 0/24 (3). vSpirit 0 (4) & 1/34 (4). vFalc 1/17 (3). vBarmy 0/28 (3)

29, RHB/RAm Allrounder / Int debut 2018 / Made Cpt of Malaysia cricket team at only 17yrs old / Brother played for Malaysia / Degree in Sports Science&Education / Will start teaching career this year / Hobbies: cooking, dogs, cycling, workouts / 27T20I 15av 1x50 HS66*v Singapore 2019 & 18w@25 / 2nd Winifred to play int'l cricket behind Winifred Leach who played two Tests for England in 1951 v Aust taking 5w @ 19

DIANA BAIG (PAK): vSaph: 0 (1) & 2/15 (4). vWar: 1/26 (4). vBarmy 0/22 (2). vSpirit 0 (3) & 0/25 (4). vFalc 0/30 (3). vBarmy 4* (5) & 2/32 (4).

26, (RHB)RAm Bowler / Int debut 2015 / Teams: Lasers / Dual international, representing Pak in both cricket and football / Opening bowler for a long time / From Gilgit-Baltistan with mtns over 7000m and has just one international cricketer in Diana / Baig means Princess! / Degree in health and physical education. 42ODI 40w@33; 28T20I 23w@23 / WC22: just three wickets in 7 games - frustrating time of it

MARYAM BIBI (HK):

18 / RHB/RAm / First change for HK / Int debut 2019 / 9T20I 2runs/2w / Hidden talent: stand up comedian - can imitate anyone in the team and very popular for it / Enjoys singing but says she's terrible at it / Sports Management Student / Like Miles, three ducks in a row v UAE in T20s / Lower-order whacker

NATASHA MILES (HK): vSaph: 2 (3). vSpirit 1(4). vBarmy 0* (1)

33 / RHB/RAm Allrounder / Teams: England Academy, MCC, Msex, Surrey, Otago / Star player in the HK Women's League / Made int. debut for HK v Pak in 2006 but then strove for England honours / Selected as one of MCC's Young Cricketers in 2007 / Her father Rodney Miles is a former chairman of HK Cricket Club / Plays guitar, loves snowboarding and film-making /5T20I 31av HS40* for HKG / Out of form: made three ducks in a row v UAE to start recently-completed T20 series before finishing with 11 / Took over at Middx from Izzy W in 2018 for a couple of seasons / Led them at Lord's in 2018 v MCC - first game at HQ for the county / Played KSL for the Thunder / Did better at No4 than opening for Middx / Came back to HK in the WC Asia region qualifiers in 2021 and did well after 15 years not playing / Crucial experience in dressing rooms being able to share what she's done - had a big impact in a short time / Mother was a really big stimulus for the development of women's cricket in HK & passed away a number of years ago - got a lot of the HK Chinese girls into cricket / They play for Anita Miles Trophy each year - HKCC v Invitational XI / Just set up the Anita Miles Foundation where players will be paired with Lottie at the Vipers playing for Hants; coaching and off-field roles will be supported with this

Team Manager: Chaitrali Kalgutkar – UAE. Coach of UAE Women's team. Past UAE player. Brought up in Mumbai but working in aviation industry in UAE for past 14 years.

Team Coach: Anju Jain – INDIA. From Delhi, 47, RHB/WK, Cpt India 2000WC 8 Tests 36av, 65ODI 29av. Head coach of Bdesh team until 2020. Now batting and WK coach for Baroda Women. Former captain of India, played between 1993 and 2005. She featured in eight Tests and 65 ODIs. Coached the Indian team between 2011 and 2013. In 2018, coach of Bangladesh and led them to their first ever win in the Asia Cup. In 2021, appointed as the head coach of Clontarf CC in Dublin.

Team Assistant Coach – Jennifer Barden. Talent Manager at Lancs CCC based at Old Trafford. Master of Science focused on elite cricket coaching. ECB Level 4 Master Coach.

www.thenationalnews.com/sport/cricket/2022/05/16/fairbreak-invitational-re-imagined-cricket-for-the-better-and-it-worked

THE NATIONAL NEWS

FAIRBREAK INVITATIONAL REIMAGINED CRICKET FOR THE BETTER AND IT WORKED

By Paul Radley 16 May 2022

It is highly likely the FairBreak Invitational will not come back to Dubai.

The new T20 tournament is a privately organised venture, run in conjunction with Cricket Hong Kong.

It only came to the UAE for its pilot edition this month because of the logistical challenges of the lengthy Covid quarantine process in that territory.

In his closing comments after Sunday's final, Shaun Martyn, the tournament's founder, said he is already looking forward to welcoming everyone to Hong Kong in March 2023.

Which is a pity. It has been a blast. But at least we can say we were there when cricket was re-imagined for the better.

In some ways, it was exactly like every other start-up tournament. Six teams with no discernible identity. Spurious names. Flashy kits.

A plain format – round-robin, then semis and a final. All played at a stadium which had seen it all before. After all, more T20 cricket has been played the Dubai International Stadium than any other cricket ground in the world.

And yet it was so, so much more. The pervading feeling among the FairBreak players could not have been anymore different to the atmosphere of the travelling circus of men's T20 cricket.

All too often, the samey shows of the franchise circuit in the men's game carry with them a strong air of entitlement. The usual players, turning up to perform on demand, and perhaps wondering: "Who is it we are playing for again today?"

Contrast that with FairBreak. For the majority of the tournament, it felt as though at least two-thirds of the players involved were pinching themselves and thinking: Am I really here? Is this really happening to me?

Take the testimonies from two of the tournament's great success stories. Sita Rana Magar, who played for the eventual winners - the Tornadoes - works in the Armed Police Force of Nepal when she is not bowling left-arm spin.

Her wicket celebrations gave the event some of its most vivid images. First, via the "Pushpa" hand gesture which went viral in cyberspace.

Then by way of a salute which brought to mind Sheldon Cottrell's trademark celebration, but more likely was in reference to her day job.

"It's been nothing less than a dream come true for me," Magar said. "A great learning experience and a lifetime of memory playing for Team Tornadoes."

Then there was Anju Gurung, a left-arm seamer from Bhutan for whom the tournament was memorable for two reasons which stick out more than most.

Firstly, her Falcons team made it to the final. And, secondly, she went to a beach for the first time.

"Me being part of the campaign, to be honest, has changed my life," Gurung said.

"I can believe, I can dream, and now I have the strength to break the barriers. I am not anymore the same."

Everywhere you looked, there were players who could echo those sentiments.

A Rwandan seamer who dismissed the world's No 1 allrounder. Argentine pace bowlers. Brazilian all-rounders. Malaysian trailblazers.

And a Palestinian engineer who was so engaging she turned her hand to conducting the pitch report before one game, too.

All of which is all very lovely and everything. But it would not have stacked up had players from cricket's nether reaches been no good at playing.

And if this tournament showed anything, it is that talent can blossom anywhere, given the chance.

With an even playing field, the best of the rest showed that they can play alongside the best of the best and thrive.

https://emergingcricket.com/insight/fairbreak-invitational-2022-review-what-we-learnt/

EMERGING CRICKET

THE FAIRBREAK INVITATIONAL 2022 REVIEW: WHAT WE LEARNT

By Shounak Sarkar 18 May 2022

What a game-changing moment the past two weeks have been for women's cricket.

With 90 women's players from 35 nations taking part in the recently concluded FairBreak Invitational, the tournament provided us with a tantalising glimpse of what a genuinely global cricket event could look like.

Certainly, the privately funded tournament put the ICC own vaunted Women's T20 World Cup 'expansion' to 12 teams (from 2026) to shame.

The Tornadoes, captained by Stafanie Taylor, were the eventual winners in the 6-team event, chasing down 151 runs with 8 wickets to spare in the Final. Falcons' Marizanne Kapp produced a batting blitzkrieg (67* off 37 balls) to set up the total, but it wasn't enough as the Tornadoes Top four of Sophie Devine, Sterre Kalis, Taylor and Sune Luus combined to canter to a victory.

With the tournament now done and dusted, Emerging Cricket reviews the big talking points that arose from the event.

1) Associate players CAN absolutely mix it with the big guns!

Batting: While some Associate players struggled to match the skill and performance levels of seasoned Full Member cricketers, there were many that excelled despite the steep learning curve. Dutch opener Kalis was particularly the standout with the bat, scoring 225 runs at an average of 32.14. She featured in seven 50+ run partnerships with her teammates Sophie Devine and Stefanie Taylor and their consistent returns at the top of the order were instrumental in Tornadoes winning the competition.

Kalis ultimately finished FairBreak as the fourth-highest runs scorer, which placed her above the likes of Devine, Taylor and Laura Wolvaardt on the runs chart. It was a highly impressive performance for the 22-year-old, who can excel even further if she can improve her ability to hit the gaps more consistently and increase her strike rate.

Kalis' compatriot Babette de Leede was equally impressive with the gloves, notching up seven stumpings to her name. She also contributed 85 runs with the bat at an average of 21.25. Fans of Dutch cricket will have plenty to smile about with regards to the duo's performances.

Scottish player Sarah Bryce also had a tidy tournament notching up five dismissals behind the stumps and scoring 145 runs with the bat. Unfortunately, her sister Kathryn (who was voted as the ICC Associate Woman Cricketer of the Decade in 2020) largely underwhelmed and failed to live up to expectations. Other notable performances included Irishwoman Gaby Lewis who only played four games but still scored 113 runs with the highlight being a spirited 62* off 57 balls against the Warriors.

Elsewhere, limited opportunities were afforded to Austrian captain Andrea-Mae Zepeda and the Brazilian duo of Roberta Moretti Avery and Laura Cardoso. Although, Moretti Avery did still feature in a 68-run partnership with the South African star batter Wolvaardt.

Bowling: On the bowling front, things were much more promising with a wider cast of Associate players putting their hand up for international recognition. Diminutive Japanese veteran Shizuka Miyaji only bowled seven overs in the entire tournament but still took six wickets, outfoxing batters with her loopy flighted deliveries. This included a match winning 4/18 against the Falcons.

Malaysian women's captain and all-rounder Winifred Duraisingam did not get many opportunities with the bat but was exceptional with the ball. She bowled almost her full quota of overs in each game and took seven wickets at an average of 24.42. Equally impressive were the American duo of left arm pacer Tara Norris and 17-year-old spinner Geetika Kodali. They both bowled with great control and took five and four wickets respectively; the pair look likely to play a significant part in the future development of USA women's cricket.

Other revelations were 19-year-old Henriette Ishimwe from Rwanda and Sita Magar from Nepal. Ishimwe was in sublime form throughout, taking four wickets at an average of 21.25 and an economy rate of 5.31. The medium pacer's most memorable moment occurred when she rattled Nicola Carey's timber with an exquisite in-swinging yorker.

2) Most of the Thai contingent had a great tournament

There was a sizable Thai contingent of players at FairBreak Invitational with five players including Natthakan Chantam, Nattaya Boochatham, Sornnarin Tippoch, Nannapat Koncharoenkai and Chanida Sutthiruang taking part. Most of the players had a great tournament, once again exposing the folly of the World Cup Qualifier debacle last year, where the Thai women were brutally excluded from both the World Cup and Women's Championship based on a flawed rankings system and membership status.

Chantam, affectionately known as 'Jeans', carried on her good batting form from the Qualifier last year, scoring 163 runs at an average of 32.60. This included a brisk 72 of 57 balls against the Warriors where she unfurled her signature range of cover drives and on drives. Furthermore, Chantam has been picked to represent the Velocity team in BCCI's T20 Challenge this year, the only Thai player to do so. This will be her second appearance in the competition and here's to hoping that she actually gets a proper opportunity this time to advertise her batting chops to an Indian audience.

Wicketkeeper Koncharoenkai also had a decent tournament; she was tidy behind the stumps, notching up four dismissals including three stumpings. With the ball, Sutthiruang and veteran Tippoch were characteristically parsimonious, taking crucial wickets and keeping the run rate down. With the Thai women next in action at the T20 World Cup Qualifiers later this year, they will be looking to carry on their cumulative form into the tournament in a bid to qualify for next year's T20 World Cup in South Africa.

3) Good broadcast quality makes a massive difference

Compare the broadcasting quality and coverage of the ICC T20 World Cup Global Qualifier A with the standards set at FairBreak Invitational and the contrast is stark. While an 'official' ICC World Cup qualifying event tried to make do with three cameras and was marred by persistent streaming issues and abysmal audio quality, FairBreak's slick TV coverage made it an attractive and engrossing product to watch and follow. The commentary was excellent and full credit goes to founder Shaun Martyn for selling the rights to fourteen broadcast partners which carried live coverage into 142 territories across the world.

The widespread penetration achieved globally was impressive and gave the cricketers a fantastic platform to showcase their skills, particularly those from Associate nations, many of whom have never had the chance to play in front of a big TV audience before. The excellent coverage was also backed up by sharp, short clips on social media highlighting the biggest moments and best performances in the game. The digital strategy was brilliantly executed, and this is something that ICC needs to improve desperately, when it comes to covering its own events.

4) Jerseys with flags are a brilliant idea

FairBreak's decision to include the country-of-origin flags across the back of player jerseys was a masterstroke. It was a bold, unique and innovative idea which had never been trialled in Cricket before, and with the exception of some Olympic events, not even in other big sports such as Football, Basketball, Rugby or Tennis. The flags served as a handy guide for casual cricket fans to get to know the Associate players better. It also showcased the true diversity that can be found in the cricket world; something which is rarely witnessed in the stratified levels of Full Member cricket. One sincerely hopes that this tradition is carried onto next year's event.

5) Recommendations for next year's event

While the tournament was a big hit, there are nevertheless a few changes that it could benefit from for next year's event in Hong Kong.

One of those would be the implementation of an IPL style playoffs system to reward the highest finishing team. It would be a just prize for consistent performances in the league stage and would essentially allow the team a couple of attempts to qualify for the final. This time, the top two teams in the league stages, Spirit and Barmy Army both lost in the semi-finals with the third placed Tornadoes prevailing in the crunch games to take out the trophy.

While the tournament coverage on TV and social media were excellent, it could benefit further with a healthy crowd attendance at the games. Mind you, this is easier said than done in Dubai, particularly for women's cricket and it is likely to be a similar challenge in Hong Kong as well. However, if possible (even if it's just the final), a live crowd would energise the tournament atmosphere significantly.

"I am grateful to have been given the opportunity to Captain the FairBreak XI in the recent tour to the UK, Scotland and Netherlands. Sport is a vehicle for progressive change, and I am a better person from it. Great to be part of a team composed of strong women from around the world."

Mariko Hill, Hong Kong

https://sportscafe.in/cricket/articles/2022/may/18/fair-break-invitational-2022-a-revolutionary-idea-in-womens-cricket

SPORTSCAFE

FAIRBREAK INVITATIONAL 2022: A REVOLUTIONARY IDEA IN WOMEN'S CRICKET

By Nishad Bapat 18 May 2022

It is often said that talent blossoms if given an opportunity and FairBreak Invitational 2022 provided a big opportunity for women cricketers, especially from associate nations. The tournament will be known as a revolutionary event as it can take the graph of women's cricket onwards and upwards.

The first season of FairBreak Invitational concluded on Sunday and Tornadoes won the inaugural edition. Of course, the winners should get credit for their hard work to earn the title, but the tournament has much more significance to it than just the results. These were not just a bunch of women cricketers playing an international match or any small league, but they were playing in the most diverse league in women's cricket. Sport is always in need of a revolution and women's cricket needed it desperately considering the scale of payments or the coverage of games they get in comparison to their counterparts.

It was the year 2014 when FairBreak's patron and Australian businessman Shaun Martyn proposed the idea of independent women's T20 league, but it was rejected as a tournament regulated by a private operator. The scenario in women's cricket also started changing as the women cricketers from full member nations were handed out professional contracts. Also, the women's leagues in Australia and England had started and so Martyn's idea wasn't unique anymore.

"We spent a couple of years where the ICC would send us off to partner with a board, the board would send us back to get permission from the ICC, and that just became a bit of a revolving door. So I backed off from doing that," Martyn had said in an interview to the Guardian.

However, Martyn made his idea unique with a focus on players from associate nations. He had a different take on the game than what many of the fans or experts might have and believed that there is also enormous talent in the players playing for associate nations.

"The women's side of the game is so diverse and so globally spread, that to think that the talent is only concentrated in a few major countries is not understanding the difference between the two games at all. There are great players in all countries," he had said regarding the issue.

Between 2018 and 2019, he organised a series of charity matches involving a single FairBreak XI, which was a mix of associate and full member players. Eventually, he gained backing from Cricket Hong King, Endorsement from ICC, and support from most of the full-member boards. With all these factors to his aid, a tournament that encouraged rising talents all over the world was on its way.

It was a gutsy decision from Martyn to start a tournament in a situation where numerous privately funded men's leagues have gone bust and some administrators still express their concern over the commercial viability of women's cricket. The tournament could become one of the most significant developments in sport bringing out a change with regards to financial context and exposure for all. The competition featured players from almost 40 countries which included 25 Associate nations making it one of the most diverse leagues in the sport.

The tournament is a part of a three-year deal with Cricket Hong Kong and the next two editions are planned to be held in Hong Kong. The tournament was one of the rarest as it featured numerous global superstars including the likes of Suzie Bates, Laura Wolvaardt, Hayley Matthews, Danni Wyatt, Marizanne Kapp, and Shabnim Ismail, and Sophie Ecclestone. Players from second-tier countries mixed up with veterans of the game as appealed to the audience and might inspire other leagues to encourage the global talent.

Right from the concept of the tournament and its teams, everything has been new but what made the competition stand apart was the performance of players from associate nations. In the group stage of the tournament, players from the Netherlands, Malaysia, Japan, Ireland, and Thailand won the 'player of the match' award. Further, Henriette Ishimwe from Rwanda produced a peach of the delivery in the tournament bowling a fabulous in swinging yorker to Nicola Carey.

Take the case of Sita Rana Magar, a Nepal player who played for the champions Tornadoes. She picked four wickets in the tournament, but one needs to look beyond the stats to know the kind of experience she got while playing with the best. She works in Armed Police Force when she is not bowling left-arm spin.

"It's been nothing less than a dream come true for me. A great learning experience and a lifetime of memory playing for Team Tornadoes," She stated.

Anju Gurung, a left-arm seamer from Bhutan considered this as a memorable experience as her team reached the finals. Gurung contributed with three wickets in the team's journey. There were a whole bunch of players like this who came from associate nations and the opportunity was one of the grandest for them.

There were Argentine pacers, Brazilian all-rounders, and Malaysian trailblazers who also got a stage to showcase their talent. The tournament handed an equal opportunity to everyone and might inspire other leagues to do so in the future.

"It has a massive effect on these people, and we feel that. It's not a small thing. They're very, very, very good players without recognition. I hope the ICC ... now sees us as a complementary piece in the development of the game. If we're growing the strength of those countries, that's only a good thing for world cricket," Martyn had said according to cricket.com.au.

Overall, the league can be seen as a start to a change in the context of more and more players getting an opportunity, more money into the sport and the global reach of the tournament's broadcast can help women's cricket thrive all over the globe. The tournament has brought attention to women's cricket and will take it further in the next two years hopefully.

https://www.allovercric.com/p/how-the-fairbreak-invitational-nailed

ALL OVER CRICKET

HOW THE FAIRBREAK INVITATIONAL NAILED IT AND HOW THEY CAN IMPROVE

By Jay Dansinghani 20 May 2022

Back when I used to travel around the world to watch associate cricket, before streaming went mainstream, I never thought this would be possible.

The recently concluded FairBreak Invitational — a tournament that featured 90 female cricketers from 35 different nations — was broadcast in more than 140 countries and territories.

Let those numbers sink in for a second.

Here are three talking points from FBI 22 — the single most global tournament in the history of the sport.

Equality through Opportunity

Can you imagine FBI 22 without Winifred Duraisingam or Sita Rana Magar? Can you imagine me asking you this question before the start of the tournament?

The Invitational proved what is possible when players from associate nations are given the same platform as full member players. Many of the associate players that featured were testing themselves against the toughest competition they'd ever faced. Many of them had more than a decade's worth of international experience. Many of them are pioneering the women's game in their respective countries.

And all of them deserved the opportunity to earn a living from a sport they're remarkably good at when you consider how the custodians of the sport have failed in their duty toward growth and inclusivity.

Associate players didn't just share dressing rooms, facilities, and hotel rooms with full member players, they were part of a professionally run tournament. A good number of players faced regular media interactions and press conferences for the first time in their careers. The broadcast was exactly what you'd expect from a global tournament, featuring eye-catching yet simple graphics and commentators well versed in the women's game.

Moreover, FairBreak Global founder Shaun Martyn's heart appears to be in the right place. It's highly unlikely that he strays from his emphasis on providing opportunities for female cricketers across the world, especially in associate nations.

Why Associate Bowlers did better than Batters

The FairBreak Invitational was more than just a series of feel-good, inspiring stories. It featured a high standard of cricket, and associate nation cricketers played a big part in this.

Five of the top 15 wicket-takers were from associate nations. More encouragingly, out of all bowlers to have delivered at least five overs in the tournament, four out of the top ten economy rates belonged to associate players Shizuka Miyaji, Henriette Ishimwe, Nattaya Boochatham, and Kary Chan.

Indeed, a bowling core comprised of Duraisingam, Sita Rana Magar, and Thailand's Chanida Sutthiruang is a big reason why the Tornadoes won the Invitational.

However, it was a different story for associate batters. Only two out of the top 15 run-scorers were from associate nations. So, why was there such a gulf between full member and associate batters?

In a lot of cases, associate batters were batting outside of their favoured positions. In their first few games, the Warriors utilized UAE opener Esha Oza in the late middle order. The Sapphires' Kary Chan never batted above five, whereas she thrives at number four for Hong Kong. Yasmeen Khan and Kathryn Bryce, also of the Warriors, were primarily used in the late middle order.

When you have players from 35 countries on show, it is hard for a captain to know a lot about each of the players under their charge. As a captain, if you throw the ball to a bowler who leaks runs, they can be taken out of the attack. Yet, there is a fear that if you send in a batter that you barely know anything about and they go on to play out a maiden, it can drain the momentum out of your innings.

Another reason for the gulf between associate batters and full member batters is their access to professional environments and regular fixtures. Full member players, on average, play more games than their associate counterparts. For many full member athletes, playing cricket is their full-time job, which means that they simply hit more balls and enjoy a dedicated weekly schedule of training and strength and conditioning.

When we spoke to Nepal's Sita Rana Magar (for an interview that will be out on AllOverCric.Com in a few days from now) she talked about how Full Member batters often have specialized training sessions. Monday could be power-hitting day, Wednesday could be strike rotation, and Thursday could be 'surviving the new ball' day. In between all of this, cardio, strength training, and appointments with nutritionists and sports therapists can give them the physiological tools they need to hit the ball further.

With associate batters, who often have to juggle cricket with their full-time jobs, they don't have the luxury of such specialized training, having to squeeze all of it into one training session.

In spite of this, however, several players showed marked improvements as the tournament went on.

After a scratchy start with the bat, Hong Kong's Mariko Hill ended her tournament scoring 21 and 30* not out against the Tornadoes. The latter was a mature innings in the high-pressure final, where she supported Marizanne Kapp in a 92-run partnership.

Two games after labouring to 8 off 22 balls on FBI debut, Kavisha Kumari struck 43 off 42 in a 116-run partnership with Deandra Dottin, which allowed the Barmy Army to gun down 151 against eventual champions the Tornadoes.

After her well-publicized struggles with the gloves in the early stages of the Invitational, Babette de Leede bounced back in emphatic fashion. Remarkably, she affected five stumpings in the Sapphires' final group game against the Falcons. Earlier in the game, she'd scored 45 — her highest score of the tournament — batting at number three to propel her team to 152.

The lesson here is simple: The more opportunities you provide to associate nation players, the more the gulf between them and the world's leading players will shrink.

How to Make FBI 23 Even Better

You have to feel for Cricket Hong Kong. Due to some of the world's harshest COVID restrictions and travel curbs, this year's tournament was shifted out of Hong Kong and hosted in Dubai. Soon after the conclusion of FBI 22, CHK and FairBreak Global announced that the next edition of the Invitational would be staged in Hong Kong. There is a fair chance it will stay that way as the Hong Kong government has finally begun to chart a path toward living with COVID-19.

Unlike Dubai, there won't be empty stands at either the Kowloon Cricket Club or the Tin Kwong Road Recreation Ground, the two potential venues for the tournament that have smaller dimensions than the Dubai International Cricket Stadium. There will be more of a community feel at the games in addition to a better aesthetic for viewers at home.

A major issue I have with T20 leagues is that quite often the teams just seem like a random hodgepodge of names. In the absence of geographical loyalties, I'd certainly like to see a degree of continuity in each of the squads. It'll help fans pick a side and stick to it. This fandom and the friendly enmity between groups of supporters will add to the allure of the tournament.

Yet, I'd also like to see players who didn't get much of an opportunity being moved to other teams. The Spirit's Betty Chan and Barmy Army duo Rubina Chhetry and Ruchi Venkatesh immediately come to mind. While Tornadoes fans will probably click away after reading this, I'd love to see Sita Rana Magar play for another team that utilizes her skills as a batter and not just her left-arm spin.

I'd also like to see two rule changes.

Firstly, I'd like to see a mandate requiring two out of team's top four batters to come from associate nations. This will prevent a situation where the only batters getting a decent hit are those from full member nations.

It would also be great if only three bowlers could bowl a maximum of four overs. This would force teams to use at least six bowlers and prevent situations where the likes of Ruchi Venkatesh, Mariana Martinez, Laura Cardoso, and Iqra Sahar barely get to utilize their primary suit.

It would also be great to see other associate stars that weren't picked this year getting a go at FBI 23. Some of the many names I'd be looking for are Malaysian all-rounder Mas Elysa, Namibian off-spinner Victoria Hamunyela, Nepal seamer Kabita Kunwar, and Scotland off-spinner Kathryn Fraser.

As much as possible, it would be great if squads, fixtures, and broadcast details were announced at least a few weeks before the tournament instead of a few days before it.

Yet, to the credit of Shaun Martyn and the tournament organizers, they were able to shift an entire tournament out of one city and into another. At the end of the day, as a viewer, whatever country you were from, there was a way to tune into FBI 22. At the time of writing, the value and the details of FBI 22's television deals are not known. Yet, even if the deals with some TV channels were not that lucrative, even if the broadcast was given away for free in some cases, the FairBreak Invitational stayed true to its promise of delivering a global and inclusive tournament.

That New Zealand legend Katey Martin wanted FBI 22 to be her final act in a storied career speaks volumes about how players have bought into the vision behind the FairBreak Invitational. Her camaraderie with Wini Duraisingam and Sita Rana Magar is one of the enduring symbols of a tournament that has the potential to disrupt women's cricket.

"The experience was a turning point for me and since then I feel I have grown as a player and as a person. I now believe dreams can come true! In Argentina, cricket is still a small game... These kinds of experiences are inspiring and show us that we can participate and compete alongside great stars of the game which would have been very difficult to imagine without FairBreak."

Mariana Martinez, Argentina

TEAM CAPTAINS

Heather Knight, Captain, The Barmy Army

Nicola Carey, Captain, Spirit

Stafanie Taylor, Captain, The Tornadoes

Suzie Bates, Captain, The Falcons

Sana Mir, Captain, South Coast Sapphires

Sindhu Sriharsha, Captain, The Warriors

FALCONS

SUZIE BATES, Captain, New Zealand
DANI WYATT, England
BRITNEY COOPER, West Indies
MARIZANNE KAPP, South Africa
MARIKO HILL, Hong Kong
THEERTHA SATISH, UAE
SORNNARIN TIPPOCH, Thailand
KAIA ARUA, Papua New Guinea
NANNAPAT KONCHAROENKAI, Thailand
CHRISTINA GOUGH, Germany
GUNJAN SHUKLA, Sweden
MARINA LAMPLOUGH, Hong Kong
CHAMARI ATHAPATHTHU, Sri Lanka
ANJU GURUNG, Bhutan
JAHANARA ALAM, Bangladesh

SAPPHIRES

SANA MIR, Captain, Pakistan
ELYSE VILLANI, Australia
NATASHA FARRANT, England
KIM GARTH, Ireland
GRACE HARRIS, Australia
GABY LEWIS, Ireland
JADE ALLEN, Australia
SHABNIM ISMAIL, South Africa
GEETIKA KODALI, USA
SHEBANI BHASKAR, USA
MARYAM OMAR, Kuwait
BABETTE DE LEEDE, Netherlands
KARY CHAN, Hong Kong
CHRISTIN LOVINO, Philippines
EMMA LAI, Hong Kong

TORNADOES

STAFANIE TAYLOR, Captain, West Indies
SOPHIE DEVINE, New Zealand
STERRE KALIS, Netherlands
ANDREA-MAE ZEPEDA, Austria
KATEY MARTIN, New Zealand
CHANIDA SUTTHIRUANG, Thailand
MARY-ANNE MUSONDA, Zimbabwe
SUNÉ LUUS, South Africa
SITA RANA MAGAR, Nepal
ALIYA RIAZ, Pakistan
DIVYA SAXENA, Canada
WINIFRED DURASINGAM, Malaysia
NATASHA MILES, Hong Kong
MARYAM BIBI, Hong Kong
DIANA BAIG, Pakistan

SPIRIT

NICOLA CAREY, Captain, Australia
BISMAH MAROOF, Pakistan
SOPHIA DUNKLEY, England
CHAYA MUGHAL, UAE
BETTY CHAN, Hong Kong
SARAH BRYCE, Scotland
NATTHAKAN CHANTAM, Thailand
DIVIYA GK, Singapore
NATTAYA BOOCHATHAM, Thailand
ANU DODDABALLAPUR, Germany
SOPHIE ECCLESTONE, England
AYABONGA KHAKA, South Africa
FATUMA KIBASU, Tanzania
SHIZUKA MIYAJI, Japan
YASMIN DASWANI, Hong Kong

BARMY ARMY

HEATHER KNIGHT, Captain, England
LAURA WOLVAARDT, SOUTH AFRICA
SELINA SOLMAN, VANUATU
DEANDRA DOTTIN, WEST INDIES
KAVISHA KUMARI, UAE
SHEMAINE CAMPBELLE, WEST INDIES
FATIMA SANA, PAKISTAN
RUMANA AHMED, BANGLADESH
TARA NORRIS, USA
ROBERTA AVERY, BRAZIL
RUBINA CCHETRI, NEPAL
LAURA CARDOSO, BRAZIL
RUCHI VENKATESH, HONG KONG
HENRIETTE ISHIMWE, RWANDA
IQRA SAHAR, HONG KONG

WARRIORS

SINDHU SRIHASHA, Captain, USA
HAYLEY MATTHEWS, West Indies
CELESTE RAACK, Ireland
GEORGIA REDMAYNE, Australia
UDESHIKA PRABODANI, Sri Lanka
MIGNON DU PREEZ, South Africa
YASMEEN KHAN, Namibia
KATHRYN BRYCE, Scotland
SHAMEELAH MOSWEU, Botswana
SHAMILIA CONNELL, West Indies
SHANZEEN SHAHZAD, Hong Kong
ESHA OZA, UAE
BELLA POON, Hong Kong
MARIANA MARTINEZ, Argentina
JENNIFER ALUMBRO, Philippines

"What you leave
behind is not
what is engraved
in stone monuments,
but what is woven
into the lives of others."

Pericles

ABOUT THE AUTHORS

Karen Motyka was born in Dublin, grew up in Wales, and was taught to write by Irish nuns. She did not excel at sport in school but read voraciously. After completing a finance degree, she headed into the City of London where she fell into global maritime trade. She has travelled extensively and knows a great deal about cargo ships and ports. Hitch-hiking around Israel and the West Bank, and keeping watch for stowaways and pirates on a containership off the West African coast are just two examples of the less conventional ways in which she has seen the world. After marrying a Sydneysider who was working in London, she migrated to Australia. They have three sons, including twins.

In 2016, she gave up her job at the Sydney office of an international shipbroker to run her husband's tax advisory business in a small town on the South Coast of NSW. In early 2022, quite by chance, she was asked to do some freelance writing for FairBreak and she discovered the exciting world of women's cricket.

Shaun Martyn has extensive experience in education, business, sport, marketing and event management. With particular emphasis on High Performance, he lectures and conducts training courses for a range of clients worldwide. He has a long history in the coaching and management of athletes across a variety of sports. He grew up close to Bradman Oval in Bowral, Australia, and, from a young age, played the sport he is most passionate about, cricket. Shaun Martyn is the founder of FairBreak.

Lightning Source UK Ltd.
Milton Keynes UK
UKHW021638110123
415098UK00011B/152